D0105152

306.
874
WAR

C.BT

Warner, Judith, 1965-

WSB
AUG 2020

And then they stopped
talking to me.

33281500086829

$27.00

DATE		

Guelph Public Library   WSB
AUG 2020

BAKER & TAYLOR

Praise for
And Then They Stopped Talking to Me

"Much has been written about our maddening middle schoolers, but little about their parents. Judith Warner remedies this omission by demonstrating—through history and horror stories, research and reflection—how by reliving our own anxieties and traumas, we wind up arming our middle schoolers for battle rather than equipping them for kindness. We swallow our kids' emotions and pain, then wonder why we feel sick. In this revelatory, original book, Warner shows there's a better way, one marked by a balance of connection, distance, and empathy—for other kids as much as our own."

—Linda Perlstein, author of
Not Much Just Chillin': The Hidden Lives of Middle Schoolers

"This book is many wonderful things: a fascinating tour of the history of early adolescence; a powerful exploration of the ways our own experiences as former adolescents can reverberate across our lives; a masterful assembly of research and insightful, propulsive reporting. Perhaps most important, it illuminates how we as adults can do the most essential work of all—raise children, at a time in their lives when we may find them alienating and infuriating, to be happy people who care about others and about creating a more just world."

—Richard Weissbourd, senior lecturer and director of the
Making Caring Common Project,
Harvard Graduate School of Education

"Warner has written the book that every parent of every adolescent needs and has not been able to find. It not only helps us decipher what's going on inside our middle schoolers' hearts and minds, but also gives us concrete advice on what to do about it. I found myself wishing I'd had it when my children were younger. Then I found myself wishing that my mother had it when I was younger. Middle school is a monstrous roller coaster ride. Warner helps us heal our own still-bruised psyches so we can actually help our children."

—Lisa Belkin, creator of the *Motherlode* blog for *The New York Times*

"It's easy to feel overwhelmed parenting a middle school child. Warner gives us the historical context to understand that we didn't get so anxious about this period for no reason. I learned a tremendous amount reading this book!"

—Rosalind Wiseman, author of *Queen Bees and Wannabes* and *Masterminds and Wingmen*

"It's been over forty years and I still get a knot in my stomach when I drive by my hometown junior high school. Warner's remarkable, compassionate, fascinating look at the terrifying abyss that is called middle school has given me a perspective and insight that I only wish I'd had decades ago. It's a must."

—Ayelet Waldman, author of *Bad Mother* and *A Really Good Day*

"Whatever you think is true about middle school, this book will make you crystal clear on two things: One is that many of your beliefs are wrong. The other is that your beliefs influence your kids in ways you hadn't realized."

—Adam Grant, author of *Originals* and *Give and Take,* and host of the TED podcast *WorkLife*

"This deeply researched and deeply empathetic book is one that every parent, every teacher, and every school counselor, administrator, and would-be reformer should read. Warner challenges us to think beyond the stereotypes, the headlines, the hype, and our own often painful memories of trying to find our footing in the adult world, and offers a compassionate portrait of what it means to grow up in America, what kids really need, and the universal drive to belong."
—Brigid Schulte, author of *Overwhelmed: How to Work, Love, and Play When No One Has the Time*

"Grounded in unforgettable interviews, with a sharp eye for the apt quotation and anecdote, and packed with fresh insights into the relevant psychological and sociological literature, this captivating book cuts across the boundaries of gender, race, ethnicity, class, and sexual orientation to lay bare the realities of pre-teen life today and the damaging imprint those experiences and memories impart upon our future identities, interpersonal relationships, and emotional expectations."
—Steven Mintz, professor of history, University of Texas at Austin, and author of *Huck's Raft: A History of American Childhood*

"If middle school is as fraught for you as a parent as it is for your child, Warner's honest, raw writing on the topic offers a dose of sanity in the midst of what often feels like fresh madness. Filled with wry humor and a reassuring sense of dealing with someone who's been in the trenches, *And Then They Stopped Talking to Me* will get you talking about the middle school experience in a way that will ease the journey for everyone in your family."
—KJ Dell'Antonia, author of *How to Be a Happier Parent*

AND THEN THEY
STOPPED TALKING
TO ME

AND THEN THEY STOPPED TALKING TO ME

Making Sense of Middle School

JUDITH WARNER

CROWN

NEW YORK

Copyright © 2020 by Judith Warner

All rights reserved.
Published in the United States by Crown, an imprint of Random House,
a division of Penguin Random House LLC, New York.
crownpublishing.com

CROWN and the Crown colophon are registered trademarks of
Penguin Random House LLC.

Library of Congress Cataloging-in-Publication Data

Names: Warner, Judith, author.
Title: And then they stopped talking to me / Judith Warner.
Description: First edition. | New York: Crown, [2020] |
Includes bibliographical references and index.
Identifiers: LCCN 2019030216 (print) | LCCN 2019030217 (ebook) |
ISBN 9781101905883 (hardcover) | ISBN 9781101905906 (ebook)
Subjects: LCSH: Parent and teenager. | Middle school students. |
Home and school. | Adolescence.
Classification: LCC HQ799.15 .W37 2020 (print) |
LCC HQ799.15 (ebook) | DDC 306.874—dc23
LC record available at https://lccn.loc.gov/2019030216
LC ebook record available at https://lccn.loc.gov/2019030217

Printed in the United States of America

Book design by Diane Hobbing

9 8 7 6 5 4 3 2 1

First Edition

CONTENTS

FOR SALLY

I HAVE GRANTED anonymity to everyone I interviewed for this book. The only people for whom I can't do that are the members of my own family. I am happy to sell myself down the river (narratively), and my husband is generally glad to come along for the ride. But my daughters deserve privacy, and so, with their permission, and with prior approval of all content involving them, I have turned them into one single composite daughter.

Beyond "her" portrait, I have created no composite characters. I did, however, change the details of people's lives to help protect their privacy—notably, their names, where they lived, and sometimes their professions. When I did so, I tried to use replacement details that were more or less equivalent—that is, if I changed a location, I did my best to swap it out for another that was demographically similar; if I changed someone's profession, I tried to match it with another that was similarly paid and regarded. I often changed the names and locations of schools as well. Since class (and class anxiety) is so integral to the stories I share here, I left everyone's socioeconomic background and current standing the same. Handling race was more complicated. When someone I interviewed talked about the role of race in his or her middle school (or parenting) story, I included it faithfully. If, however, the person I interviewed didn't discuss it, I didn't mention it either, in the interest of protecting their privacy in their communities. Because the present-day parent stories I share are meant to illustrate the foolishness of losing the boundary that separates us from our kids, they tilt strongly upper-middle-class; absurdity reliably rises with affluence. My interviewees' families of origin, however, spanned the income spectrum as well as the map.

*Trigger Warning: Middle School
May Make You Crazy (Again)*

The seventh and eighth grades were for me, and for every single good and interesting person I've ever known, what the writers of the Bible meant when they used the words *hell* and *the pit*.

—ANNE LAMOTT, *Operating Instructions*

WE'VE ALL BEEN there.

It might have happened last week.

Picking up your son outside his middle school, you watched as he stood on the sidewalk while his classmates swirled around him, leaving for sleepovers, birthday celebrations, or impromptu parties that came together right under his nose. His frozen smile as he stood there, hanging in until the last minute in the hope that an invitation might come his way, made you crumble inside. As did the knowledge that, other than try to offer up an alternative weekend plan for family fun—which he would undoubtedly dismiss as "just sad"—there was nothing you could do to help.

It might have happened last year.

You bought your daughter a too-expensive white Abercrombie dress for her eighth-grade graduation because, she said, "everybody" was wearing one, and you knew how badly she wanted to fit in. But, on the morning of the ceremony, when she went to join her classmates, you realized that "everybody" was, in fact, only the clique of rich, popular girls who had dropped her two years earlier. They were all lined up, posing as their parents snapped pictures. When they saw your daughter walking toward them, they burst into laughter. And their parents—who, not so long ago, had been your friends—laughed, too.

Or it might have happened a long time ago.

You walked into your seventh-grade homeroom on the first day of school a couple of minutes late and saw that everyone was pushing desks together into friend-group clusters. Your best friend was waiting for you, but now the two of you made just a lonely little desk dyad, and all your other friends seemed, very happily, to have moved on. As the teacher took attendance, you wondered: Had some new friendship map been drawn up over the summer? Would there ever be an opportunity to reconfigure the geometry? You didn't look at your friend, and she didn't look at you, but as you both sat there uncomfortably, you knew that she was wondering the very same thing.

Middle school is brutal. Ask just about anyone, and they'll very likely tell you it was the worst time of their life—if they'll tell you anything at all. If they don't, as is so common, simply let out a cry of *"Raging hormones!"* and cut off the conversation.

The awfulness of the middle school years—ages 11 to 14 for kids these days, 12 to 14 or 15 for adults, if they're old enough to have attended what in previous generations was seventh-to-ninth-grade junior high—is a given in our country. Suffering through is almost a rite of passage—a modern American initiation ritual marking the transition from a life mostly lived in the warm bubble of home to one that's spent in the colder, sometimes cruel, and always competitive company of peers. Scratch the surface with most people and you'll get a well-remembered anecdote, its details fresh and its telling almost automatic, the way stories told over and over again in the mind often are, particularly when they contain a form of trauma. Which, for a great many people, middle school truly is.

For a long time, I thought that there was no greater pain possible than the agonies I'd experienced in seventh and eighth grade. The whispers and giggles. The anonymous "slam books," in which everyone wrote what they *really* thought about you. Having my oh-so-private journal read out loud before French class. Having my every self-conscious habit—licking the front of my braces, chewing my lower lip, biting my nails, pulling in my stomach each time I passed a mirror—mocked and imitated. Being "dumped" by my first "boyfriend." Coming in one morning in eighth grade to find that, with no warning and for no apparent reason, none of my friends would talk to me, look at me, or even tolerate being in the same room with me—and no one would tell me why.

I can still remember how it felt: The ground disappearing beneath my feet. Not a single friendly face. Not a word of recognition, much less reassurance. It was like one of those bad dreams where you're shouting and shouting, and no sound comes out of your mouth. I felt utterly abandoned and completely powerless. I was in a black hole of pain, and it seemed like there was no outside to it.

I was fortunate in that—unusually for that time—our concerned homeroom teacher soon stepped in and brokered a conversation to try to clear the air. He put me at one end of his classroom.

At the other end sat my longtime nemesis, Marci, flanked on either side by Anna and Jill, whom I had, apparently, deeply offended.

Anna, my until-that-week very good friend, was so angry, so utterly disgusted with the mere fact of my existence, that she couldn't even lift her head off the desk where it rested between her crossed arms to look at me. Jill sat sort of blank-faced, while Marci graciously leaned forward to speak for them. Her hands were clasped daintily before her as she spoke, soft-voiced and with a sweet expression, just one bright red spot on each cheek betraying the high emotion she was otherwise masterfully keeping in check.

It was a command performance—far more subtle and sophisticated than anything I had ever seen from her before in the nine years we'd spent in the same school. On our first Girl Scout camping weekend, for example, her cheeks had flushed completely and floridly scarlet red when I'd walked into our cabin, just before dinner, and she'd led everyone else in stomping out. It had been my very first ground-disappearing-beneath-my-feet moment. It had also been my first time away from home. Marci had been my bus seatmate and had watched me try to hold back my tears as we'd pulled away from the curb and I'd waved goodbye to my mom. She was 9 or 10 months older than me—which was a lot at the time—and was a lot more sophisticated, if "sophisticated" is a word you can apply to a 9-year-old.

I never found out what I did wrong that weekend. But now, in that eighth-grade classroom, my crimes were elaborated: (1) I thought I was better than everyone else. (2) I didn't say hello in the hallways. (3) I looked through people when *they* said hello to me, like they weren't even there.

This was news to me. I thought: (1) I didn't think I was better than anyone else—I hated myself! (2) I wasn't aware of not saying hello in the hallways. (3) If I looked straight through people, it wasn't because I meant to snub them; it was just—how to explain this?—that *I didn't see them*. I was smart enough not to make that latter point out loud. I just apologized. I promised to try to do better. And I did, after that, try my hardest to remove my head from my ass long enough to acknowledge the existence of other people—a struggle that continues to this day.

In the end, thanks to our teacher's intervention, my time in the wilderness lasted for only about a week. But my very acute recollection of how that week felt lasted for decades. For many years afterward, the episode showed up in my dreams. The actors would be different—I didn't think about my middle school classmates anymore—but the experience, and above all the feeling, was precisely the same. All through my 20s, and even into my 30s and early 40s, I felt compelled to regularly ask my close friends if they were mad at me. The fear that, from one day to the next and for reasons unknown, someone could turn on me, stop talking to me, and start hating me was simply part of who I was.

My daughter never had experiences quite like that in middle school. Neither, thankfully, did she encounter the all-out horrors that some of today's middle schoolers do: Extended online bullying. Cruel insults. Sexual violence. Death threats. But she did suffer. She was different at a time of life when the secret to social success is fitting in seamlessly. And when she had her own friendship struggles in seventh and eighth grade, in the course of which she ended up going through one very long period of isolation, I learned that watching your child be rejected socially can be a form of misery that's every bit as bad as being a middle schooler yourself.

I said and did the right things most of the time: encouraged her to talk things out, to make new friends, to seek help from the school counselor, to hang out and have family time on weekends. She dismissed most of those suggestions as "useless."

She asked me to intervene and try to work things out with the other moms. I told her that parents didn't do that in middle school. But the truth was that I had tried. When the trouble had started between her and another girl in her small friend group, I had approached the girl's mom, Julie, whom I considered a friend, to ask if perhaps the four of us—the two women and our two daughters—could go out to lunch. I thought maybe she and I could team up, put our heads together and come up with a way to say to the girls: *Get it together. You have eighteen months left in each other's presence. You can make them miserable, or you can make them decent. We vote for decent. Here's how to proceed: You will be nice. You will be pleasant. You will be polite and considerate. You will co-exist—which, since you're part of the same group, means you will have to share friends.*

I had a model in mind for this. A few years earlier, one of my closest friends, Anne, had convened such a lunch when my daughter and her daughter, Isabel, were having some issues in school. Isabel was saying things that were upsetting my daughter. My daughter kept crying and going to the teacher, who was known to play favorites. Isabel kept getting in trouble for saying things that, Anne knew, were far less malicious than clueless. She suggested over lo mein that there might be better ways to communicate and handle conflicts. We made some suggestions. Everyone agreed. And that was that.

I kind of gulped out the basic idea one morning when Julie and I ran into each other on the street. In my head, it had seemed logical. Out in the air, it seemed awkward, beseeching. It was not well received.

Better to let the school handle things, Julie said, with a notable lack of warmth in her eyes. Better not to get involved. Better to let the girls sort things out. "They're all just trying to figure out who they are," she said.

I remember thinking that it was undoubtedly a mark of intellectual superiority to have been able to generate—and find meaning in—that particular sentence. But I couldn't really disagree. After all, I'd listened at Back to School Night. I knew that parents shouldn't get involved in sorting out their kids' business, especially in middle school. School business was school business, and over the years I'd actually seen the school step in with other people's kids, to good effect.

So I tried to do what I was supposed to do. I did my utmost to *take a back seat*. To promote *independent problem solving*. To *stay in my lane*. I tried not to *"interview for pain."* Julie and I encouraged the girls to seek out the school counselor, who then emailed Julie and me to "commend" us for our "wisdom" in encouraging our daughters to work out their problems at school, "with adult help, but essentially independently."

A couple of years before, when my daughter had been in fifth grade, that same counselor had almost cried while telling me about a "friendship group" meeting she had run with the girls in the class. My daughter hadn't been involved in whatever *crise du jour* had precipitated the intervention; she, like many of the others, had been required to attend so that the adults could maintain the fiction that what was going on was "everybody's" problem. In fact, at that point, she'd been somewhat young for her age and needed more time to master, or even pick up on, the social intricacies of high-level girl drama. So she had sat there, uncomfortably, wearing a cherished pair of green rubber rain boots with frog faces on the tips, while her more advanced classmates, already all but interchangeable with their straightened hair and Uggs, had eaten one another alive. The counselor had had tears in her eyes, talking about my daughter's footwear, because once upon a time, in a different era, in a different place, and with different shoes, *she* had been that froggy-booted girl, too.

By eighth grade, my daughter and Julie's daughter were running circles around this counselor, managing to be extremely busy and/or filled with nothing but the most benevolent thoughts toward each other every time she tried to make an appointment to meet with them. I was spending every moment of my driving time listening to Stephen King's *Carrie* and fantasizing about pyrokinesis. Over and over again in yoga, I set an "intention" at the start of my practice to become a positive, joyful, and comforting presence in my daughter's life. But no amount of Ujjayi breath could shake my Carrie-like vibe. Particularly once, toward the very end of the year, another mom made an offhand and well-meaning comment that truly made me feel like I, too, was back in eighth grade.

She paused alongside me for a moment just outside of school, watching my daughter chat with her friends. My daughter was "in" and "out" all the time at that point, and we happened to be observing an "in" moment.

"You know, the girls would have been *just fine,*" the woman said, "if only the moms hadn't gotten involved."

Involved?

Yes, *involved.* In every single aspect of the girls' social interactions and school lives. "The moms weighed in so heavily," she said, "and instead of giving the girls the space to work things out, they brought it up to a whole new level that almost made it impossible for them to find a way out."

She actually told me that last bit a few years later, when I was writing this book. At the end of eighth grade, however, the conversation had ended with the word "involved." And I felt like a fool. "Useless," indeed. And pretty damn mad.

But I really shouldn't have been surprised.

The parental-involvement revelation wasn't the first "I can't believe this" moment I'd had as the mother of a middle schooler. Over the years, there had been so many things that I'd experienced, witnessed, or been told about that had simply seemed crazy. There was the time I got a lecture on "social codes" from the mother of a popular girl when my daughter bought a party dress, at the height of bar and bat mitzvah season, that had already been "claimed" by her daughter. (The girl herself called me a few minutes later. "Please forget it," she said. I can still, to this day, hear her tearful voice pleading while her mother made protesting noises in the background. "I didn't want her to say anything.") There was the time another mom brought in a professional hip-hop dance coach to teach the girls in the class some choreography for the school talent show, inciting a cabal of stone-faced moms to gather to watch the dance practices and then march to the principal's office to complain that their daughters were being trained to behave like "sluts." (The girls were thrilled. The show went on. My un-dance-educated daughter gestured a bit too wildly during the number and sent all her bangles flying off the stage.) And there was the dad who bragged that he'd signed a big check to reserve a "cool" kids' table for him, his wife, and their friends at a school auction.

The weirdness wasn't just contained to parents; other adults had their issues, too. There were a couple of academic-subject teachers who had repeatedly been overheard making nasty comments about girls' "big boobs" or detestable skinniness. There was a gym teacher who often lost it with the eighth graders, making them sit silently on the floor, their backs to the wall, for entire class periods, while he berated them for letting their "drama" leak into the time they were supposed to be devoting to PE. ("All the teachers were constantly telling us how 'bad' we were as a class," my daughter recently told me. "Maybe we *were*," she reflected, "but being told that all the time didn't help.")

I had no right, really, to dole out judgments about boundaries. I had spent my middle school parenthood years cataloging hurts and snubs that my daughter wasn't even aware of: how others looked at her; whether or not they held doors for her; whether they sat with her, spoke to her, settled in next to her or scuttled away. My husband had, too. With his far more finely attuned social radar, he was constantly scanning the horizon for evidence of exclusion—and then prodding me to do something about it.

It was hell. We were all in hell. It was no accident that I was driving around listening to the story of an insane 1970s teenager with the power to channel her rage and hurt into murder. We were all going through middle school together, thinking and feeling and behaving like selfish, self-protective, and, above all, un-self-aware 12- and 13-year-olds. It was no wonder that so many of the kids—boys and girls alike—were struggling so greatly, despite all the careful social orchestrations and emotional ministrations of their attentive parents. The inmates were running the asylum. Life really was, as the women around me so often put it, "seventh grade all over again."

In the midst of all this, I was supposed to be working on a book proposal about modern women in midlife. A kind of *Perfect Madness* redux. But something else kept making noise in my head. Floundering deep in middle-school-mom misery, I yearned for good explanations for what my daughter was living through, why parents and kids were behaving as they were, and what I could do to make things better. I had no information—nothing useful to read, no relevant advice, and no insights from the parents around me, who by seventh or eighth grade were too locked into face-saving competition and proxy wars to permit any potentially damaging self-disclosures.

What I really wanted were explanations from experts who could answer the specific questions forming in my mind: Why, precisely, were the middle school years so awful? Had they always been this way? Were they this way everywhere? How much was about middle school per se, and how much was about middle school in a high-achieving—and highly competitive—American enclave? What was going on in the heads of the kids I saw parading by at school—the boys with their hair in their eyes, the girls in shoulder-to-shoulder symbiosis? *What was going on in the heads of their parents?*

Not so many years earlier, when my daughter was in the ele-

mentary grades, I would simply have asked around. Or not even—
the conversations would have started spontaneously. But in the
middle school years, there were fewer opportunities for those
kinds of easy exchanges. The kids were more independent, and
even on the occasions when parents did come together, the atmosphere was different. There was more distance and, seemingly,
more distrust.

Each school year would start with a sense of dread, as the parents girded themselves for what everyone knew would be the very
worst time in their children's lives. Well before the first day, the
sighing and anticipatory eye-rolling would begin, along with an
uptick in gossip. By the time the semester began, there would be
whispers of "drama"—not just among the kids, but among the
adults as well.

At those times, I'd email out Anne Lamott's quote about "*hell*
and *the pit*."

The moms in particular loved it. It was "perfect," they said.

And yet no one—including me—ever talked directly about
what we were feeling, or asked if there was any way to try to
change the general atmosphere. A lot of the parent relationships
by this point had started to fray. There were so many competing
agendas, so much polluted water under the bridge. Nobody was
even bothering to be fake anymore. Even at school-sponsored
grade events, the former talk of "our kids," "our classroom," and
"our community" had noticeably subsided. It was as though the
balance between adult ideals and kid realities had shifted. The
window of opportunity for teaching our children the rules of
kind and thoughtful co-existence appeared to have slammed shut.

The sense of inevitability was so deep—that sixth, seventh, and
eighth graders were destined to be mean; that middle school sucks,
sucked, and will always suck—that it was inconceivable that adults
might do anything about it. Except, of course, dig the trenches

and start arming their kids to do battle, using many of the same weapons they'd used to defend themselves during their own middle school or junior high years decades earlier.

MIDDLE SCHOOL SHOULD come with a trigger warning for parents. We all know it can be a psychologically treacherous time for kids. It's the point when old friendships abruptly end, new alliances form, and everyone is subjected to a brutal process of "sorting," as I once heard the psychologist and author Michael Thompson say, which arranges kids into unforgiving hierarchies based on looks, wealth, athleticism, and that ever-mysterious ingredient that in my day was called "cool." (A sixth-grade teacher I interviewed for this book referred to it as "social power . . . that indefinable charisma thing," and a middle school dad who normally had an easy way with words struggled to capture it, finally settling on "a strange agency.") We all want to shepherd our kids through this phase of life with as little emotional damage as possible. What we don't realize, though, is how at risk we ourselves are of being knocked off course by the overwhelming power of our own worry and concern.

The author Brené Brown has described the parental experience of witnessing—and identifying with—a child's social travails as a "secondary trauma." It's strong language that is probably not an exaggeration, particularly for today's parents, who have long demonstrated a certain vulnerability to taking on their children's experiences and emotions. They've shown a tendency toward enmeshment, whether through co-sleeping in the "family bed," or co-watching TV, or co-celebrating on high school prom night, or co-contesting bad grades in college. But there is something about middle school that has a unique power to collapse the boundaries between past and present, parent and child.

For a variety of reasons, which I will explore at length in the chapters that follow, the middle school age is the time when we feel our feelings most deeply and encode our most enduring memories. It is, in many respects, the point at which we first engage with the world in the ways that will continue to work (or not work) for us in adulthood. It's when we first activate something like the brainpower that will fuel our adult perceptions, when we start to construct the "narrative identity" through which we will describe ourselves to ourselves (and to others) for the rest of our lives. In other words, it is the time when we begin to become ourselves.

Scientists now speak of the middle school passage as a "second critical period"—a stage of rapid brain changes and also of cognitive, behavioral, and social development that rivals in consequence the much-better-recognized 0–3 age range. A chief difference, though, is that while 0–3 development plays out largely within the confines of family, the 11–14 stage unfolds in the far less controllable world of school and friends. For the current generation of parents, this lack of control can be a painful and scary challenge. For those who are already stressed and knocked off balance by their own early midlife inner upheaval—which for many falls during their kids' middle school years—this challenge can escalate into a real crisis. The power of that crisis, along with parents' inability to make sense of it, often shames and silences them. So parents who might once have sought solace from friends or advice from trusted teachers or pediatricians end up feeling very alone.

"Most people run from pain," a D.C.-area child and adolescent psychologist once told me, referring to the shut-down middle school parents she frequently sees in her practice. I, on the other hand, tend to run toward it. Which is why, at the very end of my daughter's middle school years, I began to pay a different kind of attention to the kid-and-adult dramas playing out around me. I stopped reacting and began watching and listening. It became clear to me that I was being triggered; my emotions were often over-strong, out of whack. What I still didn't know, before writing this book, was why. Nor did I realize how incredibly widespread this particular form of emotional dysregulation really is.

Middle schoolers are in many ways captives to the lives we construct for them; most don't choose where they go to school, and they certainly can't choose their classmates. They can't choose their parents, or where or how they live, either. And while they are certainly old enough to make choices about how they act toward one another, most don't have a very large repertoire of behaviors to choose from. Plagued by insecurity, unsure of who they are and where they're going, they blunder blindly into social dramas. They attack (directly or indirectly), and they retreat.

Adults, ostensibly, have far more control over how and with whom they make their lives, a wider range of behavioral responses to draw on, and an ability, when faced with a difficult situation, to step back and reason their way toward a solution. And yet, it seems to me that, as parents and as a society, we lose touch with all that potential maturity when we're confronted by kids of middle school age. This is good for no one. We need to heal and move on. After reporting and writing this book, I firmly believe that by rethinking the middle school years, we have the opportunity to become better and happier adults.

It's certainly worth a try. Because we don't want to stay in seventh grade forever.

AND THEN THEY STOPPED TALKING TO ME

CHAPTER 1

Middle School in Our Minds

The revival of the junior high school dance is, in Miss Manners'
opinion, a boon to the social development of young
adolescents. In no other way can they obtain those deep
emotional scars that make people so interesting later in life.

—JUDITH MARTIN (a.k.a. Miss Manners), *The Washington Post*

"I HAD ALL the things that made someone popular in my elementary school," Mitch, a 39-year-old campaign adviser from the Midwest, told me late one winter morning in a crowded café in Northwest Washington, D.C. It was a time of day when, through most of his adult life, he would never have been free to have coffee. He would have been downtown, in a glass-fronted office building, packing in meeting after meeting with politicos, pollsters, and other consultants, right at the center of the capital's money-and-power nexus. That had been his life for a couple of decades, and he'd been very happy in it. Until what was supposed to have been a dream job brought him under the thumb of a boss who ran her D.C. consulting firm like a middle school "mean girl," ruling by fear, ostracizing those who fell out of her favor, and using the man in question—her number two—alternately as a whipping boy and as an enforcer.

She'd berate people, then have Mitch clean up the messes. She could be kind or cruel, sane or crazy, nurturing or raging—all without warning. Mitch started walking on eggshells to avoid her displeasure—angling for her approval, jockeying to stay within the sunbeam of her power, and trying to stay as far away as possible from the purgatory in which those in the out-group waited for a reprieve. His anxiety mounted to levels he hadn't experienced since middle school, a time so dark and an emotional reality so overwhelming that it threatened to swallow his adult self whole.

Mitch came from a "good" family—neither rich nor poor, just comfortably in the middle of those who lived in his small town in the rural part of his state. He had a father who could be difficult—kind of erratic mood-wise. But his mother was steadily supportive. She was very engaged in his school. He was a great student—right at the top of all his classes. And, all the way through fifth grade, he had a lot of friends.

When middle school began and his elementary school classmates merged with kids from another, wealthier district for sixth grade, Mitch quickly made some new friends—"popular" boys from the other elementary school. He kept getting straight A's, and he kept getting invited to all the parties. But then, one Monday in March, he came to school to find that his new friends had stopped talking to him. They wouldn't sit with him at lunch or on the bus. At assemblies, there were no seats available near them.

"I was dead to them all of a sudden," he recalled. "They'd act like I wasn't there."

Panicked, he went back to his old elementary school friends. But a couple of weeks later, they stopped speaking to him, too.

The silent treatment spread from his section to other sections of the school, and from grade to grade. "It went from not talking to me to calling me a fag and other names, knocking books out of my hands, hanging signs on my back. . . . It was just endless torment," he said.

Mitch pressed hard for explanations. But no one would tell him what was going on. All of a sudden, it seemed, everything that had once been right about him was wrong. "Having an involved mother was no longer a good thing; it was a loser thing. Being smart was no longer a good thing. The boys who were more athletic, especially the football players and wrestlers, they were suddenly the favorites," he told me.

His teachers that year were all the sports coaches: middle-aged men who related naturally to boys who were just like they had been in junior high. They didn't pile on—they weren't monsters—but they didn't exactly throw a whole lot of support his way.

"Somebody like me—not athletic, not having an early growth spurt, probably exhibiting some signs of being gay—was not going to be popular," he noted dryly. "Their attitude was, *Boys will be boys*."

The girls in the class took him in. "But to be the only boy with all the girls," he said, "that didn't help the reputation of being a secret fag."

His parents knew nothing, and he told them nothing. He was ashamed. Becoming unpopular felt like a personal failure. Being called "gay"—a word no one would argue was anything other than an insult in his community in the late 1980s—brought to the surface something that he was nowhere near ready to fully contemplate, much less disclose to his parents.

The remainder of that spring was horrible. "I dreaded going to school. Every day, it was getting to three P.M. without getting the shit kicked out of you. Get to Friday. Just not get hurt and not lose my mind," he said.

Every morning, he woke up to the sound of birds singing outside his bedroom window. It came from a huge two-hundred-year-old oak tree with wide-reaching branches that each year at the start of the warm weather would fill up with nesting birds as they migrated north. The birds would build their nests just outside his window. And every day, as he woke up and got dressed, his chest tight with fear, their utter indifference as they chirped away, "just singing their heads off," as he recalled it, compounded his feeling of being all alone—out of step, a total and utter freak of nature.

For years afterward, he told me, he couldn't stand the sound of birdsong. He'd come home from high school and college and even graduate school, and the chirping would make him feel sick. Other reminders of that time also brought on a rush of sick feelings: Nintendo, 1980s clothing, even certain TV shows. He became an insecure young adult, "hypersensitive to any perceived slight, hyperaware of any perceived disapproval or displeasure," as he put it. He battled obsessive-compulsive disorder, a problem that had begun sometime in late middle school, after he'd made some new friends and then found himself engaging in rituals—odd little sayings, chants, and prayers, even a highly ritualized way of dressing to avoid repetition—all to magically guarantee that his new crowd wouldn't abandon him.

Some vestiges of his old insecurities, and even the OCD, had been set off again by the emotional yo-yo effect of his boss's silent treatment and bullying outbursts. After less than a year, he'd had to cut and run.

"It was like sixth grade. I never understood what happened. I didn't know what did it," he said, then shrugged. "It just triggered so much."

JUST SAY THE words "middle school," and the whole atmosphere in the room changes. Men shudder. Women's faces shut down, their friendly smiles fading under suddenly anxious eyes. Some people turn pale; some sort of fold into themselves and quickly walk away.

Our pop culture represents life at ages 11 to 14 either as grotesquely embarrassing (mostly when it comes to boys, as per the unfortunate Andrew Glouberman's encounters with his forever cringeworthy Hormone Monster, Maury, in the Netflix series *Big Mouth*) or as sadistic and cruel (mostly when it comes to girls, as in the goings-on of nasty Massie Block and her Pretty Committee comrades in Lisi Harrison's The Clique novels). For adult consumption, there have also been occasional forays into cinematic cruelty, like Catherine Hardwicke's sex-and-drug-fueled race to the bottom, *Thirteen,* or Todd Solondz's cult classic, *Welcome to the Dollhouse,* in which a grotesquely awkward, unattractive, and unpopular seventh-grade girl goes from one unbearably humiliating experience to another, ultimately finding companionship by hanging around with a disturbed popular boy who threatens (and then declines) to "rape" her, suggesting new times when he might pull it off. More recently, Bo Burnham's much cleaner—and much better—2018 movie, *Eighth Grade,* presents one week in the life of 13-year-old Kayla Day, a girl so low in the social hierarchy that she is all but invisible to her classmates.

In the collective imagination, the phrase "middle school" ("junior high," for older adults, "seventh grade" for just about everyone) is a form of shorthand denoting abject misery. The place itself is a nightmare institution—"the Bermuda Triangle of public education," as *The New York Times* once called it. As a phase of childhood, it's considered the pits—*The Worst Years of My Life,* as in the subtitle of the first volume in the mega-bestselling author James Patterson's Middle School book and movie series, for example. (*Get Me Out of Here!,* fittingly, is the sequel.) The words denote all that is awful, nasty, catty, gossipy, and generally deplorable— a state of being that is not necessarily the exclusive province of those ages 11 to 14. There are many parallels in adult life, as Senator Rand Paul of Kentucky made clear during the 2015 Republican presidential primary debates, when he sneered at Donald Trump's "sophomoric" behavior, then revised his assessment of the front-runner's mental age down further: "His visceral response to attack people on their appearance—short, tall, fat, ugly—my goodness, that happened in junior high. Are we not way above that?" ("I never attacked him on his look [*sic*], and believe me, there's plenty of subject matter right there," Trump retorted, true to type.)

Middle school is the time of life when bullies reign supreme. It's the age of first being "grabbed by the pussy" (and otherwise sexually harassed), a number of women pointedly recalled in late 2016. It is a trial-by-fire experience that either kills you or makes you stronger, a lifelong reference point denoting the worst kind of meanness, the worst kind of suffering, the most lasting scars. "There was nothing they could do to me on Wall Street that was as bad as seventh grade," Sallie Krawcheck, one of the country's most powerful businesswomen, once said.

Scratch the surface of just about anyone who was—and probably still is—a bit different from the horde, and you're likely to find some scars from middle school. Claire Danes was a television superstar by her mid-teens, but she was a self-described "nerdy" 11-year-old who loved schoolwork, proudly claimed the score of *A Chorus Line* as her favorite music, and was "tortured" in middle school (coincidentally enough, by the same bully who went after her future *Homeland* colleague Morena Baccarin, the actress who played Brody's wife in the series' early seasons). "She was not cool," Ariel Flavin, Danes's best friend in childhood, told the *New Yorker* writer John Lahr in 2013. "She just always said what she thought. She raised her hand every time she knew the answer, and she knew the answer every time. So people didn't like her." (Danes concurred: "I thought it was a crock of shit, all these social games. I couldn't deal.")

Even stolid Hillary Clinton has recalled junior high as a low point in her life, when her classmates teased her about her glasses and "the lack of ankles on my sturdy legs."

There is something about middle school, past or present, that brings out the very worst in people—adults and children alike. Or so a writer named Carly Pifer discovered in 2013 when *Slate* invited former "mean girls"—and boys—to submit essays describing who they'd been in school, what they'd done, and what they'd learned from their bad behavior. Pifer wrote about her time in a middle school clique called the "Magnificent Seven," which ruled the roost through "an alliance in shared cruelty." Her essay was clearly intended as a cosmic apology, but readers responded as if they themselves had been her victims. They pelted her with online insults and even made physical threats. In other words, total strangers bullied Pifer back, more than a decade after she'd left middle school behind.

"People were talking about gang-raping me," she later told me. "People are so angry. They're holding on to so much hurt."

I BEGAN MY research for this book by interviewing people who had middle school stories to tell and wanted to get them off their chests. I spoke with adults because I was interested in taking the long view, learning how the past lived on in the present, and I also wanted to benefit from the kind of information that middle schoolers themselves can't provide contemporaneously: What was going on with them and in their families at the time their middle school dramas played out? What did adults do well or badly? What insights could we all glean from their stories, given the passage of time?

I also wanted to understand what I thought of as "middle school in our minds"—the web of memories, ideas, and images that uphold the belief so many of us share that the middle school years are, have always been, and will always be a time of utter and complete wretchedness. Over the course of about two years, I spoke at length with almost 125 men and women—experts and educators, parents and non-parents—from all across the United States and a number of other nations, from a wide variety of backgrounds, and ranging in age from their early 20s to their early 60s.

I wanted to learn what people heard in the words "middle school" or "junior high" and exactly what they meant when they said things like "It's seventh grade all over again." One thing I did know, from the experience of having been a parent of an 11-to-14-year-old, was that they weren't necessarily talking about actual middle schoolers. And I quickly saw that the institution of middle school itself was something that loomed much larger than the reality of squat, sprawling buildings and ill-smelling lunchrooms. It was a place in the mind. For many adults, the middle school years contained the equivalent of a "primal scene"—only rather than being something that they had seen and couldn't forever after un-see, the primal element was a feeling that, once experienced, couldn't be un-felt.

That feeling—the middle school feeling—was one of excruciating awkwardness, painful self-consciousness, and crippling insecurity in the face of harsh and unforgiving peer judgment; a sense of being alone, on the outside, and unacceptable. At its most benign, this was the "unjoined" feeling that overcame Carson McCullers's Frankie in *The Member of the Wedding,* unmoored in her 12-year-old summer, when she "belonged to no club and was a member of nothing in the world." At its most awful, it was a "primal wound," as the journalist Peggy Orenstein, who has returned to middle school over and over again in her writing, described it to me. It was "a clutch of nausea," in the words of the novelist Ayelet Waldman, who detailed the ostracism she endured in junior high in her 2009 memoir, *Bad Mother,* and told me that her tormentors routinely show up, in various forms, in her fiction.

Middle school was "regularly scheduled torture" for Miley Cyrus (the epitome of young teen perfection when my daughter was in middle school), who wrote in her memoir, *Miles to Go,* of having spent her last year of pre-stardom in an all-too-normal Nashville sixth grade, where she was incessantly harassed by a three-bully brigade of "mean girl" classmates. For a great many of the men and women I interviewed for this book, middle school was a time of being shunned and humiliated. Of being "rated" on their faces and bodies. Of being victims of "I hate [YOUR NAME HERE]" clubs, or of being singled out—and then perhaps singling out others—for "Flavor of the Month" rejection and torment.

For them, as was the case for me, it was a time of being in, then being out, from one day to the next, with no explanation and no prior warning (*You know what you did!*), an absolutely terrifying experience that one 36-year-old analyst for a Fortune 500 company recalled to me as having been "total napalm" for her developing psyche. "I went from a happy, extroverted, confident, type A little kid . . ." she said, trailing off as she recalled the point in seventh grade when a few girls who had been her friends turned everyone in the school against her for reasons that were never made clear. "There were all these things I could have done and could have been, but then I was just destroyed."

Even when their stories were more banal—no bullying or ostracizing, but the much more common "daily casual cruelty," as a Florida magazine writer told me, people still recalled that time of life as characterized by, above all, an unshakable feeling of misery that remained as distinct and haunting and *present* to them in adulthood as it had been in middle school or junior high. The effects of that particular misery were incredibly long-lasting. A 28-year-old graduate student in Texas recalled how she turned herself inside out to join a popular clique—buying Abercrombie and American Eagle clothes that her family couldn't afford, hiding the fact that her mother was Mexican, snorting powdered candy from a striped paper Pixy Stix up her nose—only to be repeatedly dropped by the clique because she was "annoying." To be called "annoying" was an existential condemnation so shape-shifting and mysterious ("I wish I knew what it means. To this day, I don't think I know," the woman told me) that she felt she had no choice but to remake herself down to the bone: "to be perfect and better and pretty and skinnier," paying penance for her "annoying" attributes by forbidding herself to eat on certain days in eighth grade.

The middle school feeling, many of the adults I spoke to agreed, was one of being "less than," "totally other than," "like an alien"—all in all, like you were just not "who you were supposed to be," as the woman from Florida said. She had spent sixth, seventh, and eighth grades in a small middle school where she felt unacceptably different—a "straight-edged good girl . . . somebody who loved school and was a big nerd, would rather be sitting quietly in a corner reading a book than doing anything else"—and was completely at odds with the "cool girls" and "superjocks" who ruled the roost with their talk of concerts and parties, money and clothes. "In my deepest, darkest moments, that's what I go back to," she said. "Feeling so other and not even being able to put my finger on why."

The middle school feeling was "a visceral ache." Feeling "ugly and irrelevant and gross." A "long string of undifferentiated dark days and feeling just alone and abandoned"—as a D.C. lawyer in her late 40s captured the two years of misery that followed when her parents suddenly decided to take her out of a small Jewish day school and put her in an exclusive, WASP-y girls' private school instead. There, overweight, unathletic, wearing unpreppy Danskins, bearing the secrets of a home where her father ran from creditors and her mother suffered in silence, she co-existed in total and complete (if polite) isolation with girls who had names like Missy, had fathers who owned banks, had alligator shirts and Fair Isle sweaters in every conceivable color, and were taking classes together to prepare for cotillion. "My parents took me out of a warm small pond and put me into a big cold ocean," she recalled, in a statement that conveyed the feeling, for many, of the transition into middle or junior high school, even under far less dramatic circumstances. "I was really depressed. I cried every day. I often wished I was dead."

THE SENSE OF not belonging, not fitting in, not looking good, not being acceptable—being outside the fellowship of the "we" that can even include family—is what I came to think of as the essence of the middle school feeling. That feeling could take different forms for different people, according to who they were, where they came from, and how they lived. But, at base, it was the sense of their wrongness. The categories of wrongness—hair, race, sexual orientation, type of neighborhood, type of family, type of shoes—differed in magnitudes of objective importance, of course. But it was, and is, one of the peculiarities of the middle school passage that absolutely minor details could and can feel like life-or-death issues. Feeling at odds with themselves and their families, finding they'd grown apart from a childhood friend, simply having their growth spurt two or three years after everybody else in their class, all these things could and can very easily add up to feeling like the *wrong sort of person,* not just externally, but on the inside as well.

In many adults' memories, middle school was the time when the relative insouciance of childhood came crashing to an end: an existential fall from grace in which they first began to see their parents for who they were, see their family in terms of where they placed, and see themselves as they imagined themselves to be in the eyes of other people. It was the point when they developed the social identity that the early-twentieth-century sociologist Charles Horton Cooley once labeled the "looking-glass self." (Except that, in early adolescence, as the psychologist and bestselling author Madeline Levine once noted, the only looking glass that matters is "the mirror of their peers.")

These heightened powers of social perception did not lead to happy things. In fact, many of the adults I spoke with described their new awareness as sheer hell. Boys and girls who were basically all right with themselves discovered, in middle school, that they were anything *but* okay. A 35-year-old New Orleans sociologist recalled becoming aware, in sixth grade, that her thick glasses, crooked teeth, eccentric clothing, and penchant for reading through recess were no longer "cute" but "dorky." A professor whose mother had insisted that he skip the fifth grade sort of floated around in sixth, focusing only on doing well in school and pleasing his teachers. He woke up socially in seventh grade to discover that he was a hopeless loser—and that there was nothing he could do to change that. Stuck with "nerd friends," with whom he had nothing in common other than their status at the bottom of the class, he tried to find others, just as the "enforcers of the hierarchy" decided to double down on showing him where he belonged. The result, he told me, was two solid years of having his books knocked out of his arms, of "flat tires" and "wedgies," of being called (of course) a "faggot," and of games of dodgeball and "smear the queer" that left him bruised and bleeding.

Seeing parents through a new set of eyes could be just as painful. In his 2004 memoir, *My Life,* Bill Clinton wrote of having gone through a "major spiritual crisis" at age 13, when he mentally confronted the reality of being the stepson of an abusive alcoholic: "Some of what came into my head and life scared the living hell out of me, including anger at Daddy, the first stirrings of sexual feelings toward girls, and doubts about my religious convictions, which I think developed because I couldn't understand why a God whose existence I couldn't prove would create a world in which so many bad things happened." A San Francisco therapist told me of how the junior high years had brought a new awareness of the enormous—and ugly—power imbalance between her mother and father. "It put the period at the end of the sentence of my childhood," she said. Other adults recalled how the gift of greater mental acuity at age 12 or 13 had led to the unwanted realization that, in some ways, they were actually more grown-up than their parents. They'd suddenly been able to see, for example, if a parent's behavior was inappropriate—as when parents created family dramas worthy of cliquey seventh graders or over-shared, turning their junior high schoolers into newfound "best friends."

In her 2016 memoir, *The Girl with the Lower Back Tattoo*, the actor and comedian Amy Schumer painted one such scene, describing the "heavy brainwashing" by her mother that made its way into the journal she kept at age 13, during her parents' divorce. For example: "After the first five years that my parents were married my mom realized she wasn't in love and never had been." Jean, a Rhode Island educator I interviewed, spoke of the damage she suffered when her parents' marriage started breaking up, her mother started drinking, her father started sleeping around, and she found herself, at age 12, cooking and providing afterschool care for her four younger siblings, and comforting her mother on the nights when her father stormed out. She'd become her mom's confidante and the bearer of secrets for the whole family. All that was "shattering," she told me. "I went straight from childhood to adult knowledge and responsibility."

Once they developed a social sense of self with, above all, an awareness of how they looked to others, the people I spoke with weren't able to shake it. The opinions of peers, real or imagined, spoke to them incessantly, criticizing them, insulting them, exhorting them to do, look, and *be* better. Finding success with the popular crowd didn't necessarily confer protection from this sort of self-criticism. In fact, it could bring an even greater need for constant vigilance. A 24-year-old from St. Louis recalled the regimen of nonstop self-monitoring she imposed on herself as a member of her school's most popular (and notoriously mean) clique, starting in sixth grade. Every single night, she recalled, she lay awake in bed, going over her day in her mind, reviewing her every action, and thinking about ways that she might have done better. "I was almost obsessed with it, with my relationships with people," she remembered. "Whether I'd made anyone upset and done anything that hadn't gotten a positive reaction . . . thinking about how I could be better tomorrow with a boy. Or cooler tomorrow."

In the late 1960s, the child psychologist David Elkind likened this state of being to living life as a performance before an "imaginary audience" of alternately jeering and cheering critics. He also coined a phrase that to this day seems to me to perfectly capture the very specific nature of middle school self-consciousness. Young adolescents, he wrote, always feel alone in their suffering ("No one understands!") even though just about everyone else feels—or once felt—the exact same way. Elkind called that universally shared sense of being "special and unique" the "personal fable."

The stories adults told me were unique in their details and yet remarkably similar in their themes. Like my own story—and just like the dramas still playing out among middle schoolers today—there were accounts of friendships that abruptly ended in needlessly brutal ways, of ostracism, of bizarre rivalries and competition, and sometimes of incomprehensible meanness. These were crushing experiences, the pain of which, for many, had never really gone away.

For gay adults I interviewed, middle school was the time when, even if their sexual orientation wasn't yet clear to them, they realized that they were in some way profoundly different. And that difference—directly expressed or not—at the time of life when demands for conformity are the most extreme, was a huge social liability. For Mitch, it was a big barrier to acceptance by the popular boys: "I couldn't participate in talking about girls authentically," he said. And for Jean, the Rhode Island educator, who later came out as a lesbian, not being able to pull off a mainstream version of femininity had meant being completely on the outside starting in sixth grade, when the whole class split by sex: "There was the boys' side and the girls' side, and I was at the bottom of the pack and was bullied."

Black adults I spoke with told me that their feelings of difference had long predated middle school, and that the negative messages they received about themselves had begun much earlier, too. For some, this meant that they viewed at the time—and still viewed—the typical social and personal "dramas" of middle school as white people problems, far more dumb than devastating. "By the time I was nine, I was already dealing with people calling me the N-word," Tina, an African American consultant in Washington, D.C., who grew up in the South, told me. "By middle school, I didn't care about the other stuff that was coming at me." Other adults of color, however, felt somewhat differently. They had the same in-or-out, up-or-down social issues as their white classmates, they said, but there was always one additional variable thrown into the mix: a conscious awareness of race that simply didn't factor into the white kids' self-perceptions.

For some, that racial awareness was like the wind at their backs, propelling them to try to fit in as seamlessly as possible in the world of their white classmates. In a 2011 episode of the public radio program *This American Life* devoted to the topic of middle school, the author Domingo Martinez provided an ultra-extreme example of this, sharing a story drawn from his memoir, *The Boy Kings of Texas*. He told of how his sisters, Mary and Margie, had dealt with the insecurities of entering junior high in Brownsville, Texas—a place, he noted, that was "tinged with border town racism" in the mid-1980s—by reinventing themselves as Valley Girl–like personas they called "The Mimis."

The family had fallen on hard times, but that didn't stop the Mimis, who, Martinez noted, "had made their decision to be two, blue-blooded, trust-funded tennis buddies from Connecticut accidentally living in Brownsville, Texas, with us, a poor Mexican family they had somehow befriended while undergoing some Dickensian series of misfortunes." They dyed their hair blond. Their need for a designer wardrobe ate up the family's entire clothing budget. "It was really that simple," Martinez wrote. "The Mimis made a conscious decision that they would be rich and white, even if their family wasn't. In other words, Marge and Mary had a small break from reality that we all participated in to help them through junior high."

In some less out-there examples they shared with me, adults of color who'd succeeded in fitting into their majority-white middle schools spoke of being hypervigilant about making sure they had the right clothes and did the right activities in the right company. Amita, a political consultant in her late 30s, said that in the fourth grade, her mother, a recent immigrant, made the mistake of putting her in the "loser car pool." Amita fixed that fast, and by sixth grade she had progressed from the "cool kids' car pool" to the top of the popular crowd. Karen, a black woman who grew up wealthy in a white suburb and attended a private girls' school, had been a leader among the highest-status girls in her class. As an adult—a former seventh- and eighth-grade teacher turned head of a Massachusetts middle school—she looked back with some shame on the fact that she'd been one of the strictest enforcers of the rules of hierarchy and social desirability: who was in, who was out, who was mocked, who got to sit at her table at lunch, whose belongings were dumped out of their L.L.Bean tote bags onto the floor.

"As one of the few girls of color in my private school, that was my survival tactic," she said.

Both Amita and Karen had the basic components of popularity in place—money, athletic prowess, and good looks that kicked in early, while most of their classmates were still looking awkward. Kids who were just different without those markers of power and prestige had a much harder time. Tracy, a black media executive, grew up in an almost all-white, upper-middle-class neighborhood in Washington, D.C. Her parents—an English professor and his wife, a stay-at-home mother of six with a master's degree—had been the first, and for a very long time the only, African American homeowners in their immediate area. They had experienced a tremendous amount of racism from their white neighbors when they first moved into their home in the early 1960s, and then, after the 1968 riots, had feared white reprisals. After Tracy's father suddenly passed away, the family became socially and economically isolated from the city's black elite as well. They had to navigate layer upon layer of being the "wrong" kind of people, she told me—all of which had come to a head for her personally when she began junior high.

Like her elementary school, the junior high was located just a few blocks from Tracy's home. It was huge, and by the 1970s, years of busing and white flight meant that the majority of the students came from low-income "out of boundary" neighborhoods far across town. Even the teachers, Tracy noted wryly, were said to have been "bused" up from North Carolina after most of the white faculty had fled to the suburbs.

For the first time, Tracy had almost all-black classmates. And, for the first time, she was drawn into social drama. She was bullied by black kids who were richer than her, "because I was poor . . . [and] I had one parent and I didn't go to the clubs and I couldn't swim—all the things that showed you were a middle-class black person and had certain things behind you." And she was bullied by those who were poorer: It was "complete intimidation," she said. "Middle school, no matter where you are, is really about social rank. And social ranking happens everywhere," she continued. "It just becomes more complex when you slap class and race on top of it."

THERE WERE EXCEPTIONS to all these unhappy experiences, of course. In Amita's case, the mirror of her peers brought her extremely positive feedback once she hit middle school. "Everything came together," she told me. "I got contacts, the braces came off. I felt like my hair looked good. I was still super-skinny. I had an older sister with really awesome clothes I used to steal all the time." Seventh and eighth grade were a time not of social alienation but of plenitude for her. "I felt like I was in control of what I did and what everyone else did," she said.

What about the kids who were outside the circle of "everyone"? I asked out of curiosity, having ascertained that "everyone" was really about fifty people, with a core group of ten, out of a class of two hundred.

"I literally have no idea," she replied. "I don't even know who they were. They weren't into sports, they were nerdy, more socially awkward, not as attractive." She added, however, that she, too, had eventually come in for her share of social struggle. It had just come later. "I felt like I was at my social peak in eighth grade, and that sort of went down until high school graduation," she said. That pattern, a D.C.-area child psychologist later told me, is quite typical of popular girls: "They get to tenth grade, and the meanness or whatever behaviors they used to maintain their popularity don't work anymore," she said. "So they have a crisis and they come to me." A similar drop-off in popularity happens to "cool" boys by their early 20s as well.

A small but vocal minority of people I spoke with had actually found happiness in middle school, for reasons that had nothing to do with popularity. Miranda, a Westchester woman who, as the eldest of six siblings, had always been first in line when it came to suffering the effects of her parents' narcissism and unhappiness, told me of how she was made additionally miserable in her stuffy and snobby private elementary school, where she struggled with undiagnosed learning difficulties and was frequently mocked by classmates and teachers alike. The kids made snide comments about her unwashed and wrinkled uniforms. Her fourth-grade teacher showed up one day in her sixth-grade classroom to "borrow" her to demonstrate to the younger students how *not* to write. She felt "incredibly lost," she told me, both academically and socially. "I was one of those girls who got picked on because I didn't understand how the world worked. I didn't get social groups," she said. But she managed, for seventh grade, to convince her parents to send her to another school. It had a diverse student body, valued out-of-the-box thinking, and didn't care about perfect handwriting. "I fell in love with school," she recalled. "It was what kind of saved me."

Such stories were particularly notable because they were so rare. For most of the people I interviewed, the junior high or middle school years had simply been the worst of the worst: a time of unforgettable, scarring moments; of ways of thinking and feeling and being that most would have much preferred never to have experienced. As the man who skipped fifth grade put it, middle school possessed "some kind of magical quality of misery and suffering."

"All this, we never get over it," the woman who'd wished for death in her girls' prep school told me.

ONE OF THE most fascinating and curious things that I found in my interviews was that the "personal fable" quality of many people's middle school stories had survived into adulthood largely intact. The adults I spoke with believed—as had I for much of my life—that their experiences of shunning or ostracism or being "dumped" by a friend were indeed "special and unique" to them. I don't mean to say that they were self-aggrandizing. On the contrary, often accompanying the long-remembered pain was a residual feeling of shame, as though some part of them still believed that they had caused whatever mistreatment they suffered. Some seemed to be carrying the old taint of rejection forward—unless, like the woman who'd spent years fighting her way out of the mental yoke of "annoying," they'd had lots of therapy (as many had). Some cried while telling me their stories—and then beat themselves up for doing so.

After speaking to me by phone, the Rhode Island educator realized that in her eagerness to share her experiences—they might, she hoped, help educate parents so that future 12-year-olds wouldn't go through similar things—she had inadvertently triggered her PTSD. In the future, she told me, she would have to prepare herself and be mindful of how big a dose of memory she could comfortably bear. "I cannot open those boxes casually, or it really blows up on me," she said.

I found myself regularly telling people—men and women alike—who apologized in embarrassment when they were overcome by tears that they were in very good company, both in terms of what they had gone through and in the intensity of the pain their stories still caused them today. And it was true: For just about everyone I spoke with, there was something about those middle school experiences that seemed to reach right down to the very core of their being. Sometimes it seemed to them that what had happened in middle school had been a kind of preview of, or template for, life patterns to come.

Adults who went on to later be diagnosed with anxiety disorders or depression realized, in retrospect, that middle school had been the time of the first serious flare-up of their illness. The girl who felt like she'd gone through middle school with a big A on her chest for "annoying" went on to have friendships in high school and college that were similarly rejecting, and even as a young woman fell under the spell of a psychologically and sexually abusive boyfriend. "I felt like there was something wrong with me because I had been rejected," she said. "It was like my punishment to myself."

Some people were aware that even much later, into adulthood, they were still grappling with their old middle school feeling. It would get triggered when they found themselves in situations where, for whatever reason, they felt on the outside and not quite good enough. For some women, this happened in book club: "I was in a book group for twenty-seven years. For the first fifteen years, even though I was one of the charter members, I felt like I didn't belong," one recalled. For other people, like Mitch, the middle school feeling came back when they were caught in a universe they couldn't control, had to spend the bulk of their days in the company of peers they didn't particularly like, or were dependent for their most basic sense of well-being upon the whims of powerful and frequently not-so-nice people, often at work. And for many men and women alike, the middle school feeling came upon them when they entered the two-generational vortex of social and academic pressure that parenting, particularly in middle- and upper-middle-class communities, has become. Thrown into a world where everyone was competing through their kids, and where the kids themselves were being ranked by the very same markers of status that had held sway a generation earlier in junior high—money, good looks, athleticism (important just for boys back in the day, a must-have for everyone now), and, of course, that eternally magical element of popularity-conferring "it-ness"—

parents found themselves thrown back into states of misery that they consistently described as "middle school all over again."

PART OF WHAT made middle school so tough for so many people was that, at 11, 12, or 13, there was a huge gap between their powers of observation and their capacity for understanding. As junior high students or middle schoolers, they hadn't yet lived enough to be able to put their disturbing new perceptions into context or perspective. They didn't yet know that *all* families are "weird"; that many people suffer from mental illness and addiction. They might not even have been introduced to concepts like mental illness and addiction. When it came to making sense of themselves and those around them, they were largely stuck with the words and ideas that adults had given them—which, often enough, were just as harsh and judgmental, fearful and "middle-schoolerish," as their own. That is as true today as it has ever been. And it's a big part of the reason why smart, sensitive, and perceptive kids continue to have such a tough time in the middle school years.

Many of us shift into a kind of autopilot when we're around middle schoolers. They set us off, particularly if our own kids are at risk of getting hurt, and we start taking our cues from some very old scripts. Those scripts aren't just based on our own experiences. As a culture, we share a big story as well, made up of all those books and movies and news reports that, particularly in recent decades, have driven home the idea that middle school is an absolute horror show. Those stories tell us that no matter how much awkwardness or outright pain we remember from early adolescence, middle school today is much worse: Middle schoolers are growing up faster, they're in more danger, and thanks to new technology they're doing things we not only don't know about but also can't even begin to imagine. Some depict middle schoolers as practically a new breed of human: seemingly shameless and even—I came upon this word repeatedly when talking to parents—"sociopathic." *(The Slender Man stabbing!)*

This cultural narrative, with ever-updating details, has been in circulation for many decades. In fact, for as long as most of us can remember, we've invested kids of middle school age with a hefty dose of dislike, prurient fascination, and disapproval. But it wasn't always this way.

CHAPTER 2

When Familiarity Bred Contempt

The parents of 13-year-old Caitlin Teagart have decided to end
her life, saying she can now do nothing but lay on the couch
and whine about things being "gay."

— "Brain-Dead Teen, Only Capable of Rolling Eyes
and Texting, to Be Euthanzied," *The Onion*

MIDDLE-SCHOOL-AGE CHILDREN WERE not always thought of as obnoxious, horrible, cruel, sociopathic, or even extremely annoying. In fact, through much of our history, they weren't thought about in any particular way at all.

There were no middle schoolers before there were middle schools, which there were not in the United States until the 1960s. (The first junior high, the grade 7–9 predecessor of the grade 6–8 middle school, opened its doors in 1909.) And the notion that the middle school (or junior high) years constituted their own distinct phase of life—"early adolescence," or the years around puberty—really did not catch on until the 1970s.

The reality of puberty—the stage at which a person arrives at reproductive maturity (a girl's first period; a boy's first ejaculation)—has, of course, always existed. So, too, has the reality of adolescence as the period of time between when puberty occurs and when young men and women are ready to live independently of their parents and have children of their own. But these milestones haven't always happened at the ages at which they now occur, and they haven't always been seen and understood in the same ways.

In the American colonies and early United States, the physical hardships of life were so great that the average age of menarche (first period) at the turn of the nineteenth century was about 17, with boys, then as now, going through puberty about eighteen months to two years later. Unlike today, however, the arrival of puberty was seen as a very welcome thing. Even if young men and women didn't marry soon after (and many did not—economics trumped biology and frequently caused young men to have to wait until their late 20s before they were capable of supporting a family), puberty did bring other benefits to young people's parents. Once teenage boys and girls had gone through their growth spurts, they were able to do an adult's load of work, whether in the fields or in the home. They became fully productive members of their households.

And until the mid-nineteenth century, the years leading up to puberty were economically productive. Childhood in colonial America and the early Republic was short and not so sweet, and by age 11 it was usually over. Puritan children started doing their share of housework at age 6 or 7; by 11 or 12 they could be sent to live and work outside their homes as servants or apprentices—an arrangement that allowed parents to save on food and free up space for more children. Children continued being placed outside their homes to work as apprentices, farmhands, or domestic servants well into the early nineteenth century, with the result being that, by the time they hit puberty, they were often no longer entirely dependent upon their parents.

Until the 1850s and 1860s, only the wealthiest young people stayed in school past the age of 12 or 13. Many children, especially in rural areas, attended school only sporadically and left once they'd mastered the basics of reading and writing, usually around age 11. Boys in farm families who were officially enrolled in school were in reality pulled out for much of the year to work in the fields. When they went back to their one-room schoolhouses, where student seating was organized by academic level rather than by age, they often found themselves sitting elbow to elbow with little girls—a humiliation that hardly enhanced their motivation to remain longer than was strictly necessary.

Even wealthy children often lived apart from their parents for much of the year by the time they were the age of today's middle schoolers. Many well-off families sent their 11-to-14-year-olds away to boarding school—a practice that was particularly common in the antebellum South, where wealthy white planters became especially eager to put as much distance as possible between their own children and those of the people they enslaved, starting when their sons and daughters turned 10. Through the mid-nineteenth century, smart wealthy boys who had gone to school or worked uninterruptedly with tutors could leave home to enroll in college at age 12 or 13.

Enterprising boys from less-affluent families could enter some trades at this age. Firefighters, for example, often began work as boys in the mid-1800s. There were teenagers as young as 13 in the Confederate army; a 12-year-old, Johnny Walker, served as a drummer boy in the Twenty-second Wisconsin Regiment; and in his *Personal Memoirs,* Ulysses S. Grant bragged that he started working in the fields after he turned 11, when he was "strong enough to hold a plow." Though girls in the early to mid-nineteenth century did not start trades or professions like boys, they did begin to serve a productive role in their own households or in those of other families at similarly young ages.

Until the second half of the nineteenth century, there really was no opportunity, then, for young people to have what we think of now as the middle school phase of life: a period of time that's spent mostly in school, torturing or being tortured by peers, or at home, feeling miserable and making parents pay by behaving miserably, too. Kids who today would be middle schoolers weren't around their parents enough to cause them real problems. Nor did they have enough time in the exclusive company of their same-age peers to do real damage. Instead of being at home with parents or at school with friends, most of them were at work.

All of this changed, however, as the United States adjusted to two revolutions that permanently altered the worlds of work and family life, and the landscape of childhood in particular. One was industrialization, which opened up new realms of possibility for young people and ambitious parents who were eager to see their children's social standing rise. And the other was a profoundly new way of seeing children and thinking about childhood, which held that children should no longer be viewed as wicked creatures in dire need of godly discipline—as in the age of the Puritans—and should instead be thought of as pure innocents: "blank slates" whose thoughts and deeds, with proper instruction, would lead in the direction of virtue. Childhood, for the first time, was conceived of as a time of learning, play, and at-home protection. Both these developments sent parents the very same message: If they wanted to save their children's souls *and* secure their futures, they needed to keep them out of work and in school. Both had the concrete effect of extending the period during which parents and children lived under the same roof. Both greatly elevated and intensified the role of middle-class mothers, who for the first time were charged both with making sure their children stayed on track to accomplish their worldly goals (in work or marriage) and with maintaining the purity of their homes and of those living in them.

Out of that new closeness, in a burst of mutual irritation, the child we now know as the modern middle schooler was born.

In the decades after the Civil War, the industrial revolution kicked into high gear. It moved America's economic life from farms to factories, relocated masses of workers from rural towns to big cities, and created a new middle class of independent professionals, businessmen, and clerks. It moved work completely out of the household for middle-class families and led to a new ideal of the home as a sheltered, separate, and almost sacred space of peace, harmony, and parent-child good feeling.

Class status in the preindustrial world had, by and large, been fixed at birth and transmitted directly from parents to their children through, for example, landholdings, the practice of a trade, or an arranged marriage. With industrialization, all that started to change. New possibilities for social mobility became available based on education—for boys, at least, if they stayed in school into their early teens and acquired the education necessary for office or professional work. There were new sorts of class anxiety as well. Middle-class status, based on education and income, had to be re-earned with each new generation. To maintain it, children had to be trained—socialized and educated—to keep up with the demands of rapidly changing times.

Ages 12 to 14, then, became a decisive turning point in the lives of boys in particular—a moment when their destinies were largely set, either to work in the fields, enter a factory as an unskilled laborer, or stay in school and lay the groundwork for a middle-class future. Girls' destinies were not a matter of choice. Yet they, too, arrived at a crucial point of self-definition at puberty, in that the requirements of being, appearing, and remaining "chaste" and pure (i.e., being a desirable eventual partner in marriage) began to give shape to what was possible in their lives. For most middle-class girls, that meant far less freedom. From one day to the next, sisters who'd grown up playing freely outdoors with their brothers were now confined to the safety of adult supervision, almost exclusively at home. The demands of seeming a desirable mate could also mean less school. In the late nineteenth century, with girls outperforming boys in school so dramatically that they outnumbered them in public high schools by two to one, concerned physicians started issuing sterner and sterner warnings that too much education was dangerous for a girl's delicately developing reproductive system. Starting at puberty, girls were instructed to step back, scale down their activities, and focus on calmly preparing their bodies for fruitful procreation.

Even the safety of home could prove risky, however. Middle-class girls might not have been directly mixing with the treacherous working-class "youth" (as those over 14 were then collectively called) who were milling around on city streets, unmoored from their homes and the sharp-eyed adults who formerly had kept watch over them in small rural communities. But, advice writers warned, they were nonetheless extremely vulnerable to bad companions who could corrupt them with unchaste ideas. They could get involved in intense same-sex friendships that crossed the line between innocence and "unnatural" sin. And idleness was the Devil's playground, particularly in the years around puberty. In December 1887, an unsigned article in *Ladies' Home Journal*, "Concerning Some of the Pitfalls of the Way of Home Life in America," warned affluent readers not to entertain a false sense of security regarding their seemingly sheltered offspring. Middle-class urban youth's "lack of occupation at home and too much freedom for pleasure-seeking out in the streets," it said, was leading them to outright "decadence." (Ever unacknowledged, as the Emory University historian Mary Odem has noted, was the fact that the greatest sexual threat facing girls and young women came from their own male relatives.)

What all this meant was that the period of time we now think of as the middle school years started to be viewed as an utterly critical passage that parents (read: mothers) had to get *just right.* In his 1829 advice manual, *Lectures to Young Men,* for example, the Connecticut pastor Joel Hawes referred to the years around puberty as "pre-eminently . . . the forming, fixing period. . . . It is during this season, more than any other, that the character assumes its permanent shape and color." Other writers actually used terms that are strikingly similar to those used by teen brain experts today—words like "pliant" and "plastic"—in warning of the extreme potential for lifelong corruption that could come in those supersensitive and vulnerable "formative" years.

What was at stake wasn't just keeping boys and girls on track so that they might find worthy vocations and make good marriages; it was also securing children's overall moral salvation. For if the defining quality of childhood had come to be innocence, "most particularly sexual innocence," as the Temple University historian Beth Bailey has written, then the arrival of puberty could pose an existential threat if it began at an age that was considered part of childhood. And that's precisely what happened over the course of the nineteenth century. As the decades passed, the age of puberty dropped, and kept dropping so rapidly that, in the second half of the century, the average age of menarche declined one full year every thirty years, falling from just over age 15 in 1850 to 14 in 1880 to 13 by 1910.

The cause was innocent enough, even fortuitous: more and better food and, for middle-class girls, a lack of physical labor. (Working-class girls, particularly those living in isolated mountain regions, the historian Jane H. Hunter has noted, did not see this kind of rapid change.) But no matter the reason, panicked parents, physicians, and moralists of all stripes saw the age decrease as a sign of ambient sin—a new sexual precocity that was creeping from the streets of the nation's teeming urban centers into the homes of its most upright and commendable citizens.

One of the most visible, and often risible, forms this new anxiety took was a heightened concern with masturbation. In the second half of the nineteenth century, books, articles, and pamphlets from physicians, ministers, and professional moralists warning about the dangers of masturbation proliferated. Some cautioned that "onanism" could lead to the dispersal of the "energies," both male and female, that needed to be saved for procreation in marriage. Others linked masturbation to a wide spectrum of disastrous physical and mental consequences.

The physician John Harvey Kellogg, director of a Seventh-Day Adventist sanitarium in Battle Creek, Michigan (and brother of the better remembered Will Kellogg, who lent his name to the brothers' cereal venture), was particularly prolific on this subject. In an 1881 book, *Plain Facts for Old and Young* (a more chastely titled reissue of his enormously successful 1877 work, *Plain Facts About Sexual Life*), he devoted many frightening pages to the evils of the "solitary vice," invoking dwarves and "idiots" worthy of the "insane asylum" as figures to dissuade young readers from indulging in the "unnatural and abominable" habit of "self-abuse." In one particularly horrifying case study, he told of "Two Young Wrecks—Charles and Oscar B," who'd been brought by their desperate mother from their family farm out west for a stay at his clinic. Once possessed of "well-formed heads" and "beautiful faces . . . as bright and sprightly as any little boys of their age to be found anywhere," the boys had been reduced by their masturbatory habits to a "nearly helpless" state. They "reeled and staggered about like drunken men, falling down upon each other and going through the most agonizing contortions in their attempts to work their way from one chair to another and thus about the room," Kellogg wrote. "On their faces was a blank, imbecile expression, with a few traces of former intelligence still left. The mouth was open, from the drooping of the lower jaw, and the saliva constantly dribbled upon the clothing." Although Kellogg's staff tried to treat the boys and they briefly seemed to improve, in the end the doctors were forced to conclude that they were beyond medical help.

IN THEORY, THE ideal of childhood innocence and the call for its protection extended to all children. Reformers, aided by the spread of unions—which in the late nineteenth century put an end to apprenticeships for boys under age 14—pushed hard for legislation that would end child labor. They tried to protect children from adult sexual demands by campaigning to raise the legal age of consent, which in most states was set at an abominably low 10 or 12 until the 1880s. And they fought for compulsory school attendance laws.

In practice, however, the "child savers'" reforms really applied only to white middle-class kids. The vision of childhood purity and protection was never truly extended to African Americans. "Even the little child . . . before she is twelve years old . . . will become prematurely knowing in evil things," Harriet Jacobs, born a slave in North Carolina, wrote of the "acts inflicted by fiends who bear the shape of men," in her 1861 book, *Incidents in the Life of a Slave Girl*. "Soon she will learn to tremble when she hears her master's footfall," she wrote. "She will be compelled to realize that she is no longer a child."

Although the age of consent did start to rise, eventually reaching 16 or 18 in most states by 1920, such legislation was opposed throughout the South for fear of empowering black girls to bring rape charges against white men. Southern lawmakers adapted to this concern by wording their states' consent legislation in such a way that girls who were not of "previously chaste character" were exempted, because, as Beth Bailey writes, they knew that few black girls "would be presumed 'previously chaste' by white male juries." The age of consent stayed at 10 in Georgia until 1918, when it rose to 14, where it remained until the mid-1990s. The first compulsory education laws were so lax and, in the absence of adequate resources, so impossible to enforce that rural, working-class, and immigrant parents continued pulling their children out of school as needed until the 1930s. And African American children of all ages were deprived of public schooling long after the end of slavery.

Ironically, as is the case today, it was in the world of the white middle and upper middle classes—where children's lives were the safest and their education lasted the longest—that experts found their most avid consumers of books, pamphlets, and lectures about protecting childhood innocence and fighting outside "contagion." In part, this was a reflection of who had the time, resources, and education to devote to such reading and listening. But it was also a sign that middle-class mothers really needed some help. Saddled with a souped-up level of responsibility for monitoring and controlling their older children and young teens, they were becoming closely acquainted with all the disturbing changes of early adolescence—not just menstruation and wet dreams, but also mood swings, the angsty questioning of old certainties, and intellectual developments, like more independent and critical thinking, that directly called into question adult wisdom and authority.

This was not a recipe for family happiness. On the contrary, it brought a big uptick in parent-child conflict. Previously, the transitional phase between puberty and adulthood in America had been quite banal—"relatively unmarked by psychological traumas and personal crises," in the words of the scholars John Modell and Madeline Goodman. Or, at least, it had been relatively unmarked by traumas and crises involving a clash of wills between parents and children. Once children started living longer at home, and parents started focusing on their improvement more intensely, the "unconflicted passage through the teenage years," Modell and Goodman note, became a thing of the past, particularly when it came to sons and fathers.

Turn-of-the-century girls' and women's diaries show that mutual irritation was far from an all-male phenomenon. Edna Ormsby, the wife of a school principal in the suburbs of Chicago, kept a very detailed diary charting the life of her daughter, Esther, who was born in 1891. On the day of Esther's birth, Ormsby wrote that the baby was "perfect in every way." The years leading up to high school, however, were "a very trying time in her development." It was the period when Esther "did the least work and got into more mischief and gave [her mother] more trouble than ever in her life," Ormsby noted. "None of it very bad," the mother corrected herself, "but she was disorderly in her mental and personal habits." How little things have changed.

The new, extended, more emotionally enmeshed relationships between parents and their older children, combined with earlier puberty, more years of school, and more choices of future professional activity (again, for young men), created a whole new host of problems, above all for parents, in the period of their children's lives that would soon widely be known as adolescence. In fact, some scholars say that the combination of social and economic forces newly weighing on family life actually led to the "creation" of adolescence—not the actual phase of life, of course, but the phenomenon of obnoxious behavior, bad attitudes, and "raging hormones" that parents continue to complain about to this day. As the University of Texas childhood historian Steven Mintz has put it, "The term *adolescence* provided a handle that urban middle class parents used to understand the special difficulties they faced in raising teenage daughters and sons."

Out of all these tensions between opportunity and menace, ambition and perdition, the late-nineteenth-century version of what we know today as the "middle school" phase of life came into being. It was, at that point, essentially a parent-child affair. That is to say: the time in life when a (middle-class) boy or girl started the transition through puberty, made adults uncomfortable, and elicited in them a combination of regret (for childhood lost), ambition (for their future), anxiety (about everything), and, of course, annoyance.

Middle-class mothers knew how much was at stake in this critical moment of their children's upbringing. They were well aware of the supreme importance of their own influence in keeping their children morally and educationally on track. They were the most highly educated group of women in American history, many having attended high school and some even college. Eager to put their minds to work, and with servants to handle their housework and the more humdrum elements of childcare, they had plenty of time to ensure that their children transitioned out of childhood in the most propitious way. But when it came to understanding them, or even knowing how to help them, they were pretty much on their own.

The new medical specialty of pediatrics limited its focus to children under age 10. While some academics by the 1880s had started using the words "adolescent" and "adolescence" in their scholarship, the words hadn't yet made their way into common parlance. The moralistic reformers of the late nineteenth century were generally useless when it came to addressing the real-life problems of middle-class households. When male experts addressed mothers, they took a stern and scolding tone. Female "child savers" waxed rhapsodic about the joyful devotion of motherhood in vaporous terms that must have made the often annoyed or even angry mothers of real-life young teens feel terrible.

Worse still, expert opinion was often contradictory. Child welfare advocates preached the virtues of extended schooling, while (male) physicians warned that too much school could turn fertile girls into arid old maids and soften boys into sissies. A falling birth-rate among white, Protestant, middle- and upper-middle-class families, at a time of massive immigration to the United States by impoverished Catholics and eastern European Jews, was a great preoccupation of many social commentators and men of science. Theodore Roosevelt, notably, decried the trend as "race suicide."

Advice books and women's magazines were still filled with all but unreadable drivel on the heightened "temptations" of urban youth. But there were no clear indications from experts on what kind of education would make sense in the early adolescent years, or why the period around puberty was so uniquely perilous, or what, concretely and realistically, to do with pubescent kids to keep them on the right path and generally make life more pleasant for the whole household. There were no words in use, no com-monly agreed upon set of concepts to capture the unique experi-ence of going through (or parenting kids who were going through) the stage of life that soon would be called adolescence. And there was no real space yet in popular culture for stories of maternal frustration with no longer childlike older children, who, some critics were starting to say, were kind of rotting away in their modern lives of enforced leisure.

Indeed, a prominent women's magazine writer would much later reveal that it took her mother years and years to give herself permission to voice the enormous frustrations she'd felt parenting an adolescent girl at the turn of the century. And when she finally did, the then grown-up and married daughter, Alice D. Kelly, re-counted that it was "with a good deal of bitterness," pent up for decades. "She quoted verbatim my scathing remarks about her age and antediluvian ideas (she was then a pretty widow in the early thirties) before gentlemen who were calling on her," Kelly wrote of the encounter. "She spoke in tongues about the way it had aged her to think twice for three or four years every time she spoke to me lest I might weep or leave the room. She was eloquent about the lynx-like way in which I watched her when I had guests for fear she might disgrace me."

The time was right for some frank conversation.

So when a new wave of experts, members of the child study movement, started talking about child-rearing as a quasi-professional venture that even nonexperts could master by applying the latest "scientific" techniques, middle-class mothers proved an avid audience. They formed "study groups" and together began to read and discuss the latest books and articles on the burgeoning science of child development. One of their favorite authors was the psychologist G. Stanley Hall, who was soon to publish a very strange book that would help them make sense of the dust storms stirring inside their homes. At the very least, it would provide them with a new way to understand and label what had previously been a problem they could not name.

CHAPTER 3

The Hormone Monster Emerges

Psychoses and neuroses abound in early adolescent years more
than at any other period of life. This causes great emotional
strain, which some have described as a kind of repressed
insanity that is nevertheless normal at this period.

—G. STANLEY HALL, *Adolescence*

THE IDEA THAT there's something uniquely awful about middle
schoolers is now so taken for granted that it's hard to believe there
was ever a moment when adults didn't view them this way. But
the idea of 11-to-14-year-olds as obnoxious, nasty, and cruel is
really a turn-of-the-twentieth-century invention. Parents had to
spend sufficient time with their kids in order to find them that
unbearable. Young adolescents had to be around one another long
enough for the meanness we associate with the age to occur. And
a body of scientific knowledge about the normal and predictable
changes of puberty had to be built in order to justify the "raging

hormones" hypothesis. All those things happened in the decades around 1900. And they were conceptually pulled together by the work of one turn-of-the-century scientist: G. Stanley Hall.

In 1904, when Hall published his two-volume, 1,164-page magnum opus, *Adolescence: Its Psychology and Its Relations to Physiology, Anthropology, Sociology, Sex, Crime, Religion, and Education,* he was the founding president of Clark University. He'd been the first scholar in the United States to receive a doctorate in psychology, had occupied the first chair in psychology at Johns Hopkins University, had founded the first academic journal of psychology, and had pioneered the use of laboratory research methods in experimental psychology. He would go on to be the first and only American to impress Sigmund Freud enough to lure the Viennese psychoanalyst to U.S. shores, and would be known, long after his death, as both the father of child psychology and the creator of modern adolescence.

But he started life as a country boy, growing up on a series of farms in western Massachusetts, where he was involved from a very early age in the breeding of cattle, sheep, and horses. He learned about sex in this way, he later wrote, but had not found it very sexy. In school, he learned that the part of his body he'd always known as "the dirty place" had many more names, most of them terrible. By his mid-teens, he had heard of or witnessed every possible form of corruption known to schoolboys. As far as we can tell from his writing, he took no part, and he had very little contact with girls. But he did experience desire. Burning and awful desire. Puberty was torture.

Hall had been taught by his father that sexual feelings could bring lifelong disaster. "Self-abuse" or sin with a "lewd woman" could lead to catastrophic illness, in the course of which his nose might fall off. Wet dreams were a nightmare, nightfall a menace. The temptation of "self-experimentation" filled him with guilt and fear. In his earliest teen years, obsessed with controlling his desires and fearful of any evil actions he might take while asleep, he made himself a bandage-like contraption to wear each night. Unsurprisingly, this only made things worse.

Unsurprisingly, too, when this formerly agonizing pubescent boy took up his pen in midlife to write *the* book that would define what he called the "age of puberty" in the American imagination, his vision was a bit skewed. "Overdetermined," Sigmund Freud, who published his own thinking on adolescence at around the same time, might have called it. "Sex asserts its mastery in field after field," Hall wrote, "and works its havoc in the form of secret vice, debauch, disease, and enfeebled heredity, cadences the soul to both its normal and abnormal rhythms, and sends many thousand youth a year to quacks, because neither parents, teachers, preachers, or physicians know how to deal with its problems." He devoted a full nine dense and almost lurid pages to a description of the development of the sex organs. And he provided an extended discussion of the "evil" "perversion" of "onanism," noting that it could be triggered by a vast array of experiences, activities, and atmospheric conditions, ranging—and this is just an excerpt— from "idleness and laziness" to "springtime, which is a peculiarly dangerous season, warm climates, improper clothes, rich food, indigestion, mental overwork, nervousness, habits of defective cleanliness, especially of a local kind, prolonged sitting or standing, too monotonous walking, sitting cross-legged, spanking, late rising, petting and indulgence, corsets that produce stagnation or hyperemia of blood in the lower part of the body, [and] too great straining of the memory."

Despite his considerable achievements, to his contemporaries in the American academy, Hall himself was a bit of a quack and *Adolescence* something of a joke. "Chock full of errors, masturbation and Jesus" was the Columbia University psychologist Edward Thorndike's not-untypical appraisal of the book, which he termed the work of a "mad man." Other academics mocked Hall's writing style, deemed his Victorian flights of fancy old-fashioned, and for the most part rejected the theoretical framework on which he'd built his book—a variant of evolutionary theory known as "recapitulation," which held that the phases of human development embodied, or recapitulated, on an individual level, the evolution of the entire species, with adolescence representing a "savage" or "pigmoid" stage in our collective life history. Even Hall's undeniably impressive and extensive research—decades upon decades of German-, French-, and English-language readings in evolutionary theory, brain development, sleep studies, moral development, religion, education, physical and mental health, youth criminality, psychiatry, and, of course, pubertal change, plus a huge, first-of-its-kind questionnaire effort estimated to have reached 800 educators and 100,000 children—struck some as a symptom of a kind of mental imbalance. With it all, one contemporary judged, Hall appeared to have entered "the intellectual twilight zone between genius and insanity."

But the general public didn't care. Upon publication, *Adolescence* sold more than 25,000 copies—an enormous number for such a long and strange work, particularly at a time when relatively few Americans even had a high-school-level education. Its success, topped off by the publication a few years later of a heavily edited, condensed, and cleaned-up version, retitled *Youth,* made Hall the early-twentieth-century equivalent of a pop psychology superstar. "There is, perhaps, in America no one man who has made a more careful and painstaking study, extending over twenty years, of the adolescent period of boys and girls than has President Hall," *Ladies' Home Journal* gushed in 1907, before giving Hall a great deal of space in which to wake parents up to the near ubiquity of the "private vice" among their sons.

Mothers in the child study groups that had come collectively to be known as the parent education movement valued Hall's thinking so highly that they often wrote to him directly with their questions. Within just a few years, *Adolescence* had an enormous impact, not just on parents, but on educators and child welfare advocates, too. In fact, it's not an exaggeration to say that despite its occasional kookiness, Hall's book introduced the idea of adolescence that dominated the American mind for the rest of the twentieth century and has largely endured right up to the present day. He created the indelible image of a pubescent child who is disobliging, somewhat deranged, and kind of disgusting. In other words, he gave turn-of-the-century parents scientific validation for what they were already thinking but until that point had not dared say.

Hall's adolescents were besieged by highs and lows of "rapid fluctuations of mood." They were wretchedly self-conscious, confused and unmoored, and often obnoxiously rejecting of their parents' ideas and expectations (an "over-assertion of individuality," Hall called it). They were a mass of contradictions. Sometimes, in the grip of deep and dark thoughts and feelings, they appeared to have lost the ability to communicate—at least with their parents. At such times, Hall wrote, "the subject becomes dumb-bound, silent, and perhaps seems to brood, or the range of expression is very confined and narrow." Other times, however, they babbled away about absolute nonsense. "We often observe too an inverse ratio between thought and speech, so that as the former becomes scanty and indefinite the stream of words flows more copiously and smoothly," he pithily observed. Above all, adolescents were obsessed with their friends, to the point where some, he wrote, "seem for a time to have no resource in themselves, but to be abjectly dependent for their happiness upon their mates." And—in a depiction that will no doubt bring as many smiles from parents now as it did in the early twentieth century—many exhibited a curious commitment to expressing their "individuality" through utter conformity with their peers. "In this age, when everything is most uncertain," he wrote, "imitation reaches its acme."

Hall wasn't the first writer to depict the pubescent years as a swirl of contradictions and unsettledness. Highly educated adults would already have encountered a fictional version of his angsty adolescent in the late-eighteenth-century Sturm und Drang (storm and stress) novels of German Romantics like Johann Wolfang von Goethe or in the French philosopher Jean-Jacques Rousseau's 1762 book, *Emile,* which described the teen years as a "stormy revolution" or "new birth" that announced itself by the "murmuring of new-born passions" and ushered in a period of moodiness, hypersensitivity, and constant, uncomfortable change.

Earlier American authors, too, had captured the distinctive storms of feeling that Hall associated with these years. Increase Mather, the Puritan minister, wrote of having experienced a crisis of faith in the months right before he turned 16 that sounded a great deal like teen angst. "Very terrible convictions and awakenings" was how he described them: an "extremity of anguish and horror in my soul." The early-nineteenth-century parenting expert Isaac Taylor expressed the unique gloom of adolescence with the stark phrase "a tinge of melancholy pervades the mind," and the minister and social reformer Henry Ward Beecher put that inner drama into words as well: "He feels in his bosom the various impulses, wild desires, restless cravings he can hardly tell for what, a somber melancholy when all is gay, a violent exhilaration when others are sober."

In the late 1920s and early 1930s, the discovery of the sex hormones lent an even greater sense of scientific certainty to Hall's idea of puberty as a biologically based state of lunacy, driven by what came to be called "the glands." Psychoanalytic theory took over the child development field, and while the Freudians repudiated the kind of Victorian-era repression that underlay much of

Hall's sense of adolescent agony, the way that they thought about adolescence meshed perfectly with Hall's ideas. For Freud's daughter Anna, adolescence was a time of increased fighting with parents and of surging inner "conflict," deriving from the clash between biological "drives" and societal prohibitions—a completely normative kind of insanity. "The upholding of a steady equilibrium during the adolescent process is in itself abnormal" is how she once put it. She also wrote, "I take that it is normal for an adolescent to behave for a considerable length of time in an inconsistent and unpredictable manner, to fight his impulses and to accept them; to ward them off successfully and to be overrun by them; to love his parents and to hate them; to revolt against them and to be dependent on them; to be deeply ashamed to acknowledge his mother before others, and, unexpectedly, to desire heart-to-heart talks with her; to thrive on imitation of and identification with others while searching unceasingly for his own identity; to be more idealistic, artistic, generous, and unselfish than he will ever be again, but also the opposite: self-centered, egoistic, calculating."

As the early decades of the twentieth century advanced, American kids provided more and more proof for the idea that during puberty, they were destined to be normatively insane. That was undoubtedly because, in those very same decades, a majority of pubescent children in the United States began, for the first time, to spend most of their days together in school. Once they did, their bad qualities propagated like weeds—much to the dismay of the adults around them.

By THE FIRST decade of the twentieth century, middle-class American mothers and fathers had gotten the message loud and clear that the proper place for their older children was in school. But there was a big problem: The elementary schools, which contained grades K–8, were grossly overcrowded. And, by all accounts, the seventh and eighth grades were a disaster.

The curriculum was deathly boring, the teaching uninspired. Class time was spent on "wearisome and annoying repetition of subject matter and drill . . . a kind of intellectual busywork," in the words of the Illinois State Normal University professor Ralph W. Pringle, who trained teachers at the time. Unsurprisingly, the kids hated it—and many, particularly working-class or farm boys, still dropped out as fast as they could. One contemporary study estimated that in the years around 1900, only about 40 percent of children made it all the way to the end of elementary school, and after eighth grade there was huge attrition again, with only 27 percent of students continuing on to ninth grade and only 8 percent graduating from high school.

All of this, education reformers argued, needed to change. For 14-year-olds to be educated in the same building as 6-year-olds was infantilizing. The elementary schools' one-size-fits-all teaching materials and methods were completely unsuited to the fact that children ages 12 to 14 were at vastly different, and rapidly changing, levels of maturity. And the expectation that ninth graders could, from one school term to the next, immediately transition from their small and cozy elementary schools to the long, anonymous hallways of high school, was completely unrealistic, given all the other challenges they were already facing due to puberty. Having to change classrooms for each subject, keep track of separate assignments, and keep up with much harder coursework was simply too much for them. It was no wonder that so many kids dropped out. If they were having trouble, no one helped them. If they wanted to give up, no one stopped them. And this was a terrible loss, education reformers were able to state with increased vigor once Hall published *Adolescence*. Because the years around puberty, Hall argued, could be as rich in intellectual opportunity as they were difficult and disheartening.

For Hall, the start of adolescence marked a critical and unique moment in a child's cognitive development, with enormous new potential for more advanced learning and reasoning. "Never again will there be such susceptibility to drill and discipline, such plasticity to habituation, or such ready adjustment to new conditions," he wrote, noting as well that adolescent memories were particularly "quick, sure, and lasting." He cited late-nineteenth-century brain research to show that this "plasticity" was due to the fact that there was a rapid uptick in brain development in adolescence. It was not a question of overall growth—scientists knew then, as now, that the brain attained its full adult size before puberty—but rather an increase in myelination—the coating of neurons in white matter that leads to more efficient communication between brain cells and different brain regions. He also noted that the super-acuity of the adolescent mind and senses seemed to bring with it an increased vulnerability, sometimes resulting in the onset of mental illness. In other words, he rather remarkably anticipated many of the truths about the adolescent brain that would only be confirmed by modern brain science around the turn of the twenty-first century.

Hall was well before his time in identifying and understanding the nature of adolescent brain change, but he was not the first to remark on the fact that something new and unique happened to a child's *mind* at puberty—ironically enough, right around the time that kids' unlovely emotions and baser "passions" started to ignite. In the fourth century B.C., Aristotle wrote that in addition to "strong passions," "changeable and fickle . . . desires," and a hair-trigger indignation "if they imagine themselves unfairly treated," the transition into adolescence (believed to come at age 14) marked the start in youth of a salutary new kind of cognition, which he conceptualized as the beginning of the ability to make conscious choices. The seventeenth-century English philosopher John Locke also believed that a capacity for higher-level thought became possible during adolescence. Jean-Jacques Rousseau proclaimed the ages of 12 to 15 to be the dawn of the age of reason, which, he believed, marked the start of a child's receptivity to something approaching formal education.

Earlier American thinkers, too, observed that something altogether new took place in the mind of youth right around the time they went through puberty. "It is about this time, if ever, that remarkable faculties, and those rare endowments which constitute genius, if they have been latent during infancy and early childhood, begin to make themselves perceptible," Isaac Taylor told parents in 1838. William H. Burnham, a close colleague of Hall's in the psychology department at Clark, had been spreading the word for decades that the adolescent passage was a "period of functional acquisition and readjustment," when students were "open to new impressions with almost hypnotic susceptibility" and were capable of levels of pure thought they might never again attain in adulthood. "Then for a time man is capable of independent and original thinking," he declared in an 1897 address to New England educators. "Then for a brief period the fetters of habit are thrown off, and one is not a slave to his yesterdays."

Yet this positive side of the "age of puberty"—that sense of enormous and exciting potential—had never received anything like the share of attention given to the "passions" and, in particular, to the forms of "perversion" those passions might take. That lack of attention, reformers argued as the nineteenth century turned into the twentieth, was proving to be a real problem. To stem the pernicious "leakage" of untrained intellect, a growing chorus of American educators agreed, the United States needed a new kind of school, specially tailored to meet the unique needs, tastes, capabilities, and challenges of children in early adolescence. "The adolescent begins to judge, inquire, reason," Aubrey Augustus Douglass, author of the 1916 book *The Junior High School*, wrote, "and he must have the material upon which to exercise these powers."

The schools, reformers said, should be staffed by teachers specially trained in adolescent development, who could provide knowledgeable support and individualized instruction. They should accustom seventh graders slowly to the challenges of secondary school, teaching them to transition from class to class, for example, while keeping an eye out for problems, academic or otherwise. In a nod to university presidents, who since the late 1880s had been complaining that college freshmen were arriving on their campuses woefully unprepared for college-level work, the reformers said the new schools—which soon came to be called "junior high schools"—should offer some higher-level academic subject matter beginning in the seventh grade. But to keep students from finding the work too hard or too boring, the reformers cautioned, teachers should give it to them only in bite-size amounts, presented as appealingly as possible. Math, for example, might be taught in the form of accounting or bookkeeping. "If it is served to them in this way, the boys and girls enjoy the feast," declared G. Vernon Bennett, the superintendent of schools in Pomona, California, in his 1919 book, also titled *The Junior High School*.

More and better vocational education, Bennett and other reformers promised, would keep boys from dropping out. And girls, they said, would thrive with no risk of putting their reproductive futures in jeopardy once they were educated in conformity with the latest scientific findings regarding their uniquely delicate pubertal constitution. "We must keep constantly in mind the fact that we are educating the mother of the race," Bennett wrote. What this would mean concretely was "moderation in study, in social functions, in physical labor, in standing, and climbing stairs," combined with education in the "vocation" of homemaking, with special classes in "domestic science," sewing, and home economics.

The leaders of the movement to create junior high schools wanted to appeal to their prospective students' best natures. But there was a problem: Those students were the kids we know today as middle schoolers. They were . . . problematic, to put it mildly. They were boys and girls going through puberty, and the reformers believed, like Hall himself, that there were big risks inherent to trying to educate an age group in thrall to the nascent demands of what he called the "vita sexualis." That belief no doubt lay behind the American rationale for creating separate grade 7–9 schools (as opposed to, say, grades 6 or 7 through 12, as in many other countries). On the one hand, kids in the midst of puberty were seen as so sensitive and so vulnerable that they needed special, protected spaces. On the other hand, they were so awful that they needed to be essentially quarantined.

Some reformers managed to articulate this in a generally positive way, arguing for unique institutions for 12-to-15-year-olds "in order that adequate provision may be made for their peculiarities of disposition," as Thomas H. Briggs, a professor at Columbia University's Teachers College, nicely put it in 1920. Others, however, were far less kind. William H. Burnham, for one, wrote that the junior high schools needed to serve as vehicles of sublimation for a population that, without proper handling, could be entirely derailed by its sexual energies. "The function of the school is to turn this activity into legitimate channels and to develop wholesome interests," he said. "The opportunity for good is only equaled by the possibility of evil." And G. Vernon Bennett's list of all the forms of "evil" that only a cloistered junior high school could adequately check was so long and exhaustive that it had to be split into separate tallies of physical ("perverted sex habits," above all), mental ("excessive indulgence in sex thoughts and habits," among many others), and moral evils ("weaving webs of deceit . . . general outlawry against the home . . . the reading of trashy novels, frequenting bad moving picture houses . . . 'looseness' . . . 'shamelessness' ")— the last category "worse now than ever before" and "steadily getting worse still."

The first of the grade 7–9 junior high schools, Indianola Junior High, opened its doors in Columbus, Ohio, in 1909. The second opened in Berkeley, California, in 1910. And after that, the schools proliferated rapidly. By the 1920s, the majority of adolescents were, for the very first time in American history, spending more time with their peers than with their families, and by 1930 over three-quarters of U.S. students were staying in school into at least the ninth grade.

Change didn't happen at the same rate for everyone, of course. Well into the Great Depression, many junior-high-school-age children bore adult-level responsibilities as their families fought to survive. Some worked in factories or on the streets as shoeshine boys or "newsies." Others, particularly Mexican and Asian immigrants, worked in the fields alongside their parents. In fact, as late as the 1930s, it was still rare for African American children to go to school past sixth or seventh grade. By their early teens, most were working as maids or nannies, manual laborers, or agricultural workers. Partly this was because their families needed their help to make ends meet. But it was also, the historian Kriste Lindenmeyer has written, due to the fact that in many states, there weren't junior high schools for African American students to attend. In 1935, Baltimore County, for example, had no public school for black children who wanted to continue beyond the seventh grade. The city of Baltimore did, Lindenmeyer notes, but any black students from the surrounding county who wanted to go to school in the city had to jump through a whole tangle of administrative hoops, register for a "tuition plan," and take a difficult placement test that was not required of white students—all of which effectively kept them out.

For the majority of kids who did manage to stay in school through ninth grade, the experience of junior high marked a fundamental change in how the years around puberty were experienced in the United States. The young adolescents of the 1920s and 1930s, the childhood historian Paula Fass has written, were the first group of young Americans to experience early adolescence en masse, with common activities, a common pop culture (the new motion pictures and then radio), and a common institutional rite of passage. Rather than being a matter of "individual transformation," adolescence for the first time became a "social" or "group phenomenon," she notes. And, as a group phenomenon, it wasn't long before early adolescence became "the awkward, wretched, miserably self-conscious period" that we know and hate today.

A key reason, it seems, is that once most of American 12-to-15-year-olds started spending most of their time together as a group, they began to behave like today's middle schoolers. They teased one another about their looks and how they dressed. They were competitive and petty. In 1928, when Coco Irvine, a seventh grader in St. Paul, Minnesota, received a fancy new dress from her mother for her 13th birthday—"actually sleeveless (A great concession!)," she noted in her diary—the other girls her age at Friday night dancing school did what they could to spoil her joy. (They were unsuccessful. "All the girls were pea-green with envy and made derogatory remarks about sleeveless dresses," she gloated.) Not having the right clothes, even at a time when many families didn't have enough to eat, could be social suicide, painful to the point where, in the midst of the Great Depression, junior high students actually wrote to Eleanor Roosevelt begging for clothes so their schoolmates wouldn't make fun of them.

It wasn't long before parenting junior high schoolers became an experience that looked and felt a whole lot like its modern-day equivalent, too. Then, as now, 12- and 13-year-olds seemed to have a unique talent for getting under their parents' skin, with daughters possessed of a special knack for driving their mothers crazy (and vice versa). "I don't like my mother very much but I do want her to like me! I very much want her to but I will not give in," Coco Irvine wrote as a seventh grader in 1927, after one of a string of skirmishes with her mother. At 13, having matured greatly, in her own estimation, she was far more emotionally generous. "I realize now that she is growing old (she is nearly forty-four years old)," she wrote. "It is hard for her to see that things have changed since the olden days when she was my age."

There is, unfortunately, no record of her mother's view of the encounters that made their way into Coco's diary. But popular books and women's magazine articles written by experts in the late 1920s and 1930s made clear that the kind of intergenerational conflict Coco described was hardly unusual, and that her clashing feelings of love and annoyance were probably not one-sided. Much of the parental emotion those articles captured was painful and poignant. "A loving, obedient, devoted daughter becomes restless, unsympathetic, even openly rebellious. Frequently the mother is puzzled and heartbroken," an article in *Good Housekeeping* noted in 1925. The social worker Jessie Taft took a lyrical tone, writing in *Parents' Magazine* of the period "where the helpless parent and baffled child clash in blind love, fear and protest." And the magazine writer Alice D. Kelly, perhaps by way of penance for the "scathing remarks" she'd thrown her own mother's way as a young teen, painted a detailed portrait of maternal pain. "Overnight, as it were, all is changed for the mother," she wrote. "She is faced with distrust where she once found perfect confidence, with coldness where there was overwhelming affection, with argument where there was pleasant obedience. From being the most adorable, wise, lovely thing on earth she has become 'stupid,' 'old-fashioned,' 'unkind,' 'non-understanding.'" But there was plenty of straight-up bad feeling, too.

In her much-cited 1928 book, *The Psychology of the Adolescent,* the psychologist Leta S. Hollingworth wrote of "the good-natured contempt" that most junior high parents she met expressed about their kids. "Anyone who comes in contact with these in-between, half-grown children knows how assiduously they avoid all work, how prone they are to daydreaming, how indifferent they are to the grades they get in school," the pediatrician Barbara Beattie noted. Dr. Edwin Patton, an expert on boys, wrote that parents frequently observed that sons in the "awkward age" of just before 13 were "loud and boisterous and socially impossible," while the psychologist Winifred Richmond relayed a laundry list of causes for adult complaint: "the self-assertive attitude, the disobedience of parental commands and wishes, the officiousness and tendency to argumentation, the know-it-all attitude that is so trying, the open contempt for father and mother as 'old fogies.'" Fourteen, noted Gladys Denny Shultz, the childcare and training director of *Better Homes and Gardens,* was the age when boys' interest in wholesome activities like scouting would fall away, and they'd turn instead to smoking, breaking windows, and being disrespectful to teachers. Soon, they'd be "hard to control, disobedient," and, very likely, "surly and difficult." And daughters were no better. "An adolescent girl at this stage," she wrote, "is likely to pick out to do as her declaration of independence just the thing that she knows is most obnoxious to her family."

The huge generation gap that existed between junior high students of the 1920s and 1930s and their parents didn't help matters at all. It was a real gulf, a "tragedy of lack of mutual understanding," in the words of William H. Burnham. Much of this was due to new technology. "The three inventions of telephone, automobile, and moving pictures have made a totally new environment for our growing children, and have caused a real chasm between the generations," the 1925 *Good Housekeeping* article noted. Unfamiliarity bred suspicion; change bred fear. Faced with children who seemed, overnight, to have become foreign creatures— engaging in "dirty" talk and harboring "smutty" knowledge— parents railed against corrupting outside influences. "Indignant parents are complaining of having their children contaminated," the Harvard University psychiatrist Douglas A. Thom observed in a U.S. government parenting pamphlet in 1933. An obvious source of trouble was popular culture, the new "sex-saturated environment" of film, radio, and advertising, where "even cigarettes and complexion soaps base their advertising on 'sex appeal,'" as the unfortunately named Emily V. Clapp wrote for the Massachusetts Society for Social Hygiene in 1932. Parents also cast a distrustful eye on their children's junior high friends—that new, much larger, and more unknowable cohort of kids from strange homes whose strange families did strange things.

Group socialization through the institution of the junior high had actually been one of the goals of the reformers who had brought the new schools into being. Many had hoped, in fact, that young adolescents from poor and immigrant backgrounds in particular, by spending multiple years in the same classrooms as the children of the native-born, would acquire a "wholesome solidarity," as the educator Ralph W. Pringle put it. But parents had a very different reaction to seeing new ways of speaking, dressing, and thinking emerge in their kids. They saw their own influence slipping away. They scrambled to take control—of the time their kids spent out socializing, the movies their children saw, and the radio shows they listened to. But in the age of mass media, with adult love stories playing everywhere and retailers actively targeting a new category of potential shoppers called "teen-agers," they were fighting a losing battle.

CHAPTER 4

Party Hounds and Vixens

TOO MANY SUBTEENS

GROW UP TOO SOON

AND TOO FAST

Fancy Hairdos,

Adult Make-up,

Sensual Dancing,

Heavy Necking

—"Boys and Girls: Too Old Too Soon," *Life* magazine

THE JUNIOR HIGH schools had been designed, in part, to set pubescent boys and girls on the path to good character by teaching them to channel their energies in productive ways. In this, however, they were not entirely successful. Twelve-to-fifteen-year-olds, segregated into their own exclusive company, seemed simply to bring out the worst in one another.

The issue wasn't that they had embarked upon the lives of sin that G. Vernon Bennett and his contemporaries had so feared.

When *Ladies' Home Journal* polled its 12-to-18-year-old readers in 1944, the magazine found them to be reasonably conservative in what they considered age-appropriate social behavior. Fourteen was the earliest age at which boys and girls might go to the movies together, they said—provided they were part of a group. Fifteen was the youngest acceptable age for a one-on-one date. And 85 percent of the magazine's 12-to-15-year-olds said they were not interested in "going steady" (committing to a "serious" relationship with just one person, the vogue for which was strong among high schoolers in those years). The issue was, rather, that from an educator's perspective at least, the kids had turned out to be kind of uninspiring, and uninspired, as human beings.

They were dead set on applying their growing mental capacities to anything other than their studies. Rather than using their strengthened powers of judgment for the pursuit of knowledge and reason, as the early reformers had hoped, they trained their newly discerning eyes on one another. Instead of applying their new capabilities in classification and system formation to science or math, they made idiotic lists, and they sorted themselves, incessantly, into cliques and hierarchies.

At the top of the heap were kids who were good-looking and had money, who came from the "right" kinds of families, and who knew the "right" way to behave, which pretty much came down to watching the group, reading the group, moving with the group, and following the rules of the game. At the bottom were those who were socially awkward or physically unattractive, perhaps "shy, diffident, reserved . . . very introspective," as the psychiatrist Douglas A. Thom described them in his 1933 pamphlet. Doing well in school was not a plus; in fact, a 1951 study of popularity among Texas eighth graders found the two factors most negatively correlated with popularity for boys were "freedom from misbehavior in the classroom" and IQ.

The mental space that junior high schoolers might have devoted to history or literature was instead filled with social drama. Coco Irvine, for example, related with fright how some seventh-grade boys had spied on some older kids (including her beloved brother), had seen them drinking "spiked beer" and "necking" in cars, and were "writing a report on what they saw, such as who was with who and how they were getting along," and were planning to blackmail those involved. And although she and her friends were not yet old enough to drive or to date, they had their own wanna-be versions of romantic intrigue. In seventh grade, they played kissing games at parties. Coco obsessed over an alternatingly flirtatious and elusive "He" who attended her dancing school, and she relished the fact that she had a level of secret sexual knowledge that went far beyond what the adults in her life expected of a girl her age. "This sounds like a childish game but isn't," she confided to her diary about a rainy day round of paper dolls she had played with her friend Dotty in August 1928, just before beginning eighth grade. "Mother thinks it is," she went on. "She smiled benignly at us when she looked out to see we were not up to something. If only she knew! My Cassandra paper doll is pregnant though not married." Dotty, she noted, had insisted that if Coco didn't figure out a way to get the doll out of that "predicament," they were going to have to tear her up.

Julia Heller, an eighth grader growing up in a small town in southern Pennsylvania in the early 1930s, applied her list-making skills to maintaining a complex document that she called her "Boy-Friends Book." In it, she started off with a master list of thirty boys, their proper names in black cursive and their nicknames in red print, which she then sorted and re-sorted into pages of shorter lists:

Boys that have *light* hair
Boys that have *brown* hair
Boys that have *Red* hair

Boys who have bicycles of ~~there~~ their own
Boys I liked better than others
Boys I liked as they come in order of number
Boys that Dance
Boy's who live near me!

She also created single-page files for the boys who seemed to be her favorites. Each page contained a boy's name and nickname, address, color of eyes, color of hair, height, and preferred sport, followed by a short description of when and where Julia had met him and what they did or didn't do. The amorous encounters were described in language so Mae West–like that, one assumes, it had to have been lifted straight out of Julia's favorite movies or radio shows. "Dresses cute & man can he laugh cute he has the sweetest laugh could I kiss him an[d] how any time at all baby I am here for you! Just you!" she wrote of a certain Jack Gift, a seventh grader. ("He has adorable mother that the way he gets his cuteness," she added later, it would seem, judging by a slight difference in ink.) She kissed George Meyer ("Can he kiss well first get 1 sample & you'll say yes he can kiss") and chronicled having passed notes in school with him, too, which seems to have been every bit as exciting ("& were they notes. . . . Baby what a man.") In fact, she appeared to have kissed quite a few of the boys in her book—although not to have gone any further, given the distinctive way she marked one evening, four years later, with a certain Roger Immel (also known as Tom or "Tommie Immel the one & only"), whom she went on to marry: "Then the fun began when I pulled the blind down and he sat down beside me for a ——."

Had Julia Heller's mother happened upon the "Boy-Friends Book," even back in the kissing-only days when Julia was in eighth grade, she might—like Coco's mom, had she overheard the sorry saga of the pregnant paper doll—have been deeply concerned.

Like many mothers of eighth graders today who pick up their children's cellphones never again to un-see the verbal horrors found there, she might—upon encountering her daughter's bawdy language or seeing the level of boy obsession that came through in Julia's color-coded, multiply sorted lists—have put the "Boy-Friends Book" down rapidly and then obsessed for days over how to address what she'd read there without admitting to having seen it. Or she might have immediately made a scene. Either way, it doesn't take a time machine to imagine the outcome: panic in the mom, outrage (if the mother admitted to spying) on the part of the girl, an argument rapidly accelerating into a shouting match, and an ending without resolution, the daughter convinced that her mom was making a big deal out of nothing, and the mother circling the abyss.

Perhaps most disappointing of all for idealistic educators was that junior high schoolers didn't end up showing a penchant for "independent and original thinking." On the contrary, they were consummate conformists. They policed one another's behavior, keeping kids who seemed too different, "on the fringe," or "queer" (a word often repeated toward mid-century) as far away as possible. When it came to correcting classmates who broke the rules, willingly or not, they could be absolutely brutal.

In 1948, Sally Horner, an 11-year-old from Camden, New Jersey, believed to have been the real-life inspiration for Vladimir Nabokov's *Lolita,* tried to steal a notebook from her local Woolworth's in order to curry favor with a clique of girls she wanted to join. She was stopped by Frank La Salle, a known pedophile, who won her trust by pretending to be an FBI agent who could save her from jail. He kidnapped her, and she spent almost two years on the road with him before escaping. And when she came back home, her junior high classmates marked her return by ostracizing her because she was no longer a virgin. "She was viciously mocked by boys and girls alike," notes Sarah Weinman in her 2018 book, *The Real Lolita*. "Branded a slut. Shunned."

Sally's story was, of course, extreme. But her classmates' nastiness was all too typical in the universe of the American junior high school that emerged, with striking similarity, all around the country by mid-century. "What 'everybody' does, thinks and wears shakes the world," the journalist and educator Frances Drewry McMullen sadly noted in 1954. "The crowd is critical and it can be cruel."

In this, junior high schoolers were not terribly different from the adults in their lives. (Even poor Sally Horner's mother, Ella, arguably participated in the slut-shaming. "Whatever Sally has done," she told reporters very shortly after reuniting with her traumatized daughter, "I can forgive her.") In fact, in their consumerism, their moralism, and, frankly, their general lack of interest in intellectual pursuits, they were all but perfect foot soldiers for the forces of "coerced conformity" that reached their peak in the American 1950s. With their rules, hierarchies, and social codes, and above all in the overwhelmingly similar systems by which they devised who was in or out, popular or not, they reproduced the values of the adults in their world just about exactly. As the 1951 study of Texas eighth graders discovered, popular kids generally came from popular homes. Or, as the report put it, "good homes," where the parents were of higher socioeconomic status and had strong "community relations," which basically meant that they seamlessly fit in.

Junior high schoolers didn't see themselves as mini-versions of their moms and dads, of course. Adults didn't see them that way either—aside from the kinds of lifelong misfits who were likely to end up in the academy as, say, "egghead" sociologists. In fact, rather than recognizing junior high schoolers as rough-around-the-edges reproductions of themselves, adults tended to see them as foreign beings whose personal habits and behavior were, at best, kind of distasteful.

SOME EARLY SKEPTICS had anticipated that this particular group of kids might not live up to the junior high reformers' loftiest dreams. The schools, they'd said, were going to have to be really, really good if they were going to truly capture the minds (and bodies) of an age group that, not so long before, had been considered capable of going out in the world and living semi-independent and productive lives. If they didn't have something really compelling to offer, something beyond the futile busyness of running around and around in an "entertaining squirrel cage," in the memorable words of the educator Annie Winsor Allen, they were destined to be a waste of time. With body underemployed and mind underutilized, "the normal adolescent must be expected to cause much trouble for himself and others," the psychologist Leta S. Hollingworth predicted in 1928. Those words proved prescient.

As the decades passed, there were many indications that the junior high experience was every bit as mediocre as what had come before. There was no individualized attention, no specially conceived instruction geared to the uniqueness of the early adolescent mind. In fact, most junior high teachers had never received any special training at all. Seventh- and eighth-grade curricula were still full of rote learning, classroom busywork, and time-consuming, pointless homework. Ninth grade was no better.

The kids themselves remained, by and large, bored, disaffected, and alienated. "The thing that gets us down is *the way things are done,*" the *Ladies' Home Journal*'s Marjorie Lederer wrote, channeling the frustrations of the adolescent readers who'd responded to the magazine's 1944 survey. "Every week there's a new list of things to be memorized and every week we forget what we had to remember for the week before. Then there are the teachers. Some of them are so strict and old-fashioned we often want to do the wrong thing just to make them madder. . . . We get all filled up with a lot of facts that don't seem to have anything to do with us, and when we get out at three o'clock it seems like a bad dream that doesn't belong to our real lives at all." The author of the 1951 study of Texas eighth graders came to a similar conclusion: "A dislike for school by junior high school students seems to be the conventional feeling."

By the late 1950s, that feeling appeared to be mutual, as far as junior high school personnel were concerned. When Eric W. Johnson, head of the junior high division of a private school in Philadelphia, interviewed adults for his parenting book, *How to Live Through Junior High School,* he found "extreme resentment" in the way teachers talked about their students. And by the early 1960s, things had gotten so bad that William M. Alexander, the keynote speaker at a national conference of administrators convened to discuss the topic "The Dynamic Junior High," proposed getting rid of them altogether. The junior high schools, said Alexander, chair of the Department of Education at George Peabody College for Teachers, had "unwittingly hastened the disrespect for intellectual activity too common among adolescents." They had replicated the worst aspects of the American high school: "the ideals of athletic prowess (boys) and popularity (girls) over academic brilliance." He recommended replacing them with grades 5–8 or 6–8 "middle schools," which, he thought, ideally would comprise the intermediate program in an entirely new sort of K–12 public school. The new middle school programs, he hoped, would at long last make good on the junior high school's original goal of supplying an educational experience "especially adapted to the needs of preadolescent and early adolescent pupils." They would allow teachers the time to get to know both students and their parents, and to devise a flexible and individualized curriculum that could be adapted for the level of each child. Above all, he said, the schools should emphasize "intellectual growth" and "values" rather than grades.

In other words, Alexander's goals for the new middle schools were exactly the same as those of the junior high reformers at the turn of the century. And, just as soon as he announced them, a very familiar-sounding question arose: Could middle schoolers actually learn anything? Or, as one listener asked right after Alexander's speech, were kids of puberty age too in thrall to their "personal-social problems" to be worth educating at all?

The issue was not resolved. Nor would it be in the decades that followed. And a big part of that lack of resolution stemmed from the fact that no matter how many new schools were built, no matter how much they were reformed and reconceived, the way that adults looked at the students they contained remained basically the same. Indeed, right around the time when Alexander sounded the junior high's death knell, American adults' vision of junior high schoolers took a decided turn for the worse.

By THE EARLY 1960s, teenagers in the United States had been getting a lot of negative attention for quite some time. Ironically, that attention had grown out of some very positive developments. In 1938, the Fair Labor Standards Act had prohibited most paid work for anyone under age 14 and highly regulated it for 15-to-17-year-olds, officially putting an end to child labor in America. It had the effect, at long last, of pushing nearly all junior-high-school-age kids into full-time schooling and slowly increasing rates of high school attendance as well. In the post–World War II period, for the first time in American history a majority of older teens had begun not just attending but graduating from high school, and by 1960 almost 90 percent of 17- and 18-year-olds were in school.

Peacetime and prosperity meant that American teenagers in the postwar era were enjoying lives that bore little resemblance to those their parents had known growing up in the Great Depression. The all-American high school experience—football and cheerleading, saddle shoes and letter jackets, dating and driving and "going steady"—was both a source of national pride and a cause for alarm. Dating—boy-girl socializing away from adult eyes—had originated among working-class youth and had first spread to college students in the 1920s. From the start, it had been understood as a kind of transaction: The boy paid for the evening's entertainment, and the girl "granted some degree of intimacy," as the childhood historian Joseph Hawes once put it. Intimacy meant "necking" (intense making out) and could lead to "petting" (sexual experimentation that stopped before intercourse), both indulgences that, like dating itself, had become much more widespread in the 1920s, when young couples began being able to escape to the privacy of their cars. The idea of "going steady" was even more loaded, because the "steady" setup, in the domesticity-obsessed postwar era, was almost like a trial run for marriage. Once a couple was locked in, "necking and petting" weren't just possible, but expected.

The average age of first marriage dropped steadily in the postwar years—so much so that between 1940 and 1960, the percentage of 15-to-17-year-old girls who were married increased by almost 50 percent, and the percentage of boys ages 15 to 17 who were married tripled. Fully 87 percent of those teen marriages were caused by unplanned pregnancy, a 1960 study found. Media reports regularly hammered home the message that the nation's teens were on the edge of a moral abyss, drawn into early sexual activity by "Elvis' gyrations" and rock 'n' roll "leerics," and into "juvenile delinquency" by the example of bad-boy rebels like the incorrigible James Dean.

In 1954, *Time* magazine informed the nation of a "teen-age

reign of terror," as it relayed the findings of a New York *Daily News* special report on violence in the city's public schools, where "the new three R's" consisted of "rowdyism, riot and revolt," the paper said. "Within the memory of every living adult, a profound and terrifying change has overtaken adolescence," warned Dr. Robert M. Lindner, a prominent psychologist and author of the book *Rebel Without a Cause* (a case study of a "criminal psychopath" that was entirely unrelated to the eponymous James Dean movie). If adolescents in the past were engaged in "suffering-out" their "inner turmoil," he said, those of the 1950s felt free to "act out," having "abandoned solitude in favor of pack-running, of predatory assembly, of great collectivities that bury, if they do not destroy, individuality. . . . In the crowd, herd or gang, it is a mass mind that operates—a mind without subtlety, without compassion, uncivilized." By 1958, the writer Dwight Macdonald declared in *The New Yorker,* "The first association that most adults have with the word 'teenager' is 'juvenile delinquent.'" In all, the historian Peter Stearns has observed, it was in these years that American adolescence shaped up to be the "recurrent, anxiety-drenched obsession" that it has been ever since.

Parents had been worrying for decades about the potential corruption of their junior high schoolers, whether by the nation's "sex-saturated" pop culture or the contaminating influence of their friends. In the early 1940s, letters to advice writers frequently asked how to keep pubescent children more childlike. Did she approve of junior high and high school girls wearing makeup, one reader asked Eleanor Roosevelt in her *Ladies' Home Journal* "If You Ask Me" column in 1942. She did not. Was it okay for a 13-year-old girl who liked "to go out and have fun with the girls" to do so if that meant she'd have to "yell on the street and call attention to [herself] and flirt and whistle at boys" another reader asked in 1946. A definitive *no* was again the answer.

In the 1950s, those worries became much darker. Retailers,

eager to rev up their sales after the deprivations of the Great Depression and the war, had begun actively marketing a multitude of new products that invited junior high schoolers to step up, grow up, and begin to indulge in the pleasures of American teendom as early as possible. Junior high school girls in particular were offered all sorts of new ways to make themselves look and feel more like sophisticated high schoolers: their own lines of jewelry and purses, bath products and perfume, "beginning" bras, and even girdles specially made for their not-yet-bulging forms. Department stores devoted special sections of floor space to the tastes, habits, and needs of a new category of young humans—"subteens"—and smartly identified that the way to their hearts was through their "aspirational" desires. "The salesperson should always remember their insecurity, shyness, their desire to be glamorous and independent of the rules; their urge to all look alike," the trade publication *Earnshaw's Infants' and Children's Merchandiser* advised.

The wannabe desires of junior high schoolers—and even, some reports had it, of 10- and 11-year-olds—was undoubtedly a boon for manufacturers, department stores, record companies, and advertising-dependent newspapers and magazines. But many adults, watching young teens and preteens fashion themselves after 16-to-18-year-olds, weren't happy at all. In fact, they feared the worst.

By the late 1950s, they'd had a full decade of scary stories about the immoral and even criminal behavior of American teenagers. Most of these stories concerned older kids, and in particular an archetypal, hypersexual bad boy, all pelvis, leather jacket, and bad attitude, possessed of "the tight, tight jeans; the provocative gait; the conception of the basement fraternity as the scene of copulation so continuous as to defy the laws of nature," as the social critic Edgar Z. Friedenberg characterized the image in 1959. But the teen pregnancy articles did sometimes include 13-year-old girls.

And junior high school boys featured prominently in some of the worst stories of juvenile degradation to grab adult attention.

There was, for example, the story of Michael Farmer, a 15-year-old handicapped by polio, who'd been killed by a mob of knife- and machete-wielding teenage gang members as he tried to make his way to a New York City public pool in the summer of 1957. Of the eighteen boys arrested in connection with the crime, eleven were just 13 or 14. And then there were the goings-on at John Marshall Junior High School, an infamous institution in an increasingly "rough" neighborhood of Brooklyn, New York, that received national attention after a string of assaults, a knife-point rape, and multiple "hoodlum invasions" led to the opening of a grand jury investigation, which was followed soon after by the suicide of the school principal.

When George N. Allen, a reporter for the *New York World-Telegram,* went "undercover" as a substitute teacher at the school, he discovered rampant crime and chaos, drunk students asleep in class, girls sent to the bathroom in twos to avoid sexual assault, and teachers who were threatened, intimidated, and overwhelmed. His stories ("'Don't Let 'Em See You're Afraid,' Writer Told by School Official" and "'Hey Teach' Is Signal for Classroom Bedlam" were two of a sixteen-part series) became common points of reference for a growing sense that immoral youth behavior was creeping further and further downward in age.

Against this seamy and scary backdrop, and with journalists like *The New Yorker*'s Dwight Macdonald warning that "teenage terrorism" was present not just in the "wolf packs" of the inner city but also in the "preponderantly 'good homes'" of the comfortable suburbs, many adults began to fear that typical junior high school copycat behavior wasn't just a matter of clothes, music, slang, and accessories. In their social lives, adults worried, even the youngest adolescents were growing up too fast and getting up to no good.

As the 1950s turned into the 1960s, commentators warned that the drop in the marriage age was exerting a steady downward pressure on all preliminary forms of pairing off and sexual experimentation. Eighth graders were wearing "wedding-like bands," seventh graders were "going steady," and even sixth graders were turning themselves inside out over "how to get a date and how far to go in necking," women's magazines reported. With each passing year, there were more and more dire stories of junior high schoolers whose amorous activities, or mere ambitions in that area, had placed them in serious physical and psychological danger. *Ladies' Home Journal* told of a 14-year-old boy in Arlington, Virginia, who killed himself after reportedly being "jilted" by his steady girlfriend. The highly respected child psychoanalyst Selma Fraiberg wrote about a 12-year-old girl who'd been brought in for a consultation after repeatedly telling her parents she no longer wanted to live because she "felt herself a spinster." She "had never been asked for a date," Fraiberg related. "All of her girl friends had dates. Three were going steady. She had no future. There was nothing to live for. She would be better off dead."

Some parents, these articles warned, were asleep at the wheel. "I planned a special swimming-and-hamburger party so that Patty could have a 'date.' . . . I was awfully eager that she be popular," a formerly too-permissive mother confessed to the readers of *Ladies' Home Journal,* as she traced the arc that had led from her daughter's "first crush" at age 13, to "going steady" in her last year of junior high, to an (unspecified) outbreak of "scandalous behavior" at age 14. "We didn't put the lid on early enough," she wrote. "We let the crowd take over completely before we stepped in; we were too tolerant altogether." Even worse, critics charged, many parents were egging their children on: driving 12-year-olds around on their dates, shelling out for makeup and hairdressers, even pathologizing their kids if they weren't ready to date or formally socialize. " 'I don't *want* to change. I don't want to *be* changed,' "

Redbook quoted a 12-year-old boy having told a caseworker after his parents had hauled him in to social services because he was "too introverted" and preferred studying plants to going out to parties.

So many parents were complicit in their kids' pursuit of inappropriate fun that, in some communities, school administrators, and reportedly junior high students themselves, had to step in to teach them to set limits. In the Philadelphia area, they devised timetables for dating. In northern Virginia, they drafted a fifteen-point code of safe conduct. "Blackouts or lights-out games have no place in a well-ordered party," it stipulated. "Drinking or smoking at junior-high-age parties is strictly taboo."

For adults to bring such a great degree of worry and suspicion to junior high school boy-girl socializing really was a new departure. In fact, as recently as the early 1950s, expert opinion had actually inclined in the direction of *encouraging* young teens to go through the motions of pre-romantic activity. A 1953 Encyclopaedia Britannica educational film titled *Beginning to Date,* for example, had clearly aimed to teach pubescent kids the hows and whys of (well-chaperoned) early courtship.

The movie didn't specify the ages of the students it followed as they bumbled their way to their first school dance—the organization sponsoring the dance was identified only as the school's "Teen Club"—but the boys' smooth faces, squeaky voices, and diminutive stature suggested that the kids were indeed in junior high. "Oh golly, I'd be scared to death," its protagonist, George, said when faced with the prospect of asking a girl to the dance. But after his swim coach stepped in, took him in hand, and, with lots of analogies as to how it was better to start to learn to dive from the edge of the pool than from the high diving board, gently guided his "first plunge into the social swim," George did beautifully, planning his topics of conversation in advance, pre-thinking his transportation, and taking care to walk Mildred, his date— who was about two feet taller than him—right to her door.

The 1951 study of popularity among Texas eighth graders had also conveyed the sense that knowing how to curry favor with the opposite sex was a skill so essential that schools ought to play a role in teaching it. Since physical attractiveness was the one and only factor that could raise a girl's level of popularity with boys, its author noted, "homemaking classes" should stress "the importance of good grooming and help the girls choose the styles and colors which add most to their appearance."

The whole concept of popularity had not yet taken on the negative connotation we attach to it today. It was purely about being liked. And being liked was a key component of being "well-adjusted"—the formula through which optimal human functioning was understood in the postwar years. "Adjustment" was all about knowing how to fit in and being able to adapt to the world as one found it—a perfect skill for personal success in a conservative and conformist era. At its very center was heterosexuality—a goal that, in the mid-century world of Freudian-dominated psychology, was something of an obsession. Becoming a successfully functioning heterosexual was the chief developmental goal of adolescence—a potentially perilous task that had to be handled just right.

All of this is why, from the 1930s through the early 1950s, many experts actually advised parents that it was not only helpful and kind but also proper and necessary to do whatever they could to make sure that their children were popular. In the late 1950s, however, that changed. The presumption of innocence regarding junior high boy-girl activities held by adults in the *Beginning to Date* era became a thing of the past. A moralistic, quasi-punitive, almost hysterical—and parent-blaming—general outlook replaced it. And this marked a turning point in the way adults in America looked at and thought about middle-school-age kids. Children who had formerly been primarily seen as irritants, rude and awkward, and frustratedly horny (if they were boys) or snappish (if girls) now were starting to be seen as sexual agents.

In the summer of 1962, *Life* magazine ran a huge photo spread on the problem of "American subteens," describing them as "a generation whose jumble of innocence and worldly vision is unnaturally precocious—and alarming." It centered the piece on an unsuspecting 12-year-old girl named Debby Yarbrough and began with a series of innocuous-looking photos: Debby laughing with two boys in a school hallway; sticking out her hip in the school library to strike what she undoubtedly considered a glamorous pose in a tailored dress and bouffant hairdo; walking atop a fence in shorts and a blouse; and lying on her flowered bed, talking on the phone, wearing yet another fancy dress and, for some reason, a hat. A set of accompanying captions disabused naïve readers who might have thought that she and the boys in the photos looked kind of nice. Debby, "a pocket *femme fatale*," *Life* stated, was a "sultry woman of the world" who "can wrap a boy around her little finger—and works hard at it." One of the boys was "her steady"; the other, "an admirer." And both boys—typical "party hounds"— were vying for Debby's favors with "ingratiating grins."

An entire page of the magazine was then devoted to "The Bewildering Turnover of Boys in Debby's Diary":

February 5: "I love Randy. I wish we could be together always alone. He thrills me to my feet."

February 22: "I hate Randy. Tom and I are going steady. I love him. He loves me."

And then, most damning of all, a list: "Boys I went steady with in seventh grade: Hall, Scott, Gregg, Randy, Tom."

After this, *Life* went after Debby's mother, a weak if elegant woman in a black dress and pearls: " 'When Debby's daddy first heard she was going steady, his eyes got wide, his coffee cup came down,' " she told the magazine, sounding as childish as her daughter was pseudomature. "I said to him, 'Honey, don't get upset: going steady to them means holding hands and jumping across a ditch together.' But her daddy didn't adjust to it at all frankly. He's really old-fashioned.'"

Another unfortunate matron fared even worse in the article. She was photographed stuffing her face with a sandwich while two children sat holding each other not far behind her, looking suspiciously asleep. "The hostess' mother eats away, ignoring the cuddling couple on the couch," *Life* captioned the scene.

Such "adult capitulation" had to stop, experts were marshaled to say. "Sexual excitation is a potent thing which a child's psychological apparatus doesn't know what to do with," said Dr. Stuart Finch, a psychiatrist. "It's like a fuse box without enough fuses for the electrical load. Wires burn out. To relieve sexual needs they cannot gratify, they may get more involved in sex."

In truth, there was absolutely no evidence that, for all of their pseudosophisticated clothing, talk, and hair, junior high schoolers were actually *doing* the same sorts of things as 17- or 18-year-olds—who, let's recall, were frequently getting married in the late 1950s. In fact, there was no proof that rising numbers of those kids were engaging in sexual behavior at all. There were no big government studies of sexual behavior in 12-to-15-year-olds—and there wouldn't be for decades to come. There were no major scholarly studies either. *Sexual Behavior in the Human Female,* the landmark Kinsey Report of 1953, *had* contained a finding regarding preteen girls that should have been of enormous concern: 12 percent of female respondents said they had experienced some form of sexual abuse before adolescence at the hands of older men. But no one paid any attention to that. "When those findings were reported," the childhood historian Steven Mintz notes, "they evoked virtually no public interest, although Kinsey's statistics about pre-marital sexual activity and adultery provoked a huge public outcry."

For *How to Live Through Junior High,* Eric Johnson actually surveyed hundreds of public and private school students, and his findings were very much at odds with the dire story of precocious romantic involvement commonly found in the mass media. Junior high schoolers, his results showed, loved parties, hoped to be invited to as many as possible, and wanted desperately to be popular. But only 14 percent of seventh graders reported having ever been on a two-person date. Only 14 percent had ever kissed on a date, and only 5 percent had ever necked. The numbers rose as the kids got older, but it wasn't until ninth grade that a majority of students had ever kissed, necked, or been on a two-person date. The students' attitudes toward these things were overwhelmingly conservative. Eighty-seven percent disapproved of going steady in junior high. Seventy-three percent of seventh graders were against one-on-one dating and only 9 percent approved of necking.

By and large, Johnson found—as has remained true through our day—that junior high schoolers tended to engage in a lot more talk than action. And yet what they said about sexual activity was a bit imprecise, because they didn't always have a reliable handle on the subject matter. The term "necking," for example, was applied by his respondents to an enormously wide range of romantic activities that included just about anything above or involving the neck, including cheek-to-cheek dancing. "Many junior high schoolers said they had 'necked' on dates, but had not kissed," he reported.

A ninth-grade boy provided another example of verbal ambiguity when he spoke to the author about having had "a little sex" and then blasted adults for their dirty minds. "My parents seem to think that as soon as I touch or kiss a girl I'm going to go to bed with her," he said in exasperation. "I *know* about going to bed with a girl, sure, but that doesn't mean I'm going to do it. Can't we have a little sex without parents dirtying it up with their 'mature' minds? When I kissed girls in kissing games in sixth and seventh grade, I guess I got a giggly sort of thrill out of it, but there sure were a lot more giggles in it than there was sex. And when I kiss a girl now, it's sexy all right, but I'm not going all the way till I'm married." He concluded: "I think it's time parents got out of the gutter."

Johnson essentially agreed. "Too often," he wrote, "adults tend to superimpose their own point of view and fears about sex on the usually innocent activity of junior high school boys and girls."

AMERICAN ADULTS HAVE a long history of working themselves up into states of "moral panic" about children and teenagers. Behind those panics, Steven Mintz has argued, there is always a great deal of cultural displacement. "Children have long served as a lightning rod for America's anxieties about society as a whole," he notes in his history of American childhood, *Huck's Raft*. "It is not surprising that cultural anxieties are often displaced on the young; unable to control the world around them, adults shift their attention to that which they think they can control: the next generation."

Junior high school students in the 1950s were swept up in all sorts of anxiety-making adult phenomena not of their own creation: racial and ethnic turf wars in New York City neighborhoods that were adjusting ungraciously to new waves of immigration and the Great Migration, for example. In both the Michael Farmer story and George Allen's *World-Telegram* series, the boys wreaking havoc were black and Puerto Rican; *Time* magazine referred to them collectively in a 1958 article title as "These Marauding Savages." These kids had nothing whatsoever to do with the falling age of marriage and the spread of the suburban domestic ideal, both of which had everything to do with the hopes, ambitions, and anxieties of a generation of adults—their parents—who had come up during the Great Depression, lived through a world war, and wanted nothing more than security, serenity, and stability for their children. In the early 1960s, junior high kids also had no part in yet another angst-generating social trend that fatefully shaped both the world they were living in and how they were viewed: the dawn of the sexual revolution, marked by the arrival of the first birth control pill.

The Pill received FDA approval for contraceptive use in 1960, and although it did not become legal in all states until 1965—and then for married people only—many doctors found ways to prescribe it more widely, not just to unmarried women but even, on occasion, to older teenagers. Junior high school girls—only 4 percent of whom had had sex by age 15 in the early 1960s, retrospective studies would show—were not, it seems fair to say, directly impacted by the introduction of the Pill, although the *Saturday Evening Post* did manage to find one story about a junior high schooler who was on the Pill—or so she believed, having been given a package of pills, with no explanation or instruction, by her married sister. "'I take them every Saturday night when I go on a date,'" she told the family planning expert Mary Steichen Calderone, who shared the story with the magazine. "If it weren't so funny, it would be tragic," Calderone said.

The Pill did have a large *indirect* impact on junior high schoolers, however, because it profoundly changed the environment in which they were growing up. It created an enormous new sense of sexual possibility and permissibility, which a rising cohort of male writers, musicians, and filmmakers soon brought to popular culture. As a result, the Pill opened the floodgates for an onslaught of sex in writing, talk, and movies—an atmospheric change that affected Americans of all ages. One particularly unsavory, and long-lasting, aspect of that change was the degree to which it became possible—and permissible—in mainstream pop culture to depict pubescent girls as both sexual objects and seductresses.

By early 1962, a striking number of new movies had been released that pushed the envelope with their "mature" themes and content. They dealt with lesbianism (*The Children's Hour*), male homosexuality (*Victim*), incest (*A View from the Bridge*), and pedophilia (*The Mark*). One particularly bad film, *The Chapman Report*, managed to pack in adultery, rape, and "nymphomania." The most famous and influential, of course, was Stanley Kubrick's film adaptation of Vladimir Nabokov's novel *Lolita*.

Making a movie of *Lolita* would have been unthinkable in the years immediately following the book's 1958 publication in the United States. Multiple American publishers had refused to have anything to do with the novel, a tell-all confessional by the European man of letters and inveterate pedophile Humbert Humbert, who narrates how he insinuated himself into the life of 12-year-old Dolores Haze, making her his sexual and emotional captive, until she ultimately escaped. Nabokov had at first balked at the idea of bringing Humbert and his "nymphet," nicknamed "Lolita," to the screen, and had consented only after securing a promise from Kubrick that the actress playing Dolores would look, and in reality be, older than 12. "It was perfectly all right for me to imagine a 12-year-old Lolita," he said in 1962, just a few months before the movie's release. "She only existed in my head. But to make a real 12-year-old girl play such a part in public would be sinful and immoral."

Nabokov's novel unambiguously depicts Lolita as a girl who is kidnapped, raped, and subjected to insidious emotional abuse by Humbert, whose verbal attempts to justify his actions were crafted to have a distinct ring of psychopathic bad faith. Girls in the United States could begin "pubescence," Humbert told himself, at age "ten, or earlier." Lolita, he noted, had already been "debauched" by a 13-year-old boy named Charlie at summer camp, and by the time Humbert got to her, she retained no semblance of innocence whatsoever: "Not a trace of modesty did I perceive in this beautiful hardly formed young girl whom modern co-education, juvenile mores, the campfire racket and so forth had utterly and hopelessly depraved."

But Kubrick's film lent itself to a very different interpretation. Its casting had honored Nabokov's wish; actress Sue Lyon looked much older than Lolita's 12 years, and even seemed considerably older than her own real-life age of 14. Her pouty and saucy screen presence was distinctly unchildlike. With her knowing looks and clear enthusiasm for teaching her putative stepfather how to play the "particularly" fun game she'd learned at camp ("All righty then," she'd said lightly, before instructing him), it was very easy *not* to see her as a victim. And James Mason's Humbert was so charming, elegant, and funny—and so much more intelligent than the all-American dimwits in his midst—that it sometimes took an effort to remember that he was, in fact, a monster.

Some influential viewers in the summer of 1962 appeared not to see the monstrous side of him at all. *Life*'s entertainment editor, Peter Bunzel, wrote that he found Humbert "pitiable, not hateful," a man held captive by his "adoration" of and "pathetic enslavement" to Lolita. And that notion, that there could have been actual love and, even, mutuality in what Bunzel called Humbert and Dolores's "affair," belonged to a way of thinking about pubescent girls that was new and did them damage for a very long time. It was a line of thought—a rationale—that started to appear in the mass media right around the time of the release of the movie *Lolita* and followed a pattern eerily similar to the mental self-justification that Nabokov had written for Humbert.

Basically, it ran like this: Twelve-year-old girls weren't *girls* anymore. They were hitting puberty much sooner, which meant that they were ready to have sex much sooner. In fact, thanks to the vaunted sexual revolution, they were willing, even eager, to have sex. This was the signal they gave off, with their immodest clothing, too-old-too-soon language, and predilection for increasingly depraved music and dancing. Or at least this is what sexually "liberated" men could tell themselves. And if those grown men ended up succumbing to the nymphets, it really wasn't their fault. It was the fault of the girls and, more often than not, of the ambitious, social-climbing, fame-seeking, grasping, desperate mothers who inevitably hovered right over them.

The Lolita fantasy reached its zenith in the late 1970s and early 1980s when 12- and 13-year-old models became, for a time, the apotheosis of female sexiness. This was anything but "liberating." Prior to the Lolita moment, American adults had recognized that not all junior high schoolers were childlike and innocent. But Lolita was a new kind of animal. In her 1962 cinematic incarnation and moving forward, in the form of what the media studies scholar M. Gigi Durham has called "a sign of just how licentious little girls can be," she lived on long after Nabokov's very complicated book and Kubrick's black-and-white film had been relegated to the status of classics. Lolita ushered in a new way of seeing America's youngest adolescents that had virtually nothing to do with who they really were, how they felt, and what they were actually doing. But in the script of sexual liberation that was being written almost exclusively by men, it was very easy to conflate fantasy with reality and to blur the distinctions between kid provocation and adult projection. This made the 1970s and 1980s a very confusing time to be in junior high.

CHAPTER 5

Into the Abyss

Adults must recognize that the youngest teen-agers are the
uncomfortable inheritors—perhaps the victims—of the sexual
revolution. We need to understand and be sympathetic to the
new pressures they face as the first "sexually obligated"
generation in American history.

—KATHLEEN FURY, *Ladies' Home Journal*

ALL SORTS OF people were "liberating" themselves in all sorts of
ways by the time the freewheeling 1960s turned into the burnt-
out 1970s. And they were still doing so in the late 1970s, when I
was in seventh and eighth grade. Record numbers of adults were
freeing themselves from their marriages. Divorced fathers were
shedding responsibility for providing for their families. Mothers—
divorced or not—were freeing themselves of the burden, so heavy
for so long, of always having to be everything for everyone and to
put everyone else's needs first.

The air was heavy with a soured, corrupted, and commercialized trickle-down version of the idealism of the sixties. Cities were falling apart as the economy tanked, crime skyrocketed, white people fled to the suburbs, and public servants and private investors alike divested themselves of the duty to repair and revitalize. Landlords liberated themselves of unprofitable properties via arson. Trash collectors felt free to go on strike. Off-duty police officers exercised their right not to respond to official calls for help during a blackout emergency. Employers considered themselves enlightened if they hired working mothers, but cleared themselves of any need to pay wages high enough to cover childcare. For most working families, divorced or not, it was an era of latchkey children, with the relentlessly depressing *ABC Afterschool Specials* to provide company.

In all, it was a tough time to be a kid, especially an adolescent girl in a place like New York City, where I grew up. It was, as I recall, a period when, once you hit puberty, you couldn't walk down the street without inviting the most disgusting commentary possible, especially if you were engaged in such a provocative act as eating an ice cream cone. Porn was on newsstands everywhere, and my short bus ride to school (I rode the city bus, even though I lived just six blocks away, because there was a three-block stretch too dangerous for walking alone) took me past signs for "XXX" films and "peep shows." Also hitting far too close to home was the prodigious cultural output by grown men in the media who considered it the height of sexually liberated sophistication to drool publicly over very young teenagers and even preteens.

My sixth-to-eighth-grade years brought the ascent to superstardom of Jodie Foster and Brooke Shields, both playing 12-year-old prostitutes, in *Taxi Driver* (1976) and *Pretty Baby* (1978), respectively. (Shields's character, Violet, had her virginity auctioned off to the highest bidder. Even Eve Plumb, made famous by her role as the ever-beleaguered middle sister, Jan, in the squeaky-clean *Brady*

Bunch, had by 1976 succumbed to the career-enhancing lure of playing a young prostitute, in the TV movie *Dawn: Portrait of a Teenage Runaway.*)

As the late 1970s turned into the early 1980s, the producers casting the first-ever Broadway staging of *Lolita* let it be known that only an "authentic nymphet" would do for the part. In 1978, the photographer David Hamilton presented a show of his signature pubescent nudes in a Manhattan art gallery, and the *New York Times* reviewer waxed rhapsodic about the "shimmering haze of delight, half fatherly, half loverly," through which Hamilton had captured his collection of "pretty girls trembling on the verge of womanhood . . . shy, enchanting creatures," inhabiting "an ideal world." (At least three of those creatures eventually accused Hamilton of rape. He committed suicide in 2016 with a high-profile case on the horizon.) And the editors and writers of *New York* magazine distinguished themselves, time and again, with their wholehearted embrace of the new trend for extremely young models set in motion by the success of Shields—a "preteen sex symbol," the magazine called her when she was just 11. In a 1980 cover story on a group of 12-to-15-year-old "Pretty Babies," judged by the magazine to be the "Hottest Models in Town," the writers saw fit to quote Dr. H. Jon Geis, a psychotherapist identified as having "a corner on studies of love, intimacy, and so forth," who endorsed the trend. "The child-woman is a supreme temptress for the adult male," he said.

I discovered all this, or rediscovered it, I guess I should say, while trying to get a handle on how the world of 11-to-14-year-olds—both their history and the history of how adults viewed them—had changed over time. I was dumbfounded when I read the junior high reminiscences of baby boomer parents like the Nebraska psychologist Mary Pipher, who wrote in her now-classic 1994 book, *Reviving Ophelia,* of her own early adolescent years as a cleaner, simpler, more peaceful and innocent time.

She described adolescent life in her tiny rural town as having been "slower, safer and less sexualized" than the miserable and sped-up world that the junior high girls around her seemed to inhabit in the late 1980s and early 1990s. "I spent my days riding my bike, swimming, reading, playing piano and drinking limeades at the drugstore with my friends," she wrote. *The Washington Post*'s Judy Mann recalled her junior high years in a northern Virginia suburb in the 1950s with similar nostalgia: "Life was blissfully uncomplicated back then," she wrote in 1999.

I had never known a time like that. In fact, the first thing that came to mind when I tried tapping into memories of my middle school years that could capture something of the general culture of my time was an image of Brooke Shields and her mother staring out at me from the cover of an issue of *New York* magazine that had arrived in our living room during the fall of my eighth-grade year. I could still see Brooke's thick eyebrows. And I could almost remember word for word the cover lines composed just to the right of her astonishingly beautiful face: "Meet Teri and Brooke Shields. Brooke is twelve. She poses nude. Teri is her mother. She thinks it's swell."

I had to go digging around online to get those words exactly right, which was how I came across all the other late-seventies words and images that in turn confirmed that, yes, the general culture of my time had been every bit as "gross" (as I would have said back then) as I remembered. It hadn't felt good to be a 12- or 13-year-old girl in those years, at least not for me.

It had felt bad, too, I learned, for the author Rebecca Solnit, who grew up in the San Francisco Bay Area and went through junior high just a couple of years before me. "The dregs of the sexual revolution were what remained," she once wrote about the time. "And it was really sort of a counterrevolution (guys arguing that since sex was beautiful and everyone should have lots everything goes and they could go at anyone; young women and girls with no way to say no and no one to help them stay out of harmful dudes' way). The culture was sort of snickeringly approving of the pursuit of underage girls. . . . [T]here was virtually no discourse about why this might be wrong."

That was an understatement. What I discovered, clicking around in our collective past, was that in the stories that grown-up men had told themselves then, the sexual interest they showed adolescent girls was not just not-wrong, it was desired. And it was acceptable because, as the writers Mel Juffe and Anthony Haden-Guest wink-winked at readers in *New York* magazine's "Pretty Babies," "Young girls nowadays are not, in the most functional, biological sense, as young as young girls used to be." The onset of puberty had continued its steady fall, with the average age of American girls' first periods having declined in the first half of the twentieth century by about three months every decade. By the mid-1970s, it had dropped to 12 years 9 months. However, it leveled off in the following decades, and by 2011, it had only fallen by roughly another three months.

Experts had long insisted that earlier fertility did not necessarily translate into an earlier interest in having sex. "Human sexuality is governed primarily by social conditioning, rather than endocrinal stimulation," the Stanford University psychologist Albert Bandura had written, for example, in a 1964 myth-busting article he titled "The Stormy Decade: Fact or Fiction?" But that particular scientific insight—despite subsequent repetition and reinforcement by other academics—just hadn't pierced the popular imagination. In a September 1980 back-to-school feature, perfectly calibrated for a campaign season that would bring us the election of Ronald Reagan, *Newsweek* jumped on the "biological" bandwagon, too, asserting that girls' earlier puberty was propelling them into a "brave, sometimes bewildering new world of adolescent hedonism."

"Something has happened to those endearing young charmers

who used to wobble around playing grownups in Mom's high heels," the magazine's David Gelman and co-authors wrote. "Sexual adventurism among young girls has risen to an astonishing degree." He blamed the "reckless sybaritism of the young," which, he was sure to note, had "filtered down to high schools and junior high schools," on girls' earlier puberty plus all that was new in American society since the 1960s: disco music, Jordache jeans, "women's liberation, the exploding divorce rate, the decline of parental and institutional authority, the widespread acceptance of 'living together,'" and, above all, the "vast increase" in working mothers, whose absence had turned the "empty house after school" into a "favorite trysting spot." The change, Newsweek explained, amounted to nothing less than a moment of "pubescent emancipation."

I'd somehow managed to miss that particular moment of alleged girl power. Women I spoke with for this book had, too. They, like me, remembered a very different sexual reality during their junior high years. Their sexual experiences spanned an extremely wide range: Some had had no physical contact with boys whatsoever; some had interacted at the level of Spin the Bottle or Truth or Dare; one had had sex in ninth grade; one had been sexually abused by her dad; and one had been raped at a suburban high school party when she was 13.

Many, like me, remembered a world where a desire to be experienced enough to be "cool" co-existed with a very strong double standard—boys pushing to gain the status that derived from advancing through "the bases," girls sharing their curiosity but gaining the reputation of "slut" if they ran with it (or were said to have done so). Boys still called the shots, socially and sexually, and girls turned themselves inside out to win boys' approval.

Stacey, a woman who grew up on the New Jersey shore and went to junior high in the mid-1970s, remembered that being in the "cool" crowd (where she desperately wanted to be) meant drinking, drugs, and sometimes even sex. But for the girls in the crowd, this was anything but emancipation. "I remember starting to be with boys and getting my first kiss, and the pressure to do that," she said. "I remember also there was a whole thing starting to go on when girls were going all the way and getting wasted at parties and passing out . . . and five or six boys having their whatever with her. There were pregnancies," she said. "And I don't know if it was because I grew up in what was traditionally a beach, vacation, party town . . . but everybody was doing it," she paused. "Everybody *else* was doing it."

She is married to a woman now and at the time that we spoke had a daughter in middle school. She remembered that the decisions she'd made about physical contact with boys in junior high had had about as much to do with her own authentic desires as the way she'd gotten dressed in the morning for school. "A lot of what I was doing was around what I thought other people wanted me to be doing," she said. "I didn't go to my closet in the morning and put on something just because I liked it. It was always because I thought, 'This looks cool.' And it wasn't 'This looks cool to me,' it was 'I think everyone's gonna think this looks cool.'" She went on, "It never even occurred to me at that age, not once, that I was a lesbian. Not once. It was all about boys and sex."

In this environment, the rules of engagement were up for grabs, and with adults insisting that liberation was for everyone and it was all good, it was very easy to make fatal errors that could prove costly for years and years. The author Ayelet Waldman stumbled in just that way. Her story began like a version of *Are You There God? It's Me, Margaret* set in hell. Her family moved to a new town in the summer before seventh grade. Right before school started, she was invited by her next-door neighbor to a slumber party. During a game of Truth or Dare, she was asked at what age she thought she'd lose her virginity. "I said what my feminist mother had trained me to say," she told me. " 'I don't know, whenever I'm ready. It could be when I'm 23. It could be when I'm 14.' "

Before she knew it, the girls at the party had spread the rumor that she was looking to lose her virginity before the end of seventh grade. She received countless prank phone calls. "A Dixie cup of sperm was left outside my locker. When I would talk in class, people would laugh." The few friends she'd managed to make soon dropped her, via a written note in math class. "You are not allowed to sit with us at lunch anymore. You're ruining our reputation," it said. "For the rest of seventh grade, I ate in the library. The librarians were really sweet about it: I pretended I was doing work, and they pretended to believe me."

Waldman was fortunate to have encountered some school adults who were willing and able to provide her with a safe space. What I heard from other people I interviewed—all middle school parents at the time we spoke—were recollections of a pervasive feeling of unsafety during their junior high years. Boys felt unsafe because they were beaten up if they were small or unathletic, or they were harassed as "fags" if they were just different, particularly in ways that were at odds with the ethos of the popular male crowd. The whole "Free to Be . . . You and Me" spirit really hadn't extended to them, certainly not at school and sometimes even not at home. And girls had been pummeled from all sides: by horny boys (or not-so-horny boys who were overcompensating), creepy older men, and the whole range of other adults who seemed to be particularly inclined at that time to abdicate their grown-up responsibilities. And who, perhaps as their own form of seventies "emancipation" (or in jealous revenge for the perceived emancipation of the young), were allowing themselves to direct some extremely mean-spirited puerile behavior toward the kids over whom they had some control.

I think, for example, of the teacher and student council adviser who decided, for his own amusement, to take the liberty of stirring up drama inside a three-girl sixth-grade friend group. He did this first by calling two of the girls, Mandy and Lisa, into his classroom for a chat. Mandy was the fall semester class president. The third friend in the group, Sarah, was planning a run for class president in the spring. The adviser asked Mandy and Lisa what they thought about that.

"I was honest and said, 'I'm not sure she can handle it. I'm not sure she's the right person,'" Mandy told me. "I was always a girl who did the right thing," she insisted miserably more than four decades later. "I thought he was asking my assessment as a *fact-gathering* thing." Lisa had strongly echoed her reservations.

"'Come out, Sarah,'" the teacher then said. "She came out of his closet in tears," Mandy continued. "It took so long to set that right."

I had a social studies teacher who egged on the boys in my class to make fun of my nose. He also liked to tell my friend Olivia to shave her legs. He made other comments as well—zooming in on whatever of her perceived imperfections he could. I hadn't remembered this—his behavior toward her—until she mentioned it almost thirty-five years later. We were having dinner and sharing recollections, seeing each other for the first time since eighth-grade graduation. This was one of the strongest memories she'd retained from that time. And once I heard it, all of a sudden an image came back to me: I saw her shrinking behind the arm of one of those one-piece desk-chairs, shaking with something silent that looked, but surely didn't feel, like laughter.

We were alone with him, just the two of us, in his homeroom. We used to do that a lot. Hanging out with him made us feel special. He was a very popular teacher. Adults spoke of him worshipfully. Kids thought he was hilarious. "He was a very nasty man," Olivia said. "And we laughed along with his stuff. Because he was the beloved teacher. We wanted his approval."

It was only in adulthood, she told me, that she realized that what had really been going on wasn't a positive kind of special attention at all. "He was not an attractive man," she said. "He was heavy and had a bad complexion. And he was saying mean things that were not appropriate for a teacher to be saying to 12-year-old girls. He was taking out all *his stuff* on us."

That kind of adult attention was really a betrayal. An abdication of the most basic responsibility to behave like a grown-up. There was a lot of this in the 1970s. Parents who had married very young were reaching out for freedoms denied them in their own teens and even in young adulthood. Many of their marriages were coming apart. Adults were going through their own "second adolescence," it was often said. So-called adolescent behavior in grown-ups, however, was its own breed of awful. It was youthful selfishness and self-centeredness paired with the power that only adults can wield. And when parents took out their "stuff" on their kids with adolescent-style meanness, the result could be truly horrible.

Miranda, the Westchester woman with learning issues who "fell in love with school" in seventh grade, grew up in Greenwich Village with parents who came from very well-off and socially prominent families. Both delighted in flaunting convention. Her father dressed "like a homeless man," she told me. Her mother left the front door of their townhouse unlocked and welcomed in anyone who smelled food and wanted a meal. She insisted that her children swim naked in kiddie pools, then sweetly lectured those who objected about "repression."

Beyond these similarities of style, however, her parents had a "fractious" relationship, Miranda said. And she was caught in the crosshairs. "My [paternal] grandmother poured her attention on me at the expense of my younger sisters. Mom protected my sisters and resented me," Miranda explained. "So I gravitated to my dad, but he was kind of off in his own world, narcissistic, the life of the party, a raconteur." In her mother's eyes, she said, "I was 'in his camp.' I felt as if I didn't really belong at home . . . didn't belong in the nuclear family."

THERE HAVE ALWAYS been toxic parents and bad teachers. But there was something about the "societal narcissisms" of the 1970s, as the novelist Rick Moody once put it, that seemed to enable new kinds of adult acting out, impacting children in all sorts of ways. For well-off kids in the suburbs, ostensibly safe and sheltered by big houses and sprawling yards, the result might have looked like the picture-perfect emotional cesspool that Moody captured so sharply in his 1994 novel *The Ice Storm*. For those growing up without wealth in the cities, it was a matter of structural and societal collapse: of high crime rates and crumbling school buildings; angry, burnt-out teachers; and policy makers who chose to look the other way. And, as I recall from growing up in New York City at that time, of a pervasive, generalized sense of rot and decay.

Nowhere was that more palpable than in the unhappy, often decrepit hallways of junior high schools.

"Imagine walking into the meanest building on earth," Susan, a Manhattan middle school mom, began as she recounted her recollections of 1970s Brooklyn for me. "Junior high was this horrible, antiquated, awful behemoth. They hadn't changed the curriculum since day one. We went to this tiny little elementary school where life was grand, and then one day we were dumped into cell block H. . . . The social studies teacher used to stand on her desk or her chair to watch us during tests and quizzes. She'd say, 'You're all thieving, cheating little shits!' There were really tough kids giving hand jobs and smoking cigarettes in the stairwells in sixth grade. There were fights all over the place in the hallways. Some of the kids, if you looked at them in the wrong direction, you were dead."

Underneath the bravado of Susan's storytelling—a combination of great cleverness and great anger that she'd cultivated as a shield back then—there was a lot of remembered unhappiness, and fear, and resentment for having to navigate those stairwells and hallways in the first place. There was a feeling of having been neglected by all the adults who were not minding the store, who watched her fake her way through school—copying her homework off others, sneaking out of PE to smoke Parliaments in the alley, generally skating by on innate intelligence and no effort in classes that demanded nothing of her—without ever stopping to ask themselves what was wrong.

If any adults had asked, she could have told them about a lot of things. She had a verbally and emotionally abusive father. A mother who kept her marriage going, despite her husband's "temper," because that was what she had been raised to do. And who filed for divorce just as soon as Susan, her youngest child, had left the house for college, at which point a number of her friends shunned her.

Susan had a smart older brother who, like her, finagled things so that he failed out of the top-level classes where he, like her, had been "tracked" at the start of seventh grade. Maybe it was because, like her, he found the ultracompetitive "alphas and jocks" to be "the worst of the worst," as she put it to me; or maybe it was because, also like her, he wanted to make a statement of protest. "You do these things because you kind of have to stand for something, and you're given all these crazy options," she told me. "You just thought: 'If this is what the world is like, I don't want any part of it.'"

Either way, now that she was a mother herself, the degree of adult inattention—or incompetence—struck her as preposterous. "Why should a kid who's obviously bright be struggling?" she wondered aloud. "I was perfectly capable of doing better than I did, but I never did better, and nobody ever interrupted that. Obviously, I was in need of serious help. It's interesting that I was permitted to fall so far and no one bothered to catch me."

By THE MID-1970S, when Susan started sixth grade, junior high schoolers in general had been permitted to fall off the cultural radar for quite some time. As the early 1960s had turned into "the sixties"—the period of youth revolt and social change that really spanned the decade of 1963 to 1973—the first wave of baby boomers had taken the noisy spectacle of their coming-of-age with them into high school and college. The lion's share of adult attention had followed. Grown-ups continued to find 12- and 13-year-olds uniquely awful. Studies from the 1960s and 1970s found, in fact, that parents considered the junior high years particularly wretched ones for *themselves* because their relationships with their kids hit such a low point. And the schools were generally seen as disasters: "the great wasteland of the American public school system," as one junior high school teacher-turned-advocate put it in 1971.

As a cause for societal hand-wringing, however, the education and activities of 12-year-olds just couldn't compete with the Summer of Love, Woodstock, and the whole package of "turning on, tuning in, and dropping out" with which high schoolers and young adults terrified—and titillated—older Americans. In addition, the smaller cohort of kids born in the early to mid-1960s through the 1970s were easy to miss in the wake of the much larger baby boom generation born in the postwar years.

When Joan Lipsitz, the director of the Center for Early Adolescence at the University of North Carolina at Chapel Hill's School of Education, received a grant from the Ford Foundation to take a look at what was going on in the country's hodgepodge of junior high, middle, and "intermediate" schools in the mid- to late 1970s, she described the kids she found there as "a new, eerily quiet generation." The schools she saw were terrible—"dreary, unimaginative and routinized places," Lipsitz observed, staffed with "the least talented of our teachers" and run by administrators who were "obsessed with issues of control."

Despite the stated desires of education reformers to tap experts in early adolescence as teachers and administrators, many school leaders knew virtually nothing about the unique needs and challenges of 11-to-14-year-olds, and most had no desire to learn. When Lipsitz reached out to schools in all fifty states to try to get basic information about their students, she received virtually no replies. "All we can conclude is that no one cares enough to compile or to process such data," she wrote in the 1980 book that grew out of her report for the Ford Foundation. And this problem, she found, existed throughout the entire field of education. Nearly seventy years of the natural experiment of junior high had produced shockingly little by way of research or insight. It was as if no one had been interested enough to ask questions and seek answers. As a result, even educators who wanted to do better by junior high school students were operating in a "blatant void of information."

Lipsitz titled her book *Growing Up Forgotten*. She labeled the students she saw "the most overlooked age group among minors in America." And she subtitled what she had hoped would be a robust section on school reform "The Abyss."

This was very strong language, especially from an academic. And it must have sounded particularly harsh to the leaders of what Lipsitz unmagnanimously referred to as the "so-called 'middle school movement.'" At the time she was writing, that movement was over a decade old. If measured by new or reconfigured buildings, it was an ongoing success. But if judged by its original goals of creating an educational experience tailored to the unique capabilities and needs of 11-to-14-year-olds, it was shaping up to be as much of a failure as its early-twentieth-century predecessor.

Lipsitz found the same old boredom, the same alienation, foisted now on kids at even younger ages, if they were housed in middle schools. In other words, no matter how much the buildings had changed, the quality of the schooling of 11-to-14-year-olds had stayed depressingly the same. A big part of the reason, argued Lipsitz and the many other scholars who, inspired in part by her book, started to make the study of early adolescence their specialty in the early 1980s, was the very skewed way that adults continued to look at those kids.

Most middle-grade personnel, Lipsitz noted, thought of their students in the most simplistic, stereotypical, and overwhelmingly negative ways, believing, as she put it, that "adolescence is a time of tumultuous upheaval during which the best we can do is hold our breaths, wait for it to pass over, and meanwhile segregate as best we can the turbulent from the rest of society." The "deep mistrust or even dislike" of the students, she believed, meant that the schools were doomed to fail, because the adults leading them had no "sophisticated awareness" of who their students were. The authors of a 1984 review of middle school reform efforts put it even more bluntly: "These youngsters are perhaps the most maligned of any segment of the student population."

The late 1970s female version of the age-old Hormone Monster—in the form of what the journalist Karen Houppert once memorably called the "new breed of copulating schoolgirl"— was patently unhelpful. The more attention this lusty and lusted-after fantasy creature received, the less adults applied themselves to figuring out what was truly going on with her real-life peers— many of whom, it was increasingly clear by the early 1980s, were not thriving. Academics were starting to notice that many of the problems that had long worried adults about high schoolers— alcohol and drug use, cigarette smoking, violent behavior, running away, suicide, and sex—were showing up, to some degree at least, among junior high schoolers. But it was very hard to determine whether those issues were truly new and what caused them. And that was because, as the 1980s began, there was almost no data with which to establish some baseline truths about the age group.

The "blatant void"—and long-standing hard feelings—that Lipsitz had decried within the world of education existed in the field of psychology, too. Although academics like G. Stanley Hall had been studying adolescence since the end of the nineteenth century, empirical studies were sorely lacking. This was partly due to the fact that from the 1920s through most of the 1970s, empirical research on kids of any age had been lacking. Psychoanalytic theory, the way of thinking about children (and adults) and families that dominated in both the academy and clinical practice in those decades, did not engage in hypothesis testing when it came to its core theoretical concepts. "Conflict" was the central idea of the psychoanalytic theory of adolescent development. Different writers might define the nature of that conflict somewhat differently. For Anna Freud in the 1930s, it was "the struggles of the ego to master the tensions and pressures arising from the drive derivatives" (grossly simplified: the inner battle to handle both horniness and separation from parents in a socially acceptable way). For Erik Erikson in the 1950s, it was "identity vs. role confusion." But for as long as the psychoanalytic viewpoint held sway, the basic conception of adolescence as marked primarily by conflict was essentially unquestioned.

It made perfect sense to parents. It meshed beautifully with the extreme pressure toward marriage and parenthood in postwar American society, as seen in the words of the Montclair State College psychologist Jerome M. Seidman in 1953: "The adolescent 'revolt' is but a healthy preparation for marriage." And it corresponded to the experience of clinicians, who found working with teenagers fraught with frustrations, including, according to Freud, "their reluctance to cooperate; their lack of involvement in the therapy or in the relationship to the analyst; their battles for the reduction of weekly sessions; their unpunctuality; their missing of treatment sessions for the sake of outside activities; their sudden breaking off of treatment altogether."

The youngest adolescents were the most difficult of all, chiefly because they had a way of making grown-ups—even trained professionals—feel really, really bad. Theirs "is an age which is especially disappointing for the adult," the psychologists Arthur Witt Blair and William H. Burton noted in their 1951 book, *Growth and Development of the Preadolescent*. "Children at this age are hard to live with. Teachers and psychiatrists also find them uncooperative. Ordinary psychological techniques do not seem to be successful with them." The root of the problem for Blair and Burton was that, unlike younger children, the "preadolescent" posed a real threat to the adult ego: "He increasingly sees the adults in his world as they are, divested of the halo of feeling which very young children supply for their parents and teachers."

And so, bolstered by the quite remarkable theoretical view that an object of study was far too ornery and ungratifying to permit direct observation, the area of early adolescence had largely stayed a dark continent for decades. The net effect was that 11-to-14-year-olds remained an age group about whom it was singularly easy to think the worst. Adults could project whatever they wanted onto them, because there was no solid research with which to contradict what they said. Without data, it was also practically impossible to figure out, in a reliable way, how to help make their lives better. And that was a very serious problem, because by the 1980s, there were signs that a fair number of middle schoolers really did need adult help.

Two forces were converging—the tail end of the sexual revolution and the start of the Reagan reaction—and stuck in the middle were junior high school kids, who were sexualized, judged, and even demonized, and who really didn't figure at all in the equation. In fact, just about none of what was popularly said about them in the Lolita revival years had much of anything really to do with them. It *was* true that more kids of junior high age were having sex than ever before—as were Americans of all ages, outside of marriage. But the idea that this was ubiquitous or had been caused by the emergence of a new generation of sex-crazed, Sue Lyon–like nymphets was absurd. The "cool" kids (a category that, by definition, can only be very limited in number) might have been going at it—though both contemporary and retrospective surveys suggest that even in that subgroup, the reality of sex was greatly exaggerated. But the vast majority of junior high schoolers a generation ago—as is true for the vast majority of middle schoolers today—were not sexually active, not taking drugs, not drinking or smoking or getting involved in any of the other activities that parents fear the most.

What kids *were* dealing with back then was an adult world that was falling apart. Not because mothers were working (have you ever heard anyone trace their problems back to the fact that they had a working mother?), but because American society was changing, families were struggling, and nothing meaningful was being done to help them through their new challenges. There was no road map to guide grown-up behavior. Many of the beliefs and expectations that had defined the shape of adult life in the past—in ways both good and bad—had suddenly become outdated. This was particularly true for the women (and children) who were products of those very young late 1950s and early 1960s marriages that were falling apart in droves by the early 1980s. So many of the messages that women like Susan's mother had been taught about marriage and family, so many of the coping skills they'd picked up along the way to deal with the power dynamics of their relationships with men, had failed them. But there was no good expert advice for reassembling and moving on. There was no real evidence base for understanding how things like divorce or abuse or mental illness affect children, especially in the already difficult junior high years.

Many of the concepts we all needed weren't yet in circulation. We didn't have the words at our disposal that could have helped us make sense of our world and of ourselves. And neither did the adults who tried, for better or for worse, to take care of us. There was only starting to be an understanding of childhood depression, which most psychoanalysts didn't even think existed prior to the 1970s. There wasn't yet an articulation of the type of PTSD that can arise from growing up in homes and neighborhoods where toxic levels of stress are omnipresent. There was little popular awareness of common learning disabilities like dyslexia, or of other issues affecting kids' school and social lives such as ADHD. "They didn't know what to do with me," said Tracy, the African American media executive we met earlier who attended junior high in 1970s-era Washington, D.C. She'd been a star English student, she told me, but had always been bizarrely hopeless in math. She saw numbers in all different colors and found it all but impossible to work with them in any sort of coherent way. No one taught her the word "synesthesia" or suggested she might have dyscalculia. "No one knew what to do," she said again.

Journalists, then as now, covered scary and salacious phenomena occurring at the extremes—kids experimenting with drugs in fifth grade (and "some even in the third grade," as *Ladies' Home Journal* alleged in 1979)—but there wasn't a whole lot of reporting on what kids of the 1970s and 1980s really wanted or needed. What research there was, then as now, indicated that they didn't want their mothers to stop working; they wanted their mothers— and fathers, and adults generally—to *listen to them*. They wanted adults to *see them*. This desire wasn't unique to their generation, or even to the fact that they were in early adolescence. But it was coming at a time when mothers, working or not—and fathers as well—were particularly preoccupied with themselves and often not able to rise to the challenge.

That was a key part of the sense of adult abandonment that ran through quite a few of the stories I heard about being a young adolescent in the 1970s and 1980s: the lack of words and concepts from adults to help them deal with their feelings at a time when so many things felt out of control. The keeping-up-appearances approach that allowed so many *Feminine Mystique*–era marriages to last as long as they did left newly aware junior high schoolers with no way to process the sometimes awful things going on in their homes. This, too, wasn't new—and it wasn't unique to the 1970s. But the multitude of often noxious social forces bearing down on junior high schoolers *was* new and unprecedented. And it was hitting them just when they were at the point of trying to figure out who they were and where they fit—to start to weave a future identity out of the very poor material adults were providing for them.

In the decades that followed, a new emphasis on openness and authenticity between parents and children took root in American culture. It paralleled massive changes in the world of child development and psychology and dovetailed with all sorts of new worries about technology, middle-class social status, and the economy. All of this meant that when the junior high schoolers of the 1970s and 1980s became parents, they looked back very critically on their own childhood experiences. And they wanted to do things very differently.

CHAPTER 6

Mommy & Me 2.0

My daughter (my sweet, kind-hearted, shy firstborn daughter)
started middle school a year ago . . . and my heart has been
ripped out and tossed into a wood chipper.

—MELISSA TAYLOR, *SheKnows*

WHEN MY DAUGHTER started middle school, I, like all the other parents I knew, expected the absolute worst.

We couldn't really have done otherwise.

Our memories had prepared most of us to view the coming years as a tightrope walk across the abyss. We'd been primed for pretty much our entire adult lives to believe that whatever meanness or sexual grossness we remembered from junior high had, in the intervening years, gotten far worse.

In the 1990s, a new "moral panic" about middle schoolers and sex had taken up residence in the American adult psyche. By the early 2000s, it had become so extreme that it made the anxious adults of the late 1950s and early 1960s look like Zen masters. The old fears about the "sexual acceleration" of childhood, as a *Newsweek* article had put it in 1991, were back, but in an age of the 24/7 news cycle and the Starr Report, they took on a new and unique focus.

In 1997, *The New York Times* reported a shift in teenage sexual behavior: a "significant rise in the prevalence of oral sex, and a decline in the age at which it starts." A sex educator, Dr. Cydelle Berlin, noted that she'd been getting a lot of questions about oral sex from children as young as 10 or 11. They weren't engaging in it, she made clear. "Questions about oral sex start in fifth or sixth grade, not because kids are doing it, but because they've heard about it and they're curious," she explained. "By seventh grade, they want to know if it's really safer sex, and what are the mechanics. For girls, 'Do you spit or do you swallow?' is a typical seventh-grade question."

It was the sound bite equivalent of the shot heard 'round the world—an effect that Berlin undoubtedly anticipated, given her propensity, as she put it to *Times* reporter Tamar Lewin, to leave parents' groups "shocked, surprised, trembling" after speaking to them. Soon, *Time* magazine was calling middle schoolers the new "prodigies" of sex. *The Washington Post* was producing stories of middle schoolers practicing fellatio in public parks, on school buses, and even in the middle of a "crowded study hall." A Reston, Virginia, seventh grader—known to kids at school as "Mr. Pimp"—was accused of operating a "prostitution ring" for the purpose of buying and selling 12- and 13-year-olds' sexual favors. "Very bright kids, from very nice families, hit the sexual fast track in middle school," the *Washington Post* writer Judy Mann lamented, after deriving "shattering insights" from her daughter and her daughter's two best friends. "Seventh grade, I believe, is the most dangerous year of a girl's life."

By the early 2000s, Oprah Winfrey had declared an oral sex

"epidemic" and introduced her viewers to a lipstick-and-oral-sex obscenity called "rainbow parties." During those parties, middle school girls wearing different colors of lipstick lined up and serviced boys, the O magazine writer Michelle Burford claimed on Oprah's show. She termed the gatherings "pervasive."

As had been the case in the late 1950s and early 1960s sex panic, there was no hard evidence that any of these stories were based in truth. Many were sourced through middle schoolers talking about things they'd heard about other middle schoolers doing. Or they relied on adults who talked about things kids had told them other kids were doing. Or not doing. A striking number of stories were padded by anecdotes of things kids had talked about but hadn't done. What reliable statistics there were showed that sex in middle school, particularly in sixth and seventh grades, was pretty rare and actually decreased over the course of the 1990s. They also showed that, for girls at least, sex in middle school was very often nonconsensual. "Rainbow parties," agreed both academic experts and journalists who'd spent extended periods of time immersed in the world of middle schoolers, were an urban legend. "No one, least of all Oprah, seemed to question the actual logistics of any of this," wrote Peggy Orenstein, who has written about middle school girlhood since the early 1990s, in her 2016 book, *Girls & Sex*. "Exactly *how* were girls managing to complete multiple, random sex acts during the school day without an adult's notice? Were thirteen-year-old boys really up to fifteen public blow jobs in the space of a few hours? Wouldn't any rainbow effect be rinsed off or at least indelibly smudged by each subsequent partner?"

By the time I became a middle school parent, in 2008, the really crazy sex stories were gone, *Newsweek* having finally labeled fears of an "oral sex epidemic" a form of "hysteria," and *The New York Times* following a few months later with a story that dismissed "rampant teenage promiscuity" as a "myth." But more than twenty years of being on the receiving end of news that middle schoolers were horrible, sexually disgusting, even sociopathic, had nonetheless left their mark. The general sense remained that whatever loathsome behavior we might perhaps have remembered from our own junior high years was now far worse—more *out there,* more public, somehow more "degrading," as a woman who'd survived junior high (barely) in her New Jersey beach town put it to me.

We all knew that middle school was the place where girls' souls went to die. We knew that boys were in "crisis," too, falling behind girls academically and in extracurriculars, and undergoing vicious hazing and harassment if they didn't live up to the standards of the worst kind of toxic masculinity. Another legacy of the 1990s, fear of bullying, was very strongly with us as well. It had first become a major cultural concern in the wake of the Columbine massacre, which was initially erroneously reported to have been caused by Eric Harris and Dylan Klebold's desire for revenge against bullies who had made their lives hell. Then, in the early 2000s, Rosalind Wiseman's *Queen Bees & Wannabes* and Rachel Simmons's *Odd Girl Out* had popularized a new wave of academic research on "relational aggression"—the rumors and whispers and friend-turning and shunning typical of girl-style bullying. Their books were, to the parents of middle school girls at the time, what Dr. Spock had been to our mothers.

By the time my daughter was in sixth grade, the Tina Fey movie *Mean Girls,* which had been inspired by Wiseman's book, was already a slumber party cult classic. Terms such as "mean girls," "queen bees," and "alpha boys" had permanently come, in many if not most of our minds, to define the middle school experience. They'd given everyone—adults and kids alike—a ready-made vocabulary and set of concepts for making sense of the tortures to come. Teachers and school counselors weren't thrilled; such labels, they said, tended to affix blame to one designated wrongdoer when the reality was always far more complicated and the avenues of responsibility much more diverse. And it was true that the words had a way of getting weaponized, especially when wielded by parents, whose already anxious faces seemed to harden and shut down further with each passing semester.

It was a surprise, then, when my daughter got to seventh grade—always the year in news reports when girls' lives went off the rails—to see that the world in which she'd landed was *nothing* like what I'd long seen described. After all the reporting on how different, how scary, how foreign, how horrifying things were going to be once we had middle schoolers, I discovered that, in a lot of very basic ways, middle schoolers were about the same as I remembered them from way back in the late 1970s.

We'd been hearing for decades about the falling age of puberty, which was said to be plunging middle schoolers into precocious lives of sexual sophistication. But the kids I was around didn't look any different from what I recalled. They came in a big range of sizes—some huge, some tiny, some looking 9, and some looking 15. A couple of the girls (a tiny minority of two, in fact) were said to be off in Rock Creek Park doing things with "the boys." Others were watching cartoons and playing with American Girl dolls. As in the past, the most "mature" (read: socially polished, good-looking, and rich) kids tended to be the most popular. And yet, even when it came to the coolest of the "cool" kids, I heard tell of nothing that bore the slightest resemblance to the sped-up, sexed-up, morally reprehensible world that other journalist moms had described with such shock and horror a decade or so before.

This didn't mean that things were great, or that the kids were particularly *nice* to one another; they just weren't a brand-new breed of monster. They still performed and preened, checking themselves out incessantly in mirrors, real and imagined. They made one another miserable with the same old friendship machinations and in- and out-group maneuvering that I'd lived through in the late 1970s, and that my mother, recalling junior high life in the late 1940s, had assured me wouldn't last forever. The technology at their disposal *had* changed, however, and massively so. Social media was bringing a huge lifestyle shift. But middle schoolers were putting current technology to pretty much all the same uses as junior high schoolers had back in the analog days when a landline was the only phone. They were constantly online; we talked on the phone for hours and hours. (Remember busy signals? Raging parents?) They made screenshots of cruel texts to "help" their friends see who liked or hated them; we had the horrible practice of calling a friend and tricking them into bashing another friend who was listening in on another extension. They created anonymous posts and sent untraceable emails; we passed around "slam books" to express our anonymous cruelty. ("Nice body. Too bad about the face," my page said. And: "Tried to get too cool too fast.")

I quickly learned, however, that there was one thing—one *really* big thing—that had indeed changed: the world of middle school parenthood. And that change was dramatically for the worse.

For me, sixth grade had been a point when I started to have a lot more freedom. My mother knew and had to approve of my plans, but I made them, and I walked by myself or took the bus to get where I was going. She knew who my friends were and who their parents were, but I don't think it would have ever dawned on her—or on any of the other parents—to have tried to become friends with them just because *we* were friends. Her world and my world were separate spheres. She volunteered a lot at my school and so had a presence there that was much larger than was typical for parents in those days. But even then, the overlap was geographical; she resided in the world of the adults, and I was firmly in the realm of the kids.

That boundary was all but gone by the time my daughter began middle school. Parents made their kids' plans, participated in those plans, sought out and befriended their kids' friends' parents, micromanaged which groups formed and how, decided which activities their kids would do and with whom, oversaw who went to camp with whom and how and where they would bunk. Within just a few years, smartphones were ubiquitous, and parents were doing far more. They scrolled through their kids' phones late at night, stalking them (and their friends) online, seeking out—and often getting—detailed downloads of who was talking to whom and how, and what they were saying behind whose backs and when and why. And then they shared those tidbits (selectively, of course) with their mom friends.

Parents I've spoken with in recent years have stories that never cease to amaze me: Middle schoolers and their parents not only dress and talk similarly now; they also behave similarly. Moms suit up in matching outfits for their daughters' cheerleading competitions. Parents gather on school playgrounds to trash 12-year-olds for sending "slutty" pictures. Adults decide who's in and who's out for parties or even car pools based on how cool the kids will look on Facebook. ("There won't be enough room for a group picture on the front steps" was the bad-optics excuse one mother used to exclude her son's unpopular friend from a group her son had put together for an eighth-grade pre-dance hangout. Parents slide right into their middle schoolers' social obsessions—the endless dramas with friends, the contests for popularity. The more money and time parents have on their hands, the crazier this is. And the more invested parents themselves are in the trappings of power and status—an investment that tends to track the degree to which they live in a world of power and high status—the more involved they get in their kids' social ambitions. "Districts that tend to curve lower socioeconomically tend to have more faith in the school and less invasive parents," a public school official on Long Island told me. "When you turn the dial up on the wealth of the community, the parent intensity grows proportionately."

The higher up you go, the more absurd it all gets. One Southern

California mother admitted to me that she had "scoped out" a woman she saw as a "queen bee" mom and had befriended her first, in order to pave the way for her son to enter a close "triumvirate" of boys he wanted to be friends with. And then, when he ultimately was able to have the other boys to his house for a sleepover, she planned and executed a perfect pancake breakfast. "It was hyper helicopter parenting. My mom *never* would have done that," she said with some embarrassment. "I was really wanting the boys to have a positive experience and go home and say they had a good time."

When friendship-orchestrating efforts fail or much-desired relationships go bad, parents and kids agonize together. "There are some kids who are able to be friends with who they want, and there are some kids who are passed over," Cheryl, a mother on suburban Long Island, told me, miserably, of her own unsuccessful foray into the "social engineering" routinely carried out by the moms in her community.

The ubiquity of social media in the lives of middle schoolers means that parents feel compelled to live online alongside them. "That's probably the biggest question: Do you stalk or not?" said a mother of a D.C. middle schooler while a room of her peers nodded their agreement. *And do you feel guilty about it?* others chimed in. What this means is that whatever social dramas take place among the kids becomes 24/7 background noise for their parents as well. One woman told me that at a recent lunch with a friend, the other woman's cellphone buzzing had been so incessant that she'd assumed something really bad was happening. She'd asked her friend if something was wrong. Not at all, the friend had reassured her, impervious to the constant interruptions. It was just middle school drama. She required her kids to include her in all their group chats. And she had *twins* in seventh grade!

All this is done in the name of being a good parent—"doing your job," "knowing what's going on," keeping your kids physically and emotionally safe by "monitoring" their online activity. And when everything is going well, this shared online life can be a lot of fun: Kids pile into a car, and a mom or dad drops them off at the mall, proudly snapping and uploading a picture as the kids walk off in lockstep. Parents post pictures on Facebook of pre-dance preparations, post-party late-night snacks, a last-day-of-school trip to the beach. And everybody who is tagged "likes" the pictures. Everybody is happy. Everyone except the moms and dads who weren't included in the group messaging—because things have not been going well, and their children weren't invited.

Those parents are up all night, tossing in bed, turning the episodes of exclusion over and over in their minds. It's mostly—let's just admit it—moms, though not exclusively. One dad told me that he had never gotten over hearing his daughter's (soon-to-be-former) best friend telling her during a sleepover that, popularity-wise, she was at the very "bottom of the food chain." Sick with hatred, these parents ruminate, revisiting the snubs, the always-too-full carpooling arrangements, and, of course, the secrets and lies. And because they are "good" parents, because they value *being present,* because they are there all the time with their kids (emotionally and physically, in person and online), they witness all the slights and rolled eyes, the backs turned to close off a conversation, the seating rearrangements to keep best friends together (because even five minutes apart would be just too awful), the choosing of class partners in ways that always leaves one kid out. And because they are there, because there is no escape for parents, as for their kids, in 24/7 "emotionally connected" twenty-first-century family life, they feel the sting of their children's rejections and dramas with gut-wrenching immediacy.

"When Lilly gets her feelings hurt, when kids snub her, when somebody says something hurtful to her, I feel it *in my soul* like it happened to me," said a mom of a recent eighth grader.

"It's like purgatory," said Amy, a Maryland political consultant whose daughter, Caroline, had switched schools for seventh grade and was struggling mightily to make friends in a class that Amy had learned was known within the school for its cliques and meanness. "'A lot of these kids don't really know who they are yet,'" the head of the middle school had told her late in the fall in a quasi-attempt at mollification. "Not knowing who you are is not an excuse to be a total asshole," she said to me.

Amy tried her best to help Caroline make friends, hosting parent potlucks, inviting other families over for brunch or dinner. But that only meant that she had the opportunity to experience what Caroline was dealing with firsthand. "People are 'so busy' now," she told me acridly. "People are Just. So. Busy."

The multigenerational rejections threw Amy right back to seventh and eighth grade, when, as the child of a single working mother in a school and at a time when that was uncommon, she had struggled terribly to make friends. The pain of exclusion was just as bad for her daughter. The sense of powerlessness, if anything, was even worse, because she knew that if other parents would just play along with her a *little bit,* things could be very different for Caroline. And yet there was nothing she could do to change the social dynamic. "It is the definition of purgatory," she reiterated. "You're watching something over and over again. You're not able to fix it. . . . It's like death by a thousand cuts."

EARLY ADOLESCENCE HAS been a tough time for parents for as long as they've had to experience it close-up, day-to-day, with their children. But these difficulties play out in slightly different ways for each generation. Middle school parents in the 1990s often expressed real despondency as they described the feeling of watching their beloved children go through the changes of early adolescence. When Mary Pipher commented on it in her 1994 book, *Reviving Ophelia,* that grief had a very particular ring of baby boomer narcissism. Pipher told of how she and her mom friends had felt "tormented" by their daughters when the girls hit the "crucible" of junior high school and started to turn all their mothers' values inside out. For all the mothers' best efforts, their intellectually alive, "androgynous" girls with "'tomboyish' personalities" were transformed by the passage into junior high. "We had raised our daughters to be assertive and confident, and they seemed to be insecure and concerned with their femininity," she wrote. The mothers were left confused, angry, and unsure how to proceed. "Parents experience an enormous sense of loss when their girls enter this new land," Pipher wrote. She amplified that emotion a few lines later: "Everyone is grieving."

Another prominent 1990s author, the journalist Lucinda Franks, made the passage through middle school parenthood sound like her own personal expulsion from Eden. In 1993, she published the equivalent of a baby boomer parenting manifesto in the pages of *The New York Times Magazine,* in which she smugly enthused about her son Joshua, age 9, and the whole "splendid generation" that she and her contemporaries had sculpted into being: "Today's crop of under-12's, particularly in middle- and upper-middle-income families and particularly in urban America, seems to have reinvented—or even bypassed—childhood as we knew it. . . . They are proud, independent and strong-willed; they are worldly-wise and morally serious," she wrote. "They are a generation that has been raised to challenge and doubt authority, to take little at face value—in short, to enter the world of maturity long before they are mature. This was no accident. . . . We wanted to create the children we always yearned to be."

By 2000, the paradisiacal state of parenting an "under-12" had passed. Josh was 15, and Franks was making the rounds of the TV talk shows, spreading the word about "trains of girls demanding oral sex" and sixth graders competing to be admired as a "shaman" of the art of fellatio, while publicizing a piece called "The Sex

Lives of Your Children," which she'd recently written for *Talk* magazine. "I wept my way through writing this article," she told the PBS talk show host Richard Heffner. "I am not so sure that this generation has any sense of idealism."

For baby boomer parents in the 1990s, the sense of loss and of being lost, and the tinge of wounded ego that ran through all that sentiment, was so great and so widespread that the psychologist Laurence Steinberg and his wife, Wendy, devoted an entire book to it, *Crossing Paths: How Your Child's Adolescence Triggers Your Own Crisis*. The essential element of that crisis for those parents, the Steinbergs believed, was being confronted with youth and beauty not their own. A child's sexual development at puberty could actually bring on a midlife crisis in parents, they wrote, by serving as a punishing reminder of how far they themselves had come from their own (more fertile, virile, beautiful, muscled) teen years. "The physical blossoming inherent in adolescence provides a cruel contrast to our own midlife journey," they wrote. "It was difficult enough to face middle age and all its attendant side effects. But to face them alongside Adonis or Venus was absolutely excruciating."

IN THE LATE 2010s, I never heard parents express that particular preoccupation (at least not in connection with their kids). Instead, what was most painful for them, in our age of skyrocketing inequality and rampant class insecurity, was watching the middle schoolers around them sort themselves by status. The parents I spoke with were acutely aware of who was up and who was down, who lived where, had what, and came from what kind of family background. All were college educated, and many were people who lived in extremely competitive communities that they had accessed precisely *because* they had spent their lives—or perhaps had a spouse who had spent his or her life—seeking enough money and power to get there. The permutations of competition varied a bit: In Washington, D.C., it was about money plus proximity to political power. In Los Angeles, it was about money plus proximity to star power. "There's a power dynamic among the adults, and the power dynamic among [the] adults really impacts the power dynamic among the kids. It's all 'Am I in or out?' " said a mom whose three children had just finished making their way through sixth, seventh, and eighth grades at D.C.'s most prestigious private school, and all had the scars to prove it—mom as well as kids.

"Everyone wants to be close to the industry people," said Tamar, a labor lawyer in Los Angeles whose daughter spent sixth through eighth grades in a private school that draws the children of some of Hollywood's biggest stars. She had an Ivy League education but earned far less money than did most of her daughter's classmates' parents. She felt as if her own accomplishments weren't valued. She regarded the others with a combination of jealous resentment and disgust. It was not a good mix. "At the events there's a lot of fakey, fakey kiss kiss. The girls were 12 going on 25. The moms were wanting to be friends with the girls, wearing all the same stuff . . . all dressed like, my husband would like to say, 'Are you trying to pick up some extra cash?' "

Parents' social status and kids' status in their school community tended to dovetail, because what determines social status is pretty much the same for adults as it is for middle school kids: what you have, how you look, whom you're with, and how much "juice" you have of the sort that's valued in a particular community. "My son played basketball in middle school," said a doctor from Southeast Asia who spent her children's middle and high school years in a wealthy and competitive New England suburb. "He was good but not the best. He was a scrawny kid. Very good at math. The middle school parents sort of looked down on me, the way the kids looked down on him. We weren't in the fancy part of town, and he wasn't white. I was keenly aware of this—the sidelong, not-quite-there acknowledgment, the judgment and exclusion."

It was unpleasant for parents to be snubbed, but it wasn't (unless they were already feeling particularly bad about themselves) devastating. In many cases, their relative lack of money was a result of choices they had made professionally. They were academics, perhaps, or worked at nonprofits. Like Tamar, they had their own ways of looking down on parents who drove huge, fancy cars. But when their kids were snubbed for the same reasons, their pain was of another magnitude entirely. It wasn't just that it was agonizing to see the people they loved most on this earth get hurt. It also could feel to them like there had been a public referendum on the entire family and they all had lost.

That's when the old middle school feelings could boil up, turbocharged. One mother I spoke with who lives in a middle-class section of an otherwise much fancier Chicago suburb could still tap into it, just as strongly as she had when her son was in seventh grade. She was an administrator in a K–8 school; her husband was a professor. Their son, who attended the school where she worked, was a great student and a good artist, and a pretty good athlete, too. And yet, by the time he got to middle school, the other boys in the class—and their parents—had decided that he wasn't athletic enough to compete on their level. No matter the activity, they excluded him. In fact, it seemed to his mom that the other parents went out of their way not to invite him to join any of the teams the other boys played on after school, which meant, since they were an extremely athletic group of boys, he was excluded from pretty much all social activities.

"He's not really a soccer player, is he?" one mother had said to her once, when she had called her on the exclusion.

Eight years later, when she spoke to me, she was still furious.

Her son was in college and thriving, but when she thought back on all the years she'd spent locked up with those other parents in the squirrel cage of their "sweet little community," as the school always described itself, watching them judge her son as just not good enough, it still filled her with rage—"irrational" levels of rage, she admitted. Her son was not only "just not good enough" to play on their sons' soccer team; he was not good enough *globally*. Not rich enough. Not slick enough. Not cool enough.

She and her husband weren't either. Her husband had never fit in with the real estate developer or commodities trader "alpha dads" in the class. She worked full-time and sometimes had a second job in the summer, too. She wasn't around in the late morning for coffee or tennis, and she wasn't able to shuttle groups of kids around in the afternoon, when she worked in the afterschool program. That meant she wasn't in the loop. Her son had to rely on invitations, which, in the middle school years, never came. Only the biggest, tallest, most athletic, and richest boys got invitations. No one else mattered.

Sometimes it had seemed like all that rage, building and building and being pushed down into her gut, was going to eat her alive. "I felt this hatred," she said. "Hatred at these parents who were allowing children"—not just her son—"to be ostracized. Who were either blind to it or, if not overtly, tacitly ostracizing these children themselves. Who were so invested in appearance and façade and who knew who. Who were actively . . . teaching their kids to be these judgy, exclusive people."

Social status can be a fragile thing. A change can come as a result of something that occurs in either a parent's or a child's life. The loss of a prestigious job, perhaps, or a kid being pushed out of a clique. And then one generation can drag down the other. "You're high-status as a mother, but then you get divorced and you lose your fancy home, and you're looked at as a leper," said the New

England doctor, recalling the moment when her marriage fell apart. Her son was in high school then and her daughter was in eighth grade. When she moved with them to a nearby but partly blue-collar suburb, she said, "the women who used to hang out with me . . . there was a tangible shift. Maybe it triggered conflicts in them about their own marriages, but there was a shift."

For one well-off couple in the South, their eighth-grade son's lacrosse injury brought on a fall in social status that left the whole family reeling in its wake. As a future varsity player in a sports-centric school where athletes ruled the roost, the boy had spent middle school at the very top of the pack. But after his injury, he had to stop playing, and his lacrosse buddies dropped him. When it became clear that all the physical therapy in the world wouldn't return him to the level of a varsity athlete, he fell into a clinical depression—and so did his father.

The father had been a Division I athlete in college until a knee injury had forced him off the field at the end of his freshman year. He had loved his son's friends, had loved his status as a lacrosse dad, had loved the future he'd foreseen for his son as a top athlete. When it all went sour, both parents raged at their son's former friends. They hectored his coach. And they served their depressed son very poorly. "He had to find another basis for his identity," a former staff member at the boy's school told me. He needed to stop "chasing the middle school dream." But his parents just wouldn't let it go.

PARENTS HAVE LONG complained about being stuck on an endless roller-coaster ride of emotion when their kids hit early adolescence. Today, though, it seems that it's the kids who are often dragged along for the ride as they struggle to manage the crazy ups and downs of their middle school parents. Parent friendships, enmeshed with kid friendships, can become every bit as unstable during these years. Sometimes, they're even more volatile. Often, adults carry angry grudges long after the kids have moved on.

Suzanne, a Westchester lawyer and mother, had often felt isolated and out of the loop among the mostly stay-at-home moms who put in long hours volunteering at her daughter Jennie's elementary school. Over the years, though, she and her husband had found a circle of parent friends, all dual-working couples like themselves. They got together regularly for dinner. They relied on one another for carpooling. By the time their kids were in middle school, Suzanne had come to feel socially at home. But then Jennie got caught up in a tangled web of drama at the end of seventh grade. It may have had something to do with the fact that she and another girl, Sophie, had a crush on the same boy. Or it may have had nothing to do with the boy at all. There was another girl stirring things up on the periphery, too. One day, egged on by this girl to "do something," Jennie ripped up a poem that Sophie had written and illustrated and that was being displayed on the wall outside their classroom.

For this, Jennie was suspended from school. During her suspension, she had to write apology letters and "think about how to contribute to the community." On the morning she was supposed to return to school, an envelope appeared on the family's front doorstep. Inside was a hate note, signed "The 8th Graders." Another anonymous note, delivered to Jennie at school, contained dog poop.

Suzanne complained to the school; no culprit was found, and Jennie spent a couple of extremely painful months out in the cold. But then the drama stopped, and Jennie and Sophie became "best friends." When the dust cleared, however, Suzanne found that *she* had no friends. No one was calling. No one was returning her calls. Everyone, it seemed, was rallying around Sophie's mother, Ilena, who simply *could not forgive* Suzanne for not having immediately called to apologize on the very day of the poem incident.

Suzanne found this out through a woman she still thought of as a friend. She was shocked. She *had,* in fact, called Ilena, albeit some time later—she'd been pretty preoccupied, what with the suspension, the hate note, the dog poop, the weeks of ostracism of Jennie at school, and the therapy and medication that were eventually added on—but whatever gesture she had ultimately made, she learned, had been too little too late.

"Having been publicly exposed, it was up to me to make things okay again," she recalled. Except that by the time she became aware of this fact, the window of opportunity for reconciliation had slammed shut. Ilena would no longer have anything to do with her. Which meant that all of Suzanne and her husband's friends from the school were out, too. It wasn't so much that they were mad at her, the one (former) friend had broken ranks to explain, but . . . Ilena had a strong personality and . . . it was all just too complicated.

"I had made everybody's life difficult by not making the call at the right time," Suzanne said, in the stony tone of a person who is coming to terms with a trauma. "We put on the sackcloth and ashes, and then everyone behaved very badly, and it all fell on us."

Sometimes, the parent-child boundary slippage is so extreme that it's almost impossible to tell whose drama it is.

Leslie, a physician in New York City, told me of the day she received an email at work from Alicia, the mother of a "popular" boy, Grayson, who was a sixth-grade classmate of Leslie's son, Evan. Alicia wanted to schedule a phone appointment with Leslie as soon as possible to discuss what she said was an important and time-sensitive issue. Leslie made room in her schedule to hop on the phone. Alicia got straight to the point. Evan, she announced, was soon to receive an invitation to Grayson's 12th birthday party.

"Hand-delivered," she specified, as Leslie listened in disbelief. Evan's envelope had been singled out because Grayson had originally planned *not* to invite him, and so the invitation hadn't gone

out in the mail with all the others. And the reason for this intended but aborted slight was that one year earlier, Evan had had a party—*"A teeny-tiny party!"* Leslie had interrupted herself to exclaim—and Grayson had not been invited and was still, according to Alicia, deeply "offended."

Alicia told Leslie she had "overridden" her son's initial "instinct" not to invite Evan to his party. *"But . . ."* she said, pausing for effect, "I also want you to know that *he doesn't forget.* You should just make sure that your son keeps this in mind and *doesn't do it again."*

Was that a threat? Leslie wondered.

Sometimes, it's hard to tell.

Angela, a Baltimore mother of four, was no stranger to drama by the time her youngest child, Ethan, made his way into middle school. His own friend drama there started in a familiar enough way. He'd been in the popular crowd and had had a best friend named Justin. And then he wasn't—and didn't.

Following Justin's lead, all the boys in the group had turned on Ethan. He had been doing everything with them—going to parties, playing on sports teams, going camping—and now they would have nothing to do with him. Even worse, in school they tormented him endlessly, knocking books out of his hands, making mean comments, always just out of sight or earshot of the teachers. His school email was hacked; someone sent a vicious note to his one remaining good friend. A couple of girls received emails ostensibly from him threatening rape.

Justin told Ethan he had the power to cast a hex, and if he did, Ethan would be dead within a week. Overcome with anxiety, Ethan developed a tic. When the other boys headed off to sports practice after school, he began going to therapy.

Angela was furious. She had grown up under very difficult circumstances and had suffered through being the beleaguered new girl in four different junior high schools. She was not the kind of person to let things go without a fight. But when she reached out to the school on Ethan's behalf, she quickly learned that Linda, Justin's mom, was a fighter, too. And she fought dirty.

The school principal told Angela that she'd been receiving calls from a number of other parents in the grade telling her that Ethan was "too sensitive."

Back off, Angela heard.

Then someone accused Ethan of bullying. Angela approached Linda outside of school and tried to take her aside to talk. Linda made a great show of first having to call her older daughter, who was in high school. "I want you to go punch that girl in the face," she said loudly into the phone. "Call me when it's done."

"It's self-defense," she then told Angela. "I allow my kids *to defend themselves.*"

"I thought, 'Is this real, or is it all for show?'" Angela said to me.

And then things got weirder still.

Angela answered her phone one afternoon and found herself listening to what appeared to be a butt-dialed call from Linda.

"Justin, what happened at school today with that boy Ethan?" Angela heard.

"Nothing, Mom, it was fine," Justin said.

"You need to show that class how foolish that boy is." Linda's voice came through to Angela loud and clear, the words in sharp staccato. "That class *has to know.*"

"I'm willing to do *anything* so long as it doesn't affect my children negatively," Linda once told Angela.

That's when Angela realized she had been outplayed. If she took these snippets of conversation to the school principal, the principal would think she was nuts.

So she caved. She told Ethan to just "put his head down, and get through it." But it ate at her.

———

"MEAN MOMS" CAN be like "mean girls" on steroids—after all, they've had far more time to hone their skills and have many more weapons at their disposal. And "mad dads," who often lack the moms' level of social subtlety, can sometimes prove a public menace.

"I could tell you a story that would curl your hair," the public school official on Long Island told me. The tale took him back ten years, to when he'd been the young, newly appointed principal of a public K–8 school in a prosperous suburb. It was a small school, a plum assignment, he'd thought, at least in comparison with the kinds of teaching jobs he'd had in tough areas of the Bronx when he'd started his teaching career. Many of the kids back there had had huge behavioral challenges. The students in his new school were easy.

The parents were something else.

"I'm standing in the back of the holiday concert, right before winter break," he began. "I'd just been appointed principal that September. I'm standing next to the superintendent, and I look out in the lobby, and there's a scuffle going on."

He was only 35 at the time. The superintendent was a man of about the same age. "We walk out," he continued, "and there are two fathers who are having a full-blown fistfight, literally punching the living hell out of each other."

The two administrators did a quick calculation. A dad-on-dad fistfight was not something they wanted the seven hundred children who would soon file out of the auditorium to see. And so, after a moment's hesitation, they jumped in. Each grabbed a dad, wrestling him away, restraining the men as best they could, until the two men were separated.

"And they were two *big* guys," he told me. One turned out to be a city councilman, the other a respected contractor in town. "Their sixth-grade daughters were having [a] conflict," he said. "And their third-grade daughters were performing in the concert. They were walking into the auditorium together, and they started mouthing off to each other. And the next thing you know, a full-blown fistfight."

"What was the conflict between the girls?" I asked.

"There were some mean looks being exchanged," he answered. "There might have been a note or two that was passed."

"How did it resolve?" (I meant between the girls.)

"I drew the bigger guy, unfortunately," he said. "I tore my suit. And I sent the father the bill."

At best, all this is ridiculous. At worst, it can be horrific. In a suburb of St. Louis in 2007, 47-year-old Lori Drew established a fake online relationship with 13-year-old Megan Meier, who had formerly been friends with Drew's daughter but had withdrawn from the friendship when she changed schools and tried to put a dark, depressed period behind her. To take revenge, Drew created a fake Myspace profile in which she posed as a cute 16-year-old boy named Josh and worked with her daughter to make him be the answer to all Megan's dreams. Once Megan was hooked, Lori started a massive online mob takedown of Megan. In Josh's final communication, she wrote, "You are a bad person and everybody hates you. . . . The world would be a better place without you." Megan hanged herself in her closet that evening.

In 2016, just one day after the presidential election, Josie Ramon, a seventh grader in Royal Oak, Michigan, was eating lunch in her middle school cafeteria with other Latinx students when a group of white classmates started chanting "Build a wall! Build a wall!"

Josie texted a brief recording to her mother. Previous incidents of racist harassment that Josie had reported to the school, she told CNN, had been dismissed as "pranks," and in this case, she said, she wanted to have "evidence." Her mother shared the video with a few other middle school parents, and then, after one of the other parents posted it on Facebook, it spread like wildfire. At which point, angry parents turned on *Josie*. They blamed her for having besmirched the reputation of the school and accused her of having put the lives of the chanting students in danger. Some demanded that she be expelled. In school, she was ostracized. After a noose was found in a boys' bathroom, she and her friends became terrified. Within six weeks, she had to leave the school and enroll in a private school.

Even if middle school parents and children aren't teaming up to engage in out-and-out bullying, their involvement can be damaging. Leaving aside for a moment the effects on kids, it's clear that parents are suffering. Adult regression is a clear sign of distress. The return of middle school patterns of behavior means that adult mode isn't working, and all that powerful, miserable emotion takes a toll on everyone.

"I have no emotional buffer between my children's feelings and mine," Claire, a consultant for environmental groups, admitted to me. Even though two years had passed, the memory of her daughter Amelia's sixth- and seventh-grade years still caused her physical pain. She had spent her daughter's sixth-grade year watching Amelia, an anxious child who struggled academically in her high-pressure school, being pushed out of the friend group she'd had since elementary school. The group orbited exclusively and obsessively around one powerful girl who was the daughter of one of their city's wealthiest and most well-connected families.

For Amelia, the group became toxic. The girls are "classic middle school mean girls," Claire told me. "They act like they're superconfident, very precocious in the way they dress, in the way they carry themselves, in the way they are around boys. And they also are very sarcastic. It was a very tough place for an anxious kid."

Amelia started panicking about her schoolwork. She started censoring herself when she spoke, for fear of being mocked by her friends. With Claire's blessing, she slowly started to step away from the group. But it nonetheless hurt terribly when the other girls beat her to the punch and distanced themselves from her. They no longer invited her to sleepovers and often ignored her when they passed her in the hallway. Amelia began retreating into herself, becoming more and more miserable. And Claire, who volunteered at the school regularly, witnessed everything. Before long, she was doing really badly, too. So badly, in fact, that when Amelia decided, on just a few hours' notice, that she couldn't deal with attending her sixth-grade dance (a "low-key" affair in the middle school gym, for which Amelia's former friend group was planning to stage a big arrival in a limo), *Claire* had a meltdown.

She had to be at the dance no matter what because she was on the planning committee and had said that she'd help out with snacks. And so *she* had to be the one to constantly explain (without explaining too much) that Amelia couldn't attend the dance because she . . . just . . . couldn't. There was something about the whole situation that was so heartbreakingly different from the experience that her older daughter had had just three years before ("She wore this cute strapless dress and had her hair curled. She got together with a group of friends; all the moms were there and took pictures, and they were all so excited and all dressed up . . .") that she simply blew a gasket.

A barrage of thoughts pummeled her brain: *She has to go to this dance. She's pulling herself out of the mainstream. Everyone in the whole sixth grade goes to this dance. She has to go. It's the only sixth-grade dance. She's making herself so different and missing out on a shared experience and opening herself up to being the outcast.* The fear and worry spilled out as rage and frustration at Amelia. And that meant Claire, who "still had to go to the fucking dance and set up the fucking ice cream," as she recalled, also had to watch as the kids started to arrive, their parents jumping up and down in excitement and taking pictures, while she fought back tears. "All those other girls pulled up in the limo and piled out without Amelia and didn't miss her," she said. "And I was trying not to cry, because I was like, 'My poor baby, my poor anxious baby is sitting at home'—and I'd just yelled at her, because I'm the worst mother in the world—'and all these other kids are here having fun, and they just seem so lighthearted and carefree.'"

The memory made her shudder in shame. "When I look back at the moments that I wish I could redo . . . *What the fuck was my problem?*" She shook her head. "I was hysterical," she said.

The years around puberty have always required parents to make some sort of emotional readjustment. The developmental stage of pulling away has always brought with it at least a bit of emotional violence—more, perhaps, when a child felt overly close and needed to force a brutal break. A generation ago, a number of psychologists noted that part of what contributed to the brutality of a break was that parents often tended to retrench—to become more rigid and controlling—just when kids started to try to spread their wings and wander out beyond the realm of parental protection.

Much of this, of course, still goes on today. But in an age when many parents and kids see themselves as best friends, there are new dynamics as well. When parents and children form a unit, with common social ambitions and a shared way of experiencing the world around them, they have common enemies, common sources of frustration, and common agonies. This is considered not just normal now, but good—simply and naturally the way things should be.

"We all view middle school through the eyes of our kids," a D.C. lawyer said matter-of-factly to me.

The problem is, when one vision—particularly that of an 11-, 12-, or 13-year-old—prevails, adult experience and wisdom go out the window. Each generation amps the other up in a back-and-forth of emotional contagion—all of which means that parents are literally going right back to middle school with their kids, living both their children's and their own middle school feelings, and letting that whole overload of emotion guide their behavior.

The result, said the young head of a middle school in Ohio, is drama on a scale that she never saw as a middle school teacher. When she became a principal, she figured that dealing with kids' bad behavior would be part of her job. But dealing with *parents'* behavior was something else. And in recent years, she told me, those conversations had become constant.

Not long before, she'd had to give some sixth-grade parents a talking-to after they'd set up fake Instagram accounts to try to watch what kids in the class were doing online and to "entrap" those they thought were bullies in acts of aggression. They'd designated one girl in particular as a bad apple. One mom had assigned herself the job of monitoring every online move by that "mean girl" so that, at each misstep—particularly if it involved, say, parties her own daughter hadn't been invited to—she could promptly report the girl to the principal.

It had become like a "witch hunt," the principal said. And it had all come to a head when two of the mothers were gossiping about the girl via text. "We need to take her out," one mom wrote to the other.

One of the women's daughters got into her mom's phone and read the exchange. *She* still considered herself to be friends with the girl in question and told her what she had seen. The girl told her mother.

"It turned into a big thing," the principal said, and sighed. "In school leadership programs, they do not teach you how to deal with *that*."

CHAPTER 7

Looking for Control in All the Wrong Places

It's as if the child, by leaving center stage, redirects the spotlight onto the parent's own life, exposing what's fulfilling about it and what is not.

—JENNIFER SENIOR, *New York*

PARENTS, BY AND large, don't do crazy things during their kids' middle school years because they're terrible people. They do them because they're scared. They feel helpless. At their worst, they can even feel—if their children seem sad, lose friends, trigger tearful family fights, or simply disappear for long, angry stretches into the mess of their rooms—like they're failing at the most important job in their lives.

A fascinating 2015 study showed that the start of puberty is actually a trigger for marked declines in parents' feelings of "self-efficacy"—that is to say, the degree to which they feel up to the task of parenting their children in a positive way. But they tend to feel very alone. They respond by desperately trying to take control. And, as desperately controlling parents always do, they make a bad situation worse.

All of which, I think, helps explain why middle school is often the time when kids first go into therapy. It's not only because early adolescence is the age when a number of psychiatric conditions, such as depression and anxiety disorders, tend to emerge, and it's not only because middle school is the time when kids experience so much painful social drama. It's also, I believe, because middle school marks the point when parents are freaked out enough and suffering enough, and—all too often—feeling like they've failed enough that they're willing to seek out and pay for professional help.

It's a cruelly self-punishing thing to believe you have the power to create, maintain, and protect your children's happiness, just like you can protect against broken bones with wrist guards or concussions with bike helmets or skin cancer with sunscreen. In the early years of a child's life, when parents are at the center of their existence, it can feel possible to achieve this goal. The awful truth revealed by middle school is that *you can't do it*. You can't do it because life happens. The outside world exists. And it rushes in to an unprecedented degree once early adolescence begins and your control wanes (or should wane), and your kids direct their gaze away from you and toward the kids around them.

That change in orientation is inevitable. It is beyond parents' control. In fact, it's hardwired—as, in truth, are many of the things that create the miseries of the middle school years. The scales-falling-from-the-eyes social awareness, the obsession with friends, and the desperate desire to fit in and be popular: We come by all that naturally. Those terrible insults we recall so clearly sink in so deep and stay with us for so long not just because they're horrible but also because they impact our brains in a way they never have before and never will again.

We know now that puberty actually starts in the brain, when the hypothalamus triggers the pituitary gland to release the hormones testosterone, estrogen, and progesterone. These sex hormones are present in children from birth, but at puberty they begin to exert their influence in new and very specific ways. Estrogen and progesterone begin to fluctuate in girls as they start their menstrual cycle. Boys' testosterone levels increase as much as thirty times between puberty and the end of adolescence.

Estrogen, progesterone, and testosterone activate the set of dramatic physical changes we associate with puberty: the huge growth spurt, the breasts and facial hair, the drop in boys' voices, the changes in fat distribution, and the coming online of the adult reproductive system in the form of menstruation and ejaculation. They also, however, having first been set in motion by the brain, go on to change the brain in a number of ways that bring about the classic alterations in thinking, emotion, and behavior we associate with early adolescence. As the psychologist Laurence Steinberg writes in his invaluable book *Age of Opportunity,* the sex hormones essentially give the brain a kind of overall tune-up, efficiency- and acuity-wise. They make us more attentive to the world around us. We become particularly "sensitive to all sorts of environmental influences, both good and bad."

Those are extremely important, but not necessarily happy, developments. The sex hormones released in puberty affect our "sensitivity thresholds"—how reactive we are to things that happen to us, or what we feel, or what we're tempted to do. They make us far more reactive to stress in particular, due to the fact that allopregnanolone, or THP, a steroid that is normally released in our bodies in stressful situations and helps adults calm down, actually has a paradoxical effect on adolescents, making them *more* anxious. The sex hormones also make us more emotional—although researchers still caution against falling into old clichés about how they "rage" in our children's bodies. Adolescents don't have higher levels of sex hormones circulating in their bloodstream than young adults do; they just "react differently" to them, the University of Pennsylvania neuroscientist Frances E. Jensen and journalist Amy Ellis Nutt write in their 2015 book, *The Teenage Brain*. It's adolescents' environments, they and other scientists now maintain, that really determine how much of a role the sex hormones play and also how they affect teen behavior. For example, while heightened levels of testosterone in adolescence do lead to more aggressive behavior, the effect kicks in most powerfully, the psychologists Tom Hollenstein and Jessica P. Lougheed write, "under conditions of perceived social threat."

Amazingly enough, it's really just been in the past twenty years or so that neuroscientists have come to understand all this. Before that time, they believed that this sort of transformative brain growth occurred only in the womb and during the first year and a half of life. They also believed that the critical laying down of the brain's "wiring" was basically done by age five. In 1999, however, scientists at the National Institute of Mental Health, using magnetic resonance imaging (MRI) data from 145 subjects whose brains had been scanned every two years throughout their childhood and adolescence, found that right before puberty, there is a major uptick in brain development. Specifically, they learned that there is a new "overproduction" of gray matter—the bodies of nerve cells that are considered the "thinking part" of the brain—and that this new development peaks in boys right about age 12 and in girls around age 11. It happens in the frontal lobe of the brain, the part responsible for "executive functioning"—organizing, planning, maintaining self-control, and strategizing—and it is followed by a wave of synaptic "pruning," which is the process by which the brain shuts down connections it doesn't need, ultimately making the remaining connections more powerful and efficient. Another group of researchers, using the same data, found that these developments are accompanied by an increase in myelination—the coating of the brain's threadlike axons in white matter, which serves as a kind of insulation to speed up communication between the bodies of nerve cells and help different regions of the brain communicate. Myelination then slows dramatically after puberty, only reaching completion in the frontal lobe in early adulthood.

These were enormous discoveries. They demonstrated that the most rapid and wide-reaching changes to our brains after the toddler years occur right before puberty and extend through adolescence. And, for the first time, they provided a biological explanation for the age-old observation that something special seems to happen in the 12-year-old human mind. Pre-MRI technology thinkers like Locke, Rousseau, and G. Stanley Hall had been right: Kids really do become more able to reason, reflect, and engage in formal learning right around puberty. As the frontal lobe develops and comes more fully online, they gain a new ability to think abstractly, to consider a problem from various angles simultaneously, and to be more self-aware and more able to imagine other people's perspectives—all components of higher-level thinking that make them better able to learn and to do more complicated, sophisticated things.

The new discoveries brought biological explanations for some of the long-observed negative aspects of early adolescence, too. In another set of related research, a team of scientists at Harvard using functional MRI (fMRI) imaging—which shows which brain regions come online to do different tasks—found a possible reason for why social interactions in the middle school years can be so fraught with drama. The researchers monitored the brain activity of teenagers as they tried to interpret the facial expressions on a computer screen. They knew beforehand that young teens typically do far worse on this task than do older teens and young adults. Through the fMRI study, they derived some clues for the first time as to why: While older teens in the study used their frontal lobes to interpret the faces—implying the use of logic and reason—the youngest teens' brains showed activation in the amygdala, the part of the brain linked to fear and other "fight or flight" emotions. Middle school hallway fights that break out because one girl gives another girl "a look" suddenly made a lot more sense.

The realities of brain change at puberty explain why there is a quality to people's recollections of their middle school years that makes them unique: The memories really *are* more intense and detailed, the emotions evoked more immediate. We really are better able to remember songs, TV shows, and movies from this time, when, as research shows, we were particularly susceptible to cultural messages—including not-so-benign messages about what it is to be sexy or desirable. In fact, that's the central paradox of the brain in puberty: Just about every new development has the potential to be both wonderful and terrible—sometimes at the same time.

The nature of brain change at puberty explains why people who have positive middle school memories often recall those years as a time of great intellectual growth and creativity. "It was the discovery that I could actually have a conversation with the world and it would have a conversation back with me" is how Miranda, the woman who was mocked for her handwriting in fourth grade, described to me the heaven she found in a new, quirky, and intellectually exciting seventh-grade classroom after spending many miserable years in a particularly stuffy and snobby private school. It's why friendship at that time can bring not only endless misery but also unbridled joy. I recently saw a picture of my best friend and me from around 1978, and I could feel in my bones how thrilling it was to be with her.

In this period of rapid growth and development, the brain is considered more "plastic." But great plasticity also means great instability. Instability means vulnerability. The combination of so many huge changes happening at once means that there are many more things that can go wrong. All of which is why scientists in the early 2000s began to talk about early adolescence as a "second critical period." Not just "critical" in the moral, spiritual, or future-determining sense that nineteenth- and early-twentieth-century thinkers and educators understood. But "critical" in the way that neuroscientists have long understood ages 0 to 3 to be a time of uniquely important brain change and development that carries with it an equal degree of risk and potential. A transformative period of rapid brain growth and skill acquisition, in which brain connections are formed that will stay with a person—for better or for worse—for the rest of their lives. A period of new strengths and new weaknesses. A phase that, if things go well, can help kids get the foundational building blocks in place for success in their later lives. And a time when, if things go wrong, they can be set back in ways that also will live on destructively into adulthood.

In other words, a period that can be an "age of opportunity," as Steinberg titled his eponymous book, or one in which kids start to go off the rails.

In recent years, scientists have discovered more and more brain changes around puberty that bring the unique experience of the middle school moment into being. For one thing, those changes make middle schoolers care more than ever before about how other people see them. As the University of North Carolina at Chapel Hill psychologist Mitch Prinstein explains in his 2017 book, *Popular,* one of the first parts of the brain to change at puberty is the ventral striatum, a part of the limbic system that's involved in the brain's reward circuitry. Between the ages of 10 and 13, he writes, the sex hormones stimulate changes in the ventral striatum in such a way that kids crave " 'social rewards'—feedback that makes them feel noticed, approved, admired, and powerful among peers." The ventral striatum sends signals to the brain's motivational network—revving it up to *go do something* to get those social rewards. And it also connects to what Prinstein calls the brain's "emotional salience network," including the amygdala and parts of our hippocampus, which plays a key role in memory.

All of this means that we want, will strive for, and suffer over our friendships and romantic relationships more in early adolescence (and will remember that suffering more acutely) than at any other point in our lives. In fact, experts like Prinstein now understand the middle schooler obsession with popularity in part as an outgrowth of these new brain developments. "Adolescents are virtually addicted to popularity," he writes, explaining that their neurobiology is such that they physically crave hits of positive peer feedback the way people with substance use disorders crave their next fix.

That development in what scientists call the brain's "reward circuitry" occurs hand in hand with a parallel development in the realm of thinking and learning. Specifically, this newly heightened sensitivity to the opinions of others kicks in at the *exact same time* that kids develop much sharper skills for figuring out how other people are reacting to them. Psychologists call these "social cognition" skills. It's almost as though kids get a software update for the parts of their brain that help them read other people's facial expressions and interpret their peers' feelings and social cues. As a result, all the smirks, eye rolls, and sidelong glances, the nasty texts and "jk" comments hit the brain right at the point when it is biologically programmed both to notice more and to react the most.

That's undoubtedly a piece of why mental health issues like depression, anxiety, and eating disorders spike during this period. (In one 2008 study of adults with psychiatric conditions, the peak age for developing signs of a mental health disorder was 14.) Suicide attempts and successes increase then, too. When bad things happen—and they do: relational aggression and bullying, for example, peak in seventh and eighth grade—they can make a particularly deep impression, physically *and* psychologically.

A 2010 study from McLean Hospital and Harvard Medical School drove this point home. Researchers scanned the brains of young adults ages 18 to 25 who had no other history of abuse or trauma, looking to see if having been the victim of verbal attacks by peers in childhood was associated with brain changes and long-term psychiatric problems. They found that it was, and middle school was the period in which exposure to peer verbal abuse caused the greatest long-term mental health fallout. And, of course, it was the time when the amount of abusive talk peaked.

Even far less traumatic but still disruptive events—simply moving, for example—can have a disproportionate impact on kids in their supersensitive middle school years. Such were the findings of a 2016 study that looked at records for nearly 1.5 million people born in Denmark between 1971 and 1997 to see how moving from one municipality to another in childhood affected later life outcomes. The researchers found that such moves correlated with greater risks of suicide attempts, criminality, psychiatric disorders, drug abuse, and early death—with kids who moved more than once in a single year incurring the greatest degree of risk. And the kids who were most at risk of these negative outcomes were the ones who had moved between the ages of 12 and 14.

One driver of all this damage may be the fact that there's a big glitch in the way the brain develops in the years after puberty: Its different systems don't all mature at the same time. The "emotional brain"—the limbic system—ramps up fast with exposure to the sex hormones and remains in a state of high alert for years, while the "executive functioning" system, controlled by the prefrontal cortex and tasked with organization, self-regulation, and self-control (of both behavior and emotion), lags far behind. In fact, the latest research suggests that it doesn't finish developing until the mid-20s. These findings should give new meaning to our notion of early adolescence as an "awkward" age: Behind that face and body that just won't obey lies a command center at odds with itself.

A hypersensitive brain in which just about everything is conspiring to make life as challenging as possible is the stage on which the dramas of the middle school period play out. And it's not necessarily just a cosmic bad joke. In the past twenty years, new findings in brain science have gone a very long way toward explaining where the thoughts and feelings we remember from early adolescence originate and how they come about. During that same time period, extensive work in the field of evolutionary psychology has gained more widespread acceptance, offering additional explanations for the behaviors we see in middle schoolers.

For evolutionary psychologists, everything having to do with the adolescent mind and brain happens for a reason: The years around puberty are when people are meant to orient themselves toward the world beyond their families. They're meant to become social beings, to find their place among their peers, all in preparation for mating. These psychologists note that puberty is the time when primates—including, historically, *Homo sapiens*—distance themselves from their kinship groups (in the case of humans, parents). This is a biological mandate, a precondition that increases a primate's chances of mating successfully and passing on its genetic material. Human society has, of course, greatly evolved; the gap between puberty and "mating" (marrying and having children) has never been wider. But our brains don't evolve anywhere nearly as quickly as our societies—which is why they react to puberty as though we were about to leave our parents and start to reproduce.

Evolutionary psychologists argue that this is why middle schoolers' need for a friend group feels so vitally important: It provides them with a form of what the French sociologist Michel Fize has called a time of "collective autonomy"—an intermediary step between family belonging and independent selfhood. That's why friend rejection hits so hard: It deprives the newly outward-oriented middle schooler of a sense of being at home in the world. It can feel, on the deep, emotional brain level that's untouched by higher-level reason, like a threat to their very survival. And that's why "mean girls" and "bullies" are so effective: They hit their victims right where they're most vulnerable, right when it counts the most.

There are other aspects of middle school's unique miseries that appear, unfortunately, to be hardwired, too. All primates, say evolutionary psychologists, sort themselves hierarchically at puberty. They compete for mates, with the most dominant primates—the biggest, the ones with the highest status, and the ones with the best access to needed resources—getting first pick, all, once again, with the ultimate goal of having the best shot at passing along their genes.

Evolutionary psychologists believe that modern humans face many of the same challenges as our ancestors, especially in our social interactions, despite massive changes in our material culture. How we deal with those challenges developed as we adapted to our changing environments. Through most of human history, the sorting was ritualized in marriage arrangements—the whole business starting soon after puberty. Once the gap between marriage age and puberty started to significantly widen, however, our ancestral impulses adapted to more complex times. The carryover to middle school is pretty clear.

In this framework, it makes sense that the "popular" kids are generally those who are more advanced readiness-to-mate-wise: the bigger boys, the more "mature" and "sophisticated" girls. They're the ones who radiate attractiveness and healthy strength (athleticism). They're the ones with the best access to resources: that is, money. And because success for our physically small species has always rested on our unique ability to cooperate in acquiring and maintaining resources, those who are dominant in the age of puberty are also the ones with the best social skills: They are best able to cooperate and make alliances.

It also makes sense that middle-school-style "popularity"—which is all about power and status, not necessarily about being liked—is an early adolescent obsession: it's about building a hierarchy and deciding who has the right to affiliate with whom. It even makes sense that middle schoolers so viciously and committedly separate themselves into (often warring) cliques. Humans evolved living in groups where in-group vs. out-group identification was extremely important for survival, and aggression toward outsiders developed as a valuable learned behavior. And it makes sense that, as recent research has found, simply being a nonconformist in middle school is associated with very significant psychological and physical stress.

The psychologist Joseph Allen leads a team of researchers at the University of Virginia that has been following a sample of almost two hundred former seventh and eighth graders since 1998, surveying and testing them to see how their middle school behaviors, relationship styles, attitudes, and traits played out in high school and beyond. One of his most interesting findings has been that being a middle schooler who is high in "allocentrism" ("acting as a follower more than a leader, being low in assertiveness, and being readily influenced by peers . . . placing one's own desires second to those of the peer group," as he describes it) is associated with enjoying better physical health in young adulthood. This outcome may stem from the fact that, as other studies have shown, being on the outs with your friends in early adolescence can cause a degree of pain akin to physical agony; social rejection acts upon the same part of the brain as physical pain. Being a follower in middle school, Allen's work suggests, spares you the corrosive effects of too much stress, while "viewing the world differently than one's social group views it has been found at times to produce increased amygdala activation associated with unpleasant emotions—a phe-

nomenon termed 'the pain of independence.'" And, dealing another blow to the idea that kids should think for themselves, one
more study from Allen's UVA research group in 2014 found that
kids who at age 13 were successfully "autonomous"—saying no to
peer pressure for things like drinking—remained free of such
"problematic behavior" into adulthood, but also had a harder time
making and keeping good friends.

We primates are particularly vulnerable, physically and psychologically, at the moment when we're moving outside the circle of
close kinship protection. Finding a new "tribe," as the psychologist Lisa Damour puts it in her book *Untangled,* is nothing less than
a strategy for survival. Seventh graders are in a particularly bad
way because, she notes, they've typically just "withdrawn from
their home tribe" and are "often willing to be mean—or put up
with peers who are mean—in order to secure a new tribe." Given
all this, it's perfectly logical that becoming part of the popular
crowd, securing "social cachet that guarantees a place in a desirable
tribe," as Damour puts it, would carry quasi-magical importance.

The new cognitive skills that come online at puberty, experts
note, are perfectly suited for policing group behavior, keeping everyone in line with the norms and values set by the "alphas," and
expelling those who violate them. This is often described as a girl
problem. At a time when "the struggle to fit in and feel normal
is at its peak," Lyn Mikel Brown writes in *Girlfighting: Betrayal
and Rejection Among Girls,* "the price middle school girls pay for
their inclusion and social power is constant scrutiny and group
conformity—they are 'in' if they play the game and follow the
rules just right." And yet, recent research shows the phenomenon
to be active among boys as well. One 2015 study of middle schoolers in North Georgia actually found boys to be much more likely
than girls to be big perpetrators of relational aggression. Boys tend
to try to hurt other boys by excluding them from big group activities or athletics (girls, on the other hand, try to mess up other

girls' close friendships), and while girls often go after other girls whom they perceive as relationship rivals, boys tend most often to punish other boys for not showing "stereotypical masculine behavior."

This is one big reason why middle schoolers are so intolerant of difference, research suggests: At a time when identity is so very insecure, kids need *everything* in their lives—shoes, friends, Instagram posts—to project the image of self that they're working so hard to construct. Any deviation is far too dangerous to tolerate. It's also why old elementary school friendships so commonly and brutally come to an end in sixth or seventh grade—an event that can feel completely mysterious to the person who's left behind. A young woman in the Midwest who dropped her best friend from elementary school for the much faster—and more problematic— "popular" crowd as soon as she arrived in middle school was still mulling the story over in her mind more than ten years later, when she talked about her sixth-grade friend switch with me. "I feel like we are all biologically kind of on this path that's very similar until puberty hits," she said. "And then suddenly, it's like an algorithm almost. There are forks in the road, forks in the road, forks in the road, forks in the road. Decisions we make and people we can be with, and we have all these choices. Suddenly you're on a very different road from someone you were once in the same exact situation with."

All this is no doubt why middle school friendships are notoriously short-lived and unstable. In seventh grade, approximately half of them don't last a whole academic year, according to a 2015 study that followed the friendship patterns of more than four hundred kids from fourth through twelfth grades. Boys in the study tended to have more stable friendships than girls, and high-status kids who were also "prosocial" (positive, friendly, or cooperative, in social science–speak) tended to have the most stable relationships of all. As friends diverged in terms of how popular they were, how aggressive they were, and how good they were at school (or simply woke up to their preexisting differences), however, their relationships fell apart. "Differences are detrimental to friendships," the researchers concluded. They labeled their findings "The Downside of Dissimilarity."

Thinking of early adolescence in terms of evolutionary psychology—that is to say, as a time when a person "is entering the breeding pool and developing the social and physical abilities to attract mates," as the evolutionary developmental psychologist Bruce Ellis has put it—means that we can recast many of the middle school behaviors we most despise as adaptive responses to a uniquely vulnerable moment in human life. Once we do that, things start to look very different. The worrisome conformity of the middle school years, for example, becomes an adaptive response to the urgent necessity of fitting in and being accepted by a new replacement "family." This is highly unpleasant to watch but is rooted in a salutary survival skill—an idea reinforced by Joseph Allen's study finding that *not* fitting into peer norms, particularly in early adolescence when the drive to conform is at its strongest, may cause kids to develop stress-based illnesses as adults.

Middle school posturing—whether in obnoxious new forms of back talk to parents or obscene swagger online—becomes an awkward gesture toward securing a new identity at a moment of necessary disconnection from parents. The often callous way that middle schoolers make and break off friendships can be seen not as a form of social climbing, but as an anxiety-fueled attempt to handle the transition from being rooted in family to finding a new sense of belonging among peers. Middle school cliqueyness becomes a way out of the existential loneliness that results from having to leave the nest.

The fact that all the bad and painful aspects of middle school make sense from an evolutionary and neurobiological perspective doesn't mean that they're okay. Evolution, after all, isn't *nice*. The only "should" it responds to is survival. Reining in our most self-ish and brutal ancestral impulses is essentially what socialization—at school and at home—is supposed to be all about. Or so I used to think.

IF THE EVOLUTIONARY psychologists are right, middle schoolers have a big problem: *Everything* about their lives is out of whack. Their brains have evolved to set them up for mating at a point when, for any number of reasons having to do with the ways modern human beings actually live, mating is inappropriate. At the most sensitive moment of their lives since infancy, when they're the most unsure of their place in the world and most in need of solid connection, they're thrust out of their homey elementary schools and into much bigger, more impersonal, competitive, and organizationally overwhelming institutions, where they change classrooms for every subject (straining those immature executive functioning systems), have far less contact with potentially supportive adults, and have to scramble to form new friend groups. They have parents who are desperate to hold them close and protect them at a point when they are programmed to become more independent. Parents who—going through their own midlife turmoil; mourning the loss of their lovely 10-year-olds; suspiciously eyeing this same new vast expanse of unvetted teachers, kids, and families; and anxiously holding on to whatever semblance of control they can muster—aren't at their personal best.

There are decades of research now that describe this situation: Anxious and unsettled, frustrated and annoyed, aware of having reached the worst years in their parenting lives, mothers and fathers react with anger when faced with their 12-year-olds' new critical thinking skills, particularly when those skills are employed to critique *them* and, most unforgivable of all, *their parenting*. They find themselves reeling when their carefree children become serious, worried, or merely preoccupied with all the new social, intellectual, and cultural input coming at them. Back in 1994, the child development experts Reed Larson and Maryse Richards lyrically called this switch the "deflation of childhood happiness." It is entirely normal and developmentally appropriate, Larson and Richards wrote. Nonetheless, they noted, the change can make parents lose their grip on their parenting techniques, coping skills, and basic understanding of who their children are. And, unfortunately, other researchers have noted that when parents are this destabilized, they sometimes blame their kids for how they feel. They tend to handle their feelings of inadequacy and powerlessness by becoming more rigid, controlling, and emotionally explosive. The sad irony being that, in so doing, they bring on the very problems and behaviors that worry and anger them the most.

That basic dynamic—the tragicomedy of middle school parenting—hasn't gotten any better over the decades. In fact, on the parent side of the equation, things seem to have gotten worse. In 2016, the psychologists Suniya Luthar and Lucia Ciciolla analyzed the results of a wide-ranging survey that asked more than 2,200 college-educated women very detailed questions about how they felt about themselves, their marriages, their other key relationships, and their children. What they found, contrary to popular belief, was that the most unhappy mothers weren't the ones made sleepless by infants or frantic by fast-moving toddlers. They were the ones who had children in middle school. Those mothers showed the highest rates of anxiety, depression, stress, and life dissatisfaction. They were the ones most likely to experience feelings of emptiness and lack of fulfillment, guilt and "role overload."

Part of the problem, Luthar told me, is the difficulty of life day in and day out with middle schoolers, who very often tend to externalize their angst and throw it in the faces of those who love them the most. "Where do we put our pain? We give it to those who will accept it without walking out on us. You go for comfort to those who stand by you," she said. "It makes perfect sense that a child will gather all of her confusion and angst into that look she gives you." Awful though it can be, that kick-the-dog habit wouldn't hit moms as hard as it does, she believes, if they weren't already worn down, emotionally and physically exhausted, by the parenting demands American mothers place on themselves today. Moms are "first responders to their kids' pain," she said, and when that pain reaches middle school proportions, it can suck mothers right down into the abyss.

White middle-class American mothers have been called upon to play an impossibly exalted role in their children's lives since the late nineteenth century. But now those expectations extend to mothers of all races and classes and, increasingly, to fathers, too. We tend to be particularly harsh taskmasters with ourselves in the area of "emotional labor"—in this case, making our children happy. Much of this, I've found from talking to late boomer and early Gen X parents over the years, grows out of the feeling of having been emotionally untended-to, especially during the junior high years. Parenthood is for many of this generation a chance for a "do-over," as a California mother called it, contrasting the life she has tried to make for her children with her own childhood, in the course of which she had to leave her home at age 10 and move in with a much older sister because her mother's gambling addiction had made life too scary and unstable.

The mother who shared with me her hellish recollections of junior high school in 1970s Brooklyn became so invested in making sure her son got into one of New York City's top public middle schools that she spent thousands of dollars on test prep, micromanaged and obsessed over his school visits and choices, and then essentially fell into a state of nervous collapse. "Two days before the results came—when we knew the results were in the mail—I literally took to my bed," she said.

For Luthar, the competitive aspect of middle school, hitting parents right when they're going through their own "midlife stuff," is one of the top reasons middle school mothers are so un- happy. "It's in middle school that the element of competition really comes out," she told me. "That's when the kids get tracked academically. That's when the sports get really competitive. That pushes our own buttons. Some of that gets triggered in us."

That triggering couldn't happen at a worse time. Middle age is the point in life when most people take a hard look at themselves and go through a period of status worries, identity doubts, and unhappy self-questioning that feels a lot like middle school. This means that parents embarking upon middle age are in a funny sense at the same developmental level as their kids, sharing similar obsessions, similar insecurities, all of this similarly complicated by the biological fact that their bodies, after a long period of rela- tive stasis, are once again changing—and specifically, at least for mothers entering perimenopause, in ways that concern their re- productive functioning. (Although, unlike with kids, the more "mature"-looking mothers *don't* derive high status from it.)

For most parents, early middle age marks the point when they have ostensibly arrived where they're going and have to come to terms with where they are. For many, this isn't fun, to put it mildly—and for those who haven't achieved all they'd hoped to achieve or haven't earned what they'd hoped to earn, seeing their own relative class status recapitulated in their kids' status within a middle school class (as so often happens) makes them more miser- able still.

One generation ago, a "midlife crisis" was generally understood to be a moment of almost teenagerish rebellion—a great cry of *Basta!* to the duties and limitations imposed by marriage and fam- ily, a demanding reassertion of self. Now, for many, the crisis seems to come when those duties and limitations start to be lifted. After all, if you've spent more than a decade defining yourself by your good work as an ever-present, high-performance parent, having kids of middle school age brings on a change in identity that can be very destabilizing, particularly for adults who especially like the identities they've constructed for themselves as parents. Mothers and fathers who, for example, pride themselves on being "connected parents" can be thrown off balance by the sight of the closed bedroom door cutting them off from their children's universe. Parents who loved being a part of their children's extended community of soccer moms and dads or Suzuki families may have social losses to deal with as well, as their children's interests and friendships change. Parents who formerly basked in the reflected glory of a high-status popular kid may find it extremely painful to find that their own star has fallen when he or she ends up on the outside—as so many popular kids at some point do. In short, the "who am I and where do I fit in" mental meanderings of the middle school years are now often a two-generation phenomenon.

The enormous preoccupation with status that many middle- and upper-middle-class parents in particular now bring to middle school is just the latest layer in a pileup of stress that many have been carrying for decades. It didn't just start with parenthood. And it's about far more than the dramas engulfing their kids. It's a grinding, incessant worry about money, financial security, and family rank, about holding things together in the present and positioning the next generation to move up, rather than fall behind, in the future.

The fact is, today's parents of school-age kids have gotten the short end of the stick, stability-wise, for pretty much their entire adult lives. They're by and large Gen Xers, which means that in the early 1990s, they were the first generation of college graduates to see their earnings actually fall during their first years in the workforce. They went on to become the first college-educated generation to progress through adulthood dogged by widespread fears of downward mobility. They were harder hit by the Great Recession than any other age group, were the most likely to have bought homes during the housing bubble that preceded the recession, and by early middle age were more burdened with debt than any other generation. They are also extremely fearful about their children's future prospects. By the mid-2010s, 85 percent of those ages 45 to 59 and 75 percent of those ages 30 to 44 were telling pollsters they believed that life would be more difficult for the next generation than it had been for their own. All but the very wealthiest Americans are now running scared—facing a future in which they're pretty sure life is going to be tougher for their kids than it has been for them (and, in many cases, than it was for their parents).

What's more, today's parents inherited from the baby boomers before them a hubristic belief in their ability to shape and control their children's destinies. But while the boomers grew up during a period of historic economic growth that built and bolstered a solid middle class, today's parents grew up in a world where increasing gaps in income and wealth were starting to translate into enormous disparities in educational opportunities, health and well-being, and life outcomes overall. The trend was so sharp that by the time Gen Xers themselves had kids, inequality had reached levels that had not been seen in our country since the Gilded Age. Increasing numbers of middle-class people were being left behind, priced out of housing markets and incurring massive debt to finance a college education. Belief in the American Dream—the promise of fairness and meritocracy that had united and inspired so many generations—was vastly declining. By 2014, nearly three-quarters of Americans no longer believed that people who worked hard could get ahead, and an even greater number thought there was a different set of rules for people who had money and were well connected.

The impact of growing up in this age of extreme inequality has been huge for middle schoolers and their parents at all income levels. On a practical level, it means that parents are extraordinarily stressed—and often relatively absent. In the upper middle class, eager to hold on to top jobs with high pay, high status, and extensive benefits, they're working longer hours than ever before, with a constant awareness that if they falter, there is an endless supply of hungry candidates for their positions waiting right outside the door. In the middle class, many now work second jobs to supplement salaries that, one generation earlier, could support entire families. And in our increasingly contingent labor economy, low-income parents often have two or three jobs, on unpredictable schedules, without sick days or family leave.

All kids now receive the message that money equals success. But the higher up the income ladder you start, the more money that has to be, and the narrower the path to success. For kids in the upper middle class, college per se is not enough. To stay at the top, and to rise even higher, they feel they need to attend the "best" (i.e., the most selective) college possible, then graduate school. And that means starting preparation for college as early as middle school.

Academically ambitious parents and kids quickly learn that if they're going to exhaust their high school's math offerings by twelfth grade, they really have to pack as much ninth- and tenth-grade math into their seventh- and eighth-grade years as possible. With college coaches recruiting middle schoolers for future athletic scholarships, parents are told, kids have to seriously start upping their game in sixth grade at the latest. Naviance, the online college search and application prep service, is now on offer in seventeen hundred middle schools. The U.S. Department of Education, via its Federal Student Aid website, has been pushing middle school students and parents to start stressing for college early and often. "Talk to your child about his or her interests and help match those interests with a college major and career," its online check-list for parents of middle schoolers urged in 2019. "Start saving for college if you haven't already," it advised beleaguered tweens.

What all this means for college-bound kids is that the most de-structive tendencies of the middle school mindset—the obsession with status, the endless comparisons with peers, the self-questioning and often cruel levels of (self- and other-) criticism—are now being fed by a new "imaginary audience": college admissions commit-tees. Which, kids are told at earlier and earlier ages, have the power to brand them winners or losers for the rest of their lives. As a re-sult, these kids are getting a running head start on the stress, com-petition, insecurity, and worry that used to just accompany the college application process in the last two years of high school—and, unsurprisingly, they are showing more of the stress-related mental health issues that are now considered epidemic on college campuses. By the mid-2010s, clinicians and school personnel alike were reporting that they were seeing more widespread and intense anxiety in kids of middle school age than ever before. Death rates from suicide, for example, nearly doubled in 10-to-14-year-olds between 1999 and 2014.

I don't think that most middle school parents are consciously thinking about college when they pay for their kids to participate in travel sports teams or middle school Model United Nations, quiz their kids for spelling bees, drive them to ethics bowls, or shell out thousands of dollars for college summer programs for "gifted" middle school students. Neither do I believe that they consciously, for the most part, think about their kids' popularity or unpopularity as a harbinger of future wealth and well-being. But they do know that relationships are important, and for reasons that go beyond short-term happiness. "How you pick your friends is how you pick your significant others and form other relationships. It's not an isolated event," said Leslie, the New York doctor drawn into high drama over a 13th birthday party invitation for her son.

We parent to prepare our children for the society in which we live. And, at base, raising children to be successful in the future isn't a bad or unreasonable thing. But in a world marked—as ours is now—by extreme inequality, this natural parental impulse gets distorted. Extreme anxiety makes it ugly. The pressing need to achieve—or hold on to—wealth and social status turns everything into a nonstop competition.

In our "winner-take-all society," parenting to win means something very different from teaching kids to work hard and play by the rules. It means emphasizing skills that confer advantage in a world where the game of life is rigged, including teaching kids to work the system to their advantage; to grab hold of every bit of privilege they can; to get to know the right people, position themselves well, and navigate power dynamics; to be narrowly focused on their own personal goals; and to always remember that if they don't grab the top prize, someone else will.

And if that means encouraging some not-very-nice behavior toward those who either impede their self-development or hold them back, well, then, kids have got to do what they've got to do. And parents do, too.

As Suniya Luthar, who spent decades prior to her motherhood research focusing on adolescent development in both low- and high-income communities, said to me, "There's only room in the mirror for one, and we are all trying to get that one spot in the upper middle class. My gain is your loss; your gain is my loss."

If we want to see where this madness may lead, we might look at what many consider to be the world's most competitive educational system. In China, middle school—grades 7 through 9, called "junior secondary school"—culminates in a national examination, the Zhongkao, which determines where kids will go to high school. Only a tiny sliver of candidates make their way into the country's top high schools, which prepare them to try to test into the most prestigious universities. And that, a number of young adults who attended China's most elite public schools told me, means that the world of Chinese middle school rivals our own in competition, envy, and cruelty. (With one very key difference: The "alpha kids" in Chinese middle schools are the top-ranking students, and they are publicly ranked after monthly exams.)

In fact, while social science research on popularity and children's social behavior in China has long tended to stress the influence of the country's "communitarian" values, the former Chinese middle schoolers with whom I spoke recalled a junior secondary school climate straight out of *Lord of the Flies*—an atmosphere of unbridled and brutal struggle for status, rife with power abuses by parents, teachers, and students alike.

"For academic pressure, grades 7 through 9 are particularly tough," said one young woman, recalling the five to seven hours of homework a night she juggled at age 13 while preparing for her all-important high school entrance exams. The competition, she said, could be intolerable. Suicides of middle school and even primary school students, due in large part to excessive school pressure, are so frequent, and so undeniably a public health problem, that in recent years the Chinese government has been willing to officially acknowledge them. Parents behave like "control freaks," this young woman said, and teachers are hell-bent on "making teenagers into machines of competition, rather than caring for them as human beings." Students whose families are less wealthy or who are perceived as not being "smart enough" are bullied, she said. Class presidents, charged with keeping order in the classroom when teachers are out, "use such power to isolate students they don't like and to rule others." She likened the way students under pressure sometimes treat one another to the behavior of participants in "the Stanford prisoner experiment."

Another early twentysomething who attended some of the country's most elite schools spoke of teachers ridiculing lower-performing kids in front of their peers and pressuring their parents to lean on them more; parents bribing teachers for better grades and letters of recommendation for their kids ("If you're not doing it, you're almost left behind," she said); and some parents even quitting their jobs to focus full-time on their middle schoolers' high school exam prep. The nightmare that can result, she noted, is of another order of magnitude than the typical high-pressure parent-child dynamics in competitive American communities. "You have parents who beat their kids up because they've already invested so much time, money, attention in their kids. So they blame their kids," she said. "They have so much stress and anger."

Do toxic schools, exclusionary values, and a competitive culture essentially guarantee that all the worst aspects of the early adolescent experience will come to the fore and define the age? There's very good reason to think so. In recent years, the United States has had the dubious distinction of being the most unequal of any high-income country in the world, while its middle schoolers have ranked among the world's most unhappy. In one 2015 study of the United States and peer nations, American 11-, 13-, and 15-year-olds were third from the top in terms of feeling "pressured by schoolwork"—and third from the bottom in "finding their classmates kind and helpful." A 2007 study of World Health Organization data found U.S. middle schoolers to be the least likely kids their age to say their schools were "nice" or "fair," to say they liked school, or to say they felt like they belonged. They also ranked among those most likely to say they felt socially isolated—"left out, alone, lonely, helpless, and bullied." American students whose parents did not finish high school scored lowest on such measures of connectedness and support. But even the most privileged American students, some of whom were in private schools, declared themselves more miserable than kids in other comparable nations, wrote Jaana Juvonen, a professor of developmental psychology at UCLA who led a team of colleagues in analyzing these results. "Negative views of school and sense of isolation are not universal problems of young adolescents across cultures," she concluded.

Adults I spoke with who grew up in Poland, India, Spain, and Peru all backed up the research finding that middle school isn't experienced everywhere as the tenth circle of hell. "That's such a tough age," a Vietnamese-born woman who has made her adult life in the United States instantly said at the mention of the words "middle school." Was it tough in Vietnam as well? I asked. "Oh, no," she replied, just as quickly, "not at all." In other countries, the kids we think of as middle schoolers are known to be particularly annoying, and sometimes enraging, but it is their parents (and siblings), rather than their peers, who chiefly suffer. In France, I learned, early adolescence is viewed as a time of extreme self-consciousness, private angst, and wretched behavior at home. It's known as *l'âge ingrât,* which translates literally as "the ungrateful age," but could also be understood as the "displeasing," "graceless," "unattractive," or "ugly" age. (I think "the ugly age" sums it up best.) In Costa Rica, early adolescence is thought of as a real headache—again, chiefly for parents. That's why, I was told, age 13 in particular is called *el edad del pedo,* or "the age of the fart": It stinks.

What these international examples drive home is that biology is not destiny. Middle schoolers are not fated to be competitive and cruel. That insight is, perhaps, the most important and empowering takeaway from almost four decades of scholarship on early adolescence. Despite the fact that kids come to middle school with the same hardwired givens—the biological changes that are "inevitable and ubiquitous (except in rare medical conditions)," as Tom Hollenstein and Jessica Lougheed have put it—there is huge variation in how kids going through puberty behave and feel. And that is determined by a combination of biology and the environment they're in—nature plus nurture.

The two realms are not perfectly separate. In fact, the brain and its environment are intertwined, one constantly acting upon and impacting the other. That's why the dominant paradigm for human development now is this: Biology loads the gun; environment pulls the trigger. We can't do anything about the hardwired factors that our children bring with them to the moment of puberty: their genes; their neurobiology; the elements of personality, taste, and temperament that have shown up in them since infancy. But if we think of the biological as *possibility,* what we have to work with, and the environment as a series of *opportunities,* then we open up a lot of options for creating a better life for our kids. And for ourselves, too.

CHAPTER 8

What We Value

American parents want their kids to be a social success.
Academic success is nice, but social success is something that
American parents really want. That's why I have to tell American
parents—I don't always say it because it's so in your face—*don't
go back to middle school*. Your kids have to go through it, but
don't go back to it yourself.

—MICHAEL THOMPSON

THE WINNER-TAKE-ALL MENTALITY—applied not just to achievement,
but to all aspects of life—was at the heart of many of the stories I
heard while reporting this book. Parents who didn't naturally share
that zero-sum orientation were shocked, horrified, and often hurt
when their expectations of basic kindness and consideration—
expectations based on the way they themselves had been raised in
a less competitive era—were violated by other parents, especially
ones they considered friends. It was a clash, they felt, between an

increasingly old-fashioned notion of bringing up children to be considerate of others (the essence, really, of good manners) and a new social order where everyone just did battle according to the demands of their children's self-interest.

In such a world, there is no room for accommodation or compromise or emotional generosity, much less compassion. And there isn't much by way of good role-modeling. I saw this over and over again in my years as a middle school mother, and I heard about it frequently in interviews, too—as, for example, when a mom named Deborah told me what happened when her daughter Ruth had a panic attack at her friend Rachel's 11th birthday party. It was an unpardonable offense, after which both mother and daughter found themselves out in the cold.

The party had been an iffy proposition for Ruth from the start. She'd been having a rough time with her anxiety. And she'd never made it through a sleepover before. But Rachel was her best friend, and she really wanted to be with her to celebrate. So she gamely headed out with her sleeping bag and pillow. She lasted through dinner and a movie (although Rachel's mother, Gail, made sure to let Deborah know she had shown some "very possessive" behavior at the theater). But then, right before cake, when it was dark out and Ruth was getting tired, she just lost it. She had a hysterical, humiliating, out-of-control anxiety attack.

Deborah was struck right away by how cold Gail's voice sounded on the phone when she called to say that Ruth wanted to go home. She apologized extra hard, and then Ruth repeatedly apologized, too, crying as her mother led her out the door. Deborah wasn't quite sure why they were apologizing so much, both that night and in the days and weeks that followed. After all, Ruth hadn't *chosen* to have a meltdown. It had been horribly painful and embarrassing for her. And, as time passed, it became increasingly clear that it had cost her her best friend.

Rachel, it seemed, was simply unable to forgive Ruth for falling apart on *her* special day. And Gail, whom Deborah had also considered a friend, backed up her daughter completely. " 'Well, it was really *disruptive*. It really messed up the flow of the birthday party and having the cake,' " Deborah recalled, spitting out the words Gail had spoken during their post-party conversation. "I always thought part of being a friend is knowing how to put up with people when they're annoying or sad or just not doing so well," she continued. "It's the difference between having some standard you adhere to, and expect your child to adhere to, and validating every feeling your child has."

Standards are a tricky thing in a world where the only value that really matters is looking out for number one. That outlook, I have found, can make parents who pride themselves on being "good people" behave in pretty bad ways.

Tamar, the labor lawyer in Los Angeles, told me at length how much she despised the materialism of the kids and parents in her daughter Emma's middle school. So Tamar was absolutely thrilled when she was able to find a progressive sleepaway camp—"a really moral place"—where the values aligned with her own. "There's an all-gender cabin, and a transitioning girl in a boys' cabin. It's very 'Free to Be You and Me,' and a lot of counselors don't shave their legs, which I love," she explained.

She was more delighted still when Emma enjoyed her time there so much that she wanted to return for a second year. There was just one hitch: Gaby, a close friend from Sunday school, had gone with Emma the first year and wanted to go back, too. But Gaby had been a real bummer. "She was going for the first time, and she was clingy and complained, and I think that Emma just felt it had brought down her *camp experience*," Tamar said.

Gaby's parents were splitting up, and she wasn't in a good place. Her mother, Lisa, wasn't in a good place either. In fact, she had cried when Tamar called to tell her that the girls would need to attend separate sessions. Gaby, apparently, had cried, too. And even Emma, who had copiously vented to Tamar about Gaby the summer before, seemed to disapprove of her mother's call. But none of them seemed to understand what was really at play. "I felt this was going to be really high-stakes for her," Tamar said. "This was going to be her camp for life. She could spend years going there, be a CIT [counselor in training] there."

If that made Tamar a "mean mom"—as the general reaction seemed to suggest—she could live with that. She had to do what was right for her child. "It's really good for her," she told me. "She comes back really *grounded*."

By the next school year, the girls were best friends again—and they've remained so ever since. At least as far as Tamar knows. Emma doesn't share much with her anymore. "She's afraid I'll interfere," she said.

The fact that, in a number of parent stories—as in similar situations I witnessed during my time in the middle school trenches—it was the kids themselves who spoke up to beg adults to back off is a very hopeful thing. It demonstrates something that happy middle school teachers and administrators have told me many times: Part of what emerges, intellectually, in the critical middle school years, part of what—they believe—makes this age so wonderful to teach, is a powerful sense of fairness and a real nose for injustice. But those aspects of the early adolescent psyche—like all the talents and skills we go out of our way to teach and train—have to be cultivated and practiced. As with everything else that resides in middle schoolers' brains, if we really want things like kindness, inclusion, and empathy to take root and reach their full expression, we have to reinforce them.

MIDDLE SCHOOL PARENTS—like all parents, in all phases of their children's lives—worry about their kids and want nothing more than to protect them. But as the history of American 11-to-14-year-olds repeatedly has shown, in looking for the dangers they most fear, parents consistently pay attention to the wrong things.

The American obsession with adolescents and sex has long had adults chasing after demons that don't exist, or that exist to a far lesser extent among middle schoolers than we tend to think. The hype about middle schoolers' perilous precocity makes for good entertainment. But the truth is that the world of early adolescence in recent years has been far cleaner, safer, more nurturing, and more innocent than it was when today's moms and dads were in junior high school. Eighth graders now engage in fewer activities like going out unsupervised, dating, having sex, and drinking than kids their age have in decades—possibly, experts say, because they're spending so much time online. And though parents—including me, until I did this research—are convinced that sexting is ubiquitous, good research shows that it's really a pretty marginal activity among sixth to eighth graders. (Especially when it comes to sending "nudes." Lots of gross words go around, but not so many pictures.)

In fact, I don't think it's an exaggeration to argue that the greatest danger facing middle schoolers right now isn't their phones or their peers. It's us—or, more specifically, it's the common values that hold sway in our world: selfishness, competition, and personal success at any cost. Research shows that those values are psychologically damaging for all people, at all ages, and in all communities, rich, poor, and in the middle. But, precisely because early adolescence is such a critical period, they hit middle schoolers extra hard.

Parents generally don't strive to make their kids super-attuned to status or super-selfish, of course. Most, at all income levels, say that in addition to wanting to make their kids "happy," they want to bring them up to be "good" people. Yet actions speak louder than words—by either omission or commission—and adolescents are especially well attuned to the sound of adult hypocrisy. In

2013 and 2014, Rick Weissbourd and Stephanie Jones, co-directors of the Making Caring Common Project at the Harvard Graduate School of Education, surveyed more than ten thousand socioeconomically and ethnically diverse middle and high school students in a wide variety of schools across the country, and they interviewed hundreds of teachers and administrators as well. Previous research had told them that the vast majority of parents—"almost all," they wrote—said that they cared profoundly about raising kids who were "caring, ethical" people. But what they found was that about 80 percent of the kids in their survey reported that their parents were "more concerned about achievement or happiness than caring for others." When the researchers surveyed teachers, administrators, and school staff, they found again that about 80 percent of those adults said that parents prioritized their children's achievement and personal happiness above caring for others.

For Weissbourd and Jones, what this showed was a profound "rhetoric/reality gap" between what parents said mattered to them and what values they conveyed to their kids through their attitudes and behaviors. "It's the steady diet of messages that children get, such as when parents let children quit teams without considering their obligation to the team, or don't require their children to reach out to a friendless kid on a playground, or allow children to talk too much, taking up too much air time with other children or adults," Weissbourd and Jones wrote. "Many other cultural observers have chronicled parents' micromanaging their children's happiness, including catering to children's every need in ways that can make children concerned about little other than themselves."

Being raised with a narrow achievement orientation, they found, correlated with kids' developing less empathy, consideration for others, and basic kindness—the necessary preconditions for creating a better social environment among peers. Citing related research by the Frameworks Institute, a Washington, D.C., think tank, Weissbourd and Jones also noted that the way many

American parents conduct themselves as community members and as members of society at large—showing great concern for and investment in what is going on in their children's schools, playgrounds, and the like, while showing no particular commitment to "larger collectives and the common good"—is directly (if inadvertently) teaching kids to divide the world into in-groups and out-groups.

In other words, when we think and behave like middle schoolers all our lives, it doesn't make for a very nice world: "When children and youth are too concerned with their own happiness, and when parents are too focused on children's happiness, children are less likely to do what's right, generous, and fair both in making mundane decisions such as whether to pass the ball to a friend, and when in the throes of high-stakes conflicts between their own welfare and that of others, such as when deciding whether to risk standing up for a friend who is being bullied," Weissbourd and Jones wrote.

All of this is no doubt why middle schoolers—and their parents—in upper-middle-class communities appear to some observers, including research psychologists, to be the meanest, most unhappy group and to be the most likely to do unkind things. Competitive people can never let their guard down. Competitive, insecure, status-obsessed communities operate like lifelong middle schools.

It's been thirty years since the psychologist Jacquelynne Eccles first published an enormously influential wave of research on the problems with American junior high and middle schools, boiling their issues down to a major problem of "stage-environment fit." It is now clear that not much has changed. The mere transition to middle school is still linked to a whole host of problems for incoming students, including lower self-esteem, less motivation, and a decline in academic achievement. These schools are still being publicly denounced as "educational wastelands," and middle schoolers are still being written off as all but uneducable. For example, in 2011 a former middle school science teacher from Chicago expressed on public radio his belief that "you're sort of wasting your time trying to teach middle school students anything." In recent years, the most commonly envisioned fix for what ails middle schools and middle schoolers appears to be putting sixth through eighth graders in K–8 schools, as districts in Baltimore, Milwaukee, Philadelphia, and New York have. (Boston, as this book went to press, was about to start experimenting with both K–8 and K–6 plus 7–12 schools.) In other words, we seem to be starting over from scratch, returning to the pre–junior high setup from the turn of the twentieth century.

Maybe eliminating middle schools entirely will help. But, as we know from our whole long and sorry history, you can't get meaningful change from new buildings if you don't profoundly alter what goes on inside them. What happens in our middle schools is in many ways a microcosm of our larger society. The truth is, we can't make middle school better for our kids if we don't make our culture less middle-schoolish.

That's a big ask. In the meantime, however, there is a lot that schools and parents can do. After all, psychologists make no secret of what middle schoolers need in order to thrive: good relationships, a sense of belonging, and the feeling of being competent and skilled. Those are the keys to happiness for people of all ages, for that matter, and for lifelong resilience. I've spoken to many teachers, camp directors, counselors, and administrators who are eager for more opportunities to provide kids with those essential elements of well-being. Parents can teach their kids the skills they need to navigate the inevitable ups and downs, frictions and factions, of middle school life, too. Like educators, they can empower their children to start to solve their problems productively by themselves and find their way toward better friendships.

That doesn't mean that adults should step back, throw up their hands, and claim powerlessness in the face of inevitable "boys will be boys" or "that's just the way girls are" behavior. On the contrary, it means that parents, like teachers, have to lean in more—but in entirely different ways.

In every positive story someone shared with me for this book—and there *were* positive stories—there was always an adult at the center who, without naming it as such, set out to provide a kid or a group of kids with at least one of the building blocks of long-term happiness and resilience.

There was the middle school principal who took the time to get to know every student's name, carved out ways to recognize everyone's achievements, and even taught a required study skills class where he laid down the rules of "inclusive friendship—although he didn't use the word 'inclusive,' he just got it across," a woman who recalled middle school as the best time in her school life told me.

There was the English teacher with college football player "cred" who'd made belonging a reality—indeed, an imperative—in his classroom by lifting up the kids who otherwise fit nowhere: the "weird, smart kid" from a conservative Christian family whose friend group had just dumped her, the mixed-race boy who was gay but wasn't yet out, the refugee from Vietnam, and the poor white boy whom everyone looked down on. The teacher couldn't, and didn't try to, make them popular, but he did bring them respect by celebrating them as exemplars of academic excellence and making clear that others, too, could win his favor through extraordinary effort. By being who he was and using his own social capital to set a new norm for what was considered valuable, even admirable, he turned the social hierarchy of a big southern public middle school on its head, at least within his classroom. And that was enough to make a really big difference for kids who otherwise would have been bullied. "Kids wanted to earn his respect and love and attention, so they would behave themselves," the self-described "weird, smart kid" said. "By the end of eighth grade, I thought I could do anything."

There was the principal at a small, alternative public school in Providence, Rhode Island, for "at risk" kids whose connection with his students, and his commitment to giving them the tools they needed to succeed, was so strong that he'd stayed late one evening so that a 14-year-old girl could make up a test she missed while she was out having a baby. As a result of that evening makeup, she'd been able to maintain her 3.0 GPA. This had qualified her for a field trip to Harvard, to visit a lab that was doing genetic research on fruit flies. After struggling in other schools, she was now in an accelerated program and for the following year had been accepted into a specialized high school, where she was going to pursue her dream of becoming a nurse. She paused to show me a picture of her baby as she took me on a tour of her current school—the gym, with its high ceiling and big windows; a newly renovated science lab; a classroom where the desks were arranged in a square, college seminar style. "I love this," she kept saying.

There was the black afterschool program teacher who'd gone out of his way to mentor a boy who was one of the only African American students in a Jefferson, Missouri, middle school. And once he'd found "someone who looked like me and was there for me," the former middle schooler recalled, he went from feeling "lost" to feeling more at home in the world. He discovered a sense of purpose: to become the director of a Boys & Girls Club and mentor other kids through middle school. "When I found the perfect person I could connect with in middle school, I thought, 'How do I go to college to be exactly like him, to be a role model?'"

he said. When I met him, he was the program manager in a D.C. afterschool program that offered free classes in chess, magic, and fashion design to a community of middle school students who were 99 percent black and nearly all low-income.

And there was the mother who'd sat up with her daughter and her daughter's middle school friends when they had sleepovers late at night, helping them interpret their world. She knew they had a reputation as the school "mean girls," but she played the role of a nonjudgmental sounding board nonetheless, trying to lead them to rise above themselves and take a mile-high view. "She would help us figure out what was going on with our friends," her now-grown-up daughter recalled. "We'd tell her literally everything, and she would explain how self-esteem and the need to be liked were really the things driving most of these weird/bad choices our friends were making—dating multiple boys at once, making out. . . . She urged us to have compassion for the girls we were so ready to write off as 'skanks.' "

That daughter went on to become an eighth-grade teacher and then train other middle school teachers as part of her work in an organization that helps low-income middle schoolers get ready for high school and college. "We expect middle schoolers to be total bastards to each other," she told me. "But that doesn't have to be the case."

The mother-daughter example perfectly captures one of the most important insights of all the research into happiness, early adolescence, and resilience: We have to see our children—and other people's children—as works in progress. We have to help them develop the social tools they need to live fulfilling lives. And, if we genuinely want our children to be caring and ethical people—not to mention happy—in middle school and after, we have to think hard about the values we're teaching them. This is not just a matter of "be nice" stuff. Shifting away from a narrow focus on self to an orientation that takes in the realities of others—learning to "*zoom in,* listening closely and attending to those in their immediate circle, and to *zoom out,* taking in the big picture and considering multiple perspectives," as Weissbourd and Jones put it—actually leads to long-term emotional health and well-being. Taking action to benefit other people makes kids feel and conduct themselves better. And when their parents are on board with this, too, kids do better still, even academically.

What ties all this together?

Solid moments of connection—moments that teach a better, kinder, smarter, more compassionate way of being. Not fancy curricula that are taught in a single assembly or a one-off training for teachers (because these usually don't work). Not pretty buzzwords that prove hollow when put to the test. What does work are gestures that convey that the adults in a middle schooler's world are paying attention and really care, especially about the sorts of people and actions and qualities that normally don't have much cachet in middle school. Those kinds of efforts can truly change the climate in which middle schoolers learn and live. And they benefit everyone, not just those who happen to be currently on the outside. All adolescents who feel their school is inclusive do better long-term.

When *Queen Bees & Wannabes* author Rosalind Wiseman travels the country consulting with middle schools that want to change their climate, she'll work, for example, with student council members who are planning a dance and get them to think hard about details like how they publicize it and how they choose the music, to see if they're unintentionally excluding certain members of the school population. She'll train them to ask questions such as "'How do we give information about this dance? Where do we put up our posters? Let's do an inventory of where the posters traditionally are put up. Do all different kinds of kids see that? Or are we putting posters in places that only certain types of kids are going? Do we need to put posters in places where we don't normally put them?' Because kids think—we all think this way—'If I don't go somewhere, I don't think to put a poster where I don't go,'" she explained to me. "But by doing that, you're sending a message to the kids who don't populate that place that *you're not invited*. If you want different kinds of kids to show up at the dance, then they need to be able to have their music there. There's this incredible opportunity," she said, to teach kids how considerations like this can make other kids, who may be different from them, feel welcome at a dance. To make them realize "that what I do as a leader matters," and, "through the process of the dance thinking," ask themselves, "'How do I represent the people who are part of my community?'"

Creating a plan like this makes kids aware of the ways they typically choose to include or exclude others, even in—especially in—situations where they're unaware of making a choice. It puts into action Weissbourd and Jones's appeal to adults to teach kids to "zoom out" and expand "their immediate circle" to others not like them. And it imparts social skills—something we tend to forget that kids really do need to be taught, particularly when it comes to the kinds of situations that we ourselves often still don't know how to handle.

Some schools do this through community service projects, ideally conceived to aid kids in really understanding the lives of the people they're helping, rather than to generate Instagram-ready moments of high-minded good deeds. Many K–8 schools achieve this by having older children "buddy" with younger ones—kids they'll see every day and keep an eye on over the years. One K–8 school in suburban New York City that shares a property with a special ed school for children with high levels of need practices "reverse inclusion" by sending its middle school students to regularly eat lunch with the special-needs kids. There, too, the middle schoolers have "buddies" to look out for. "It really softens them a lot," the principal told me.

Some teachers find ways to impart skills through teachable moments. One figured out how, in very casual, impromptu, and private ways, to give an eighth-grade girl who was having trouble connecting with her classmates same-day praise when she handled herself well and gentle suggestions about how, when things went poorly, she might try a different tactic in the future. Another took it upon himself to discreetly—and nonjudgmentally—steer a popular seventh grader in a more positive direction whenever he witnessed the boy being unkind. "Why did you respond that way?" the teacher would ask, in as close to real time as possible. "What did you mean? Could you have done things differently?"

Schools can't eradicate bad middle school behavior. They can't force all kids to like one another or to hang out with one another. They can't alter the fact that kids will, almost inevitably, sort and categorize themselves and construct hierarchies. But in addition to teaching skills, schools can make decisions about what the culture within their walls will be. "They can squeeze the top and the bottom so they're not so far apart socially," the child psychologist and author Michael Thompson told me. The adults in a school can set social norms—the kinds of strictures that determine what's okay and what's not—which middle schoolers are naturally eager to enforce. They can make it a norm that isolating people is unacceptable, and they can enforce such norms through the ways that they themselves behave.

Doing all this, once again, doesn't require fancy interventions, adopting the perfect curriculum, or—God forbid—new standardized testing to measure students' progress in "social-emotional" learning. (That's right where some test-crazy California school districts went in 2016 after adopting a new curriculum to teach children skills like perseverance, empathy, and self-control.) What it does mean, however, is that teachers have to cultivate a decent degree of what one called "with-it-ness"—the ability and willingness to watch carefully and get a handle on what's really going on with the kids. It means they have to think concretely about things like what they're allowing to play out in their classrooms if they let kids pick their own group-work partners. Often this reinforces cliques and results in hierarchies being replicated over and over again, with, more often than not, one odd kid out who winds up in the bathroom crying instead of working on a lab. Assigned seating, on the other hand, creates a more "egalitarian classroom environment," where "a rising tide lifts all boats," according to a 2015 literature review by Smith College educators.

All this requires asking simple yet sometimes uncomfortable questions: Does a school really celebrate all sorts of students, even those the faculty doesn't necessarily love? Does it tend to replicate the preferences of the popular crowd (and their parents), supporting their activities and neglecting others? Do faculty members who have "cred" convey that it's perfectly all right for clique members to stay glued together 24/7, because "everyone" does that, they themselves did in the past, and you can't "force" anyone to do anything? Or do they convey that it's not so cool to need to be with your posse all day long? And is it really so terrible to assign lunchroom tables?

Setting the norm that everyone matters isn't just about recognizing a specific child who has been ignored or denigrated. That effort, like all social engineering, often backfires. Rather, when successful, it can involve creating a new "cool" activity around which kids can come together differently, see one another differently, and perhaps even discover new parts of themselves.

I saw this in action in a small New England K–8 school, when a group of middle schoolers led an assembly that they'd proposed and conceived themselves. I was struck by the particular eloquence and self-possession of a small boy who turned out to be an eighth grader. I remarked upon him to the head of the middle school, who proudly filled me in. In fifth and sixth grades, the boy had been "nerdy and marginalized," she said. He looked down all the time. He wore the same pants every day. But he was also "really smart and funny," and in seventh grade a new opportunity arose for him to show it. Seventh grade was a writing-heavy year, and a key part of the curriculum involved having kids share their writing and receive feedback. "He got a lot of juice and respect because he's an awesome writer, and that became what was important in that class," the middle school head said. "I see him in school now carrying his head much higher, and I think he can be more of his authentic self, because it's being validated now."

TAKING ON ENTRENCHED hierarchies and changing school culture is not necessarily easy to do—particularly if educators are trying to fight the good fight in a community ruled by affluent "alpha parents," who are generally used to calling the shots and getting their way and, in too many cases, also have the unfortunate tendency to treat school personnel like hired help. Living a shiny, happy life in these communities generally means keeping up a good face— which requires admitting to no weakness, or failure, or even vulnerability. Parents' (and middle schoolers') investment in projecting a perfect façade makes digging deep to achieve real problem solving very difficult. And powerful parents tend to have a vested interest in making sure their rich, athletic, expensively dressed children remain the top dogs.

A Connecticut public middle school principal told me he faces constant pushback from parents in his school's affluent community when he stands up for what he views as core values and disciplines kids who violate them. Two recent cases that were particularly ugly concerned episodes of racist speech (a problem that, I heard repeatedly, greatly increased in middle schools during and after the 2016 presidential election). In one case, the parents "fought us, screamed at us," he said, after their son, a popular sixth grader, had received a two-day suspension for having told a Korean classmate to "go eat some rice" and "go home." In the other case, four popular eighth-grade boys were suspended after repeatedly "teasing" one of their friends—another popular boy, who just happened to be the only African American student in the class—with mentions of "fried chicken" and "watermelon." By the time the principal became aware of the situation, it had gone on for weeks. The words had practically become a "nickname," he told me.

The African American boy had laughed it off, but the principal didn't think it was funny. After he made the decision to suspend the boys, he said, the "circus" began. The parents fought the suspension all the way up to the district superintendent. They argued that the black student had "allowed it to happen" by laughing along. In meeting after meeting, the principal found himself forced to spell out the most basic community standards to parents who had suddenly become intellectually incapable of grasping them: "This is not how we treat people, and this is not language that should become the norm because somebody thinks it's funny or no one is correcting it," he'd say. In the end, he told me, after the four boys' parents had "bullied" the black boy's mother, even she called to say that perhaps the punishment was too severe. But the principal wouldn't budge. "That was shocking," he told me. "Everybody claims to be so inclusive, and really when it comes down to their kid, they're quick to find an out."

Creating spaces where everyone feels equally valued can be especially tricky in private schools, with their in-your-face annual fundraising and governance by a board of trustees that usually includes wealthy current parents and has the power to set school policy—even fire the head of school.

Whether or not the power of wealthy donor parents and board members is palpable for other, less-wealthy parents (and their kids) depends on the culture of the school. At one New York City school known to draw mega-rich families, I was told, there was a middle school head who wasn't willing to sit back passively and let the popular kids decide everything from who hung out with whom on the weekends to who sat where at lunch. After observing them in action and noticing that one sixth-grade girl had no choice but to sit by herself every day at lunch, he decided to put a curb on the "alphas'" power to isolate and announced that the entire middle school had to sit by homeroom in the cafeteria.

The "popular" girls hated this—and so did their moms. By the time the next academic year started, he was gone.

"All the powerful moms who'd written big checks . . . these are the ones running the school and these are the girls running the classrooms," the mother of the isolated girl told me.

In another truly mind-boggling incident, when the head of a small, progressive K–8 private school decided to take a stand with his teachers and push back against some "alpha" parents and kids in a very troublesome sixth-grade class, things got nasty very quickly.

Two new teachers had been hired over the summer. This was unusual; it meant that the rising class of parents and kids hadn't been able to meet them before the final hiring decision was made. That was wrong, everyone said. It was the first strike against the teachers.

The headmaster had written glowingly of the teachers in an email to parents just before school began. They were experienced educators, he'd said, committed to working with middle-school-age kids and well versed in the kind of progressive education that the McKinley School community endorsed and embraced. But the *kids* didn't see that email. What they saw, when they showed up for the first day of sixth grade, were two new adults who were just . . . different.

They were older than almost all the other teachers at the school. They weren't given to high fives or liberal use of the word "awesome." The male teacher wasn't American. He drank coffee in class, and he was a smoker (outside the school building).

This was a small school where the homeroom teachers also taught reading, writing, math, and social studies and got to know the kids extremely well over the years. And this sixth-grade class, everyone had long known, was a bad one: super-cliquey, super-mean, and super-hierarchical. Hell-bent, it sometimes seemed, on mutually assured psychological destruction. There were a couple of "alpha boys" and a plurality of "alpha girls," all of whom were, for 11- and 12-year-olds, unusually attuned to the perks and power of money. They were obsessed with clothes and the size of their houses, who their parents knew and where they'd gone to college. They were obsessed, already, with getting accepted at the "right" college, and in particular with surmounting the first hurdle between them and Harvard: getting into a competitive high school. And then, outside the "alpha majority," there were some kids who were routinely snubbed and either mocked if they tried to fit in, or consigned to invisibility if they knew their place and shut up.

The new teachers considered all of this a problem. They didn't want those dynamics playing out in their classrooms. So—to use a word that wasn't yet a cliché—they decided to disrupt things. There was a girl who never spoke in class or did her homework. They insisted that she participate in class discussions and told the friend who'd long been doing her schoolwork for her to cut it out. They refused to let the "alpha kids" go on eating up most of the attention in class. They highlighted the schoolwork of the invisibles. They broke up the cliques for group work. They told the rich kids to stop bragging. They told the joker kids to stop trading in "just kidding" insults.

Soon, a number of the "popular" kids were coming home crying. Word started circulating around the school that the teachers were "mean." That they didn't understand "the McKinley School way"—an amorphous thing that no one had ever really heard of before these teachers started to "betray" it. All of this was accompanied by much vigorous parental head-shaking and pointed looks in the direction of the headmaster's office, and a general sense that if things didn't change soon, *something* would have to be done.

About two weeks into the school year, the teachers were summoned to a meeting in the headmaster's office to meet with a parent who, avoiding eye contact and with a silent friend by her side for "moral support," said she wanted to let them know (without naming names) that "everyone" felt that things were out of control in the teachers' classrooms. That the kids were learning nothing. That they weren't being prepared for the upcoming rigors of seventh and eighth grade. The teachers were dumbfounded. Up until that point, they'd had nothing but smiles from parents (they didn't know enough yet to realize whose smiles really mattered), and they'd thought things were going quite well.

But now they were learning that "everyone" was unhappy. With no names, however, they couldn't figure out why. So they went back to doing what they had been doing. On students' birthdays, they made the whole class sit in a circle and say, one after another, what they liked about the person being celebrated. When students read their written work to the class and asked for feedback (as the teachers regularly made them do), the teachers insisted that their classmates respond, first with a compliment and then with a suggestion. They used the same strategy with, and gave the same amount of effort and care to, everyone.

In early October, a delegation of sixth graders marched into the headmaster's office. They presented a list of grievances. They demanded that the teachers be fired. He quietly demurred.

A few days later, however, at Back to School Night, that normally affable and soft-spoken man practically shouted as he filled all of the parents in on what had transpired in his office. Some erstwhile invisible parents gasped. The parents of the kids in question stared at him, stone-faced.

"There *is* such a thing as over-empowering your kids," he all but snarled.

And then he exited the room, and the teachers took over.

PARENTS AREN'T TRAINED as educators. But they can do a lot to improve the climate in which their middle schoolers live. Like teachers, they can set norms and do their best to teach by example.

They can, for instance, put even a minimal amount of thought into how they handle the mechanics of their kids' social lives. They don't have to make a big, noisy show of rounding up a group of kids for a party or sleepover while the uninvited look on. They don't have to print up sweatshirts with their kid's name and bar or bat mitzvah party date on them if they've only invited a select few to the reception—or, worse, all *but* a select few. They don't have to advertise their kids' activities on Instagram.

I get extra-cranky on the subject of social media because there's so much hypocrisy around the topic of middle schoolers' online lives. It's considered good parenting to secretly scroll through your children's texts but beyond the pale to say that phones need to be put away at, say, a birthday party, despite the fact that the guests may be paying more attention to texting than to celebrating the birthday kid. Unilateral parent action on screen use can be social suicide for a middle schooler, as one mom told me she discovered after collecting a group of girls' phones in a basket at the start of a gathering in her home—only to have it turn out to be the last her daughter would host. But *communities* can set norms around phone use. Schools can—and increasingly are—demanding that they be put away during the school day. Prominent parents in Silicon Valley are publicly sharing that they're saying no to phones and social media before the teen years. (Melinda Gates told *The New York Times* she wished she'd continued the ban even longer.) Parents of middle schoolers, who are so uniquely at risk for toxic FOMO (Fear of Missing Out), need to question whether their own addiction to being able to reach their kids at the drop of a hat is standing in the way of the kids' well-being.

Parents can, after all, learn to be present in other ways. Like the mom in the story about the middle schooler who grew up to become a middle school teacher, they can learn to listen to their kids without wallowing in their drama. They can elevate, rather than lower, problematic conversations. They can do the emotional work to raise gossip, or complaints, or just plain old neutral after-school car conversations to a better and more productive level. For example, instead of rushing in to agree that "Tiffany is *such* a bitch, and not even that pretty," and then agreeing to gape at the poor girl's embarassing (and illegal) Tinder, they can ask something like, "Why do you say she's a bitch? What does she do?" Not: "WHAT DID SHE DO TO YOU?"

In other words, a parent can pose a gentle query that essentially says, *Tell me what it means to you for someone to be a bitch,* without using such obviously pedantic, ponderous, and pathetic language. They can try to find out what's going on in the girl's life that might explain why she's on Tinder in the first place and express some sort of sadness about whatever that turns out to be. I see this as a way of essentially playing a bit dumb to extract more and better information (a tried-and-true reporting technique). It's also a matter of seeming not to pay too much attention while, in fact, attending very closely. I know, from personal experience, that these techniques do work.

It's hard not to regress when our kids go through hard times in middle school. When parents do, I've noticed, their whole demeanor changes. Their language shifts. Perfectly reasonable adults start using words like "sociopath" and "monster" to talk about 11- or 12-year-olds who have been mean to their kids. Sometimes they use the exact same terminology that their children do—or, more precisely, that they themselves used for other kids when they were their children's age. They talk about their kids being "dumped" or "broken up with" by ex-friends who want to engage in "social climbing." They refer to boys as "dicks." I once heard the phrase "dud kids" used by a mother about children—including one of her own—who, she believed, had been grouped in the same section at school precisely because they weren't popular or cool. She said, "I went into the class, and it was the kid with the neck brace and the kid with the limp and the kid with the shorts. All the dud kids. All the mothers of the cool kids had arranged to make sure all those kids were put together." Another mom used the phrase "the little island of misfit toys" in a similar way.

Parents who had no adult guidance in thinking through their own junior high school experiences (and no books or movies to suggest helpful language or add some levity) often don't have the skills to help their kids figure out what's going on in the present and, even more important, what to do about it. They are knocked off their feet as they imagine their children asking the kinds of questions they've never been able to answer for themselves: *Why did they stop talking to me? What did I do? Is there something wrong with me?* Their own pain and rage can reappear in a split second. And at those times, it's very hard to think, much less behave, like a grown-up.

This is not helpful for anyone. We don't have to echo our middle schoolers' language or mirror their emotions to hear and acknowledge what they have to say. In fact, there's nothing more annoying and, as the kids say, "cringey" than a parent who slips into middle school mode. When parents speak about "cool" kids and "annoying" or "babyish" kids, "mean girls" and "bullies," "popular" and "unpopular" kids—the latter categories, in parent-speak, still seemingly possessed of magical qualities far beyond the realm of human comprehension—they kind of talk themselves into a hole. And there's a danger to it as well: They very often lose sight of exactly which middle schooler they're addressing. In other words, as Paige Trevor, a D.C.-area parenting educator, once said to me, "Parents are going back in time and trying to fix their [own] problems. We tend to parent ourselves rather than the children we have."

Those are important words to heed. The truth is, we parents potentially have a lot of tools at our disposal that can guide us in making sense of middle school and helping our middle schoolers make sense of it, too. And we need to use those tools. If—as I know from experience—we can't access *feeling* like the adults that we are supposed to be, we have to fake it 'til we make it. One thing I've found really helps: channeling other adults with cooler minds. I learned to do this myself over time by tapping into the voices of experts whose words and ideas I found the most compelling.

I often think, for example, of the psychologist Michael Thompson's advice to avoid "interviewing for pain." That means resisting the urge to start a school-day postmortem with "How was ['mean kid's' name here] acting today? What did they do? That's *horrible*—you must be so upset!"—which immediately sends your kid the message that if they're not already upset (or already ruminating over the other kid's actions), they should be. A better plan: Let the stories come in their own time. And if they don't come, don't go looking for them. If they do, listen, empathize, but don't dwell. And pivot quickly to asking your kid what they think *they* could do to make things better.

I also like to think of the words of William Stixrud, a neuropsychologist, who warns parents against imposing the effects of "secondhand stress" on their kids. In his recent book, *The Self-Driven Child,* he explains how mirror neurons in the brain make kids almost uncannily able to pick up on their parents' vibes. This means that excessive parental emotion over a middle schooler's social ups and downs—even if masked—can almost be a kind of communicable disease, one that can provoke new and heightened distress in children. Perhaps that's why one 2010 study found that how well parents managed their own stress was more important than any other parenting factor (except showing love and acceptance) in their children's level of happiness.

Another psychologist told me she recommends that parents work with their kids to "deconstruct" some of the words that have the most power in their worlds. For middle schoolers, of course, one of the most powerful is "popular"—a word so important that it now almost has its own field of social science research. Experts break "popularity" down into two types: "sociometric" popularity (when kids are actually well liked) and "perceived" popularity (when kids are high-status and powerful, but very often disliked). They know that kids who are well liked tend to have a distinct set of skills: They're good at understanding other people's perspectives, are high in empathy and impulse control, have a good sense of humor, and know how to be "prosocial"—a "positive and desirable peer companion," in social science–speak. They also tend generally to radiate the pleasantness that comes from maintaining an overall "positive affect."

Kids with high status—who are frequently feared rather than liked—have the aforementioned skills as well, though they often choose not to use them. In addition, they have other skills that are less admirable, including a talent for getting what they want and for getting others to *do* what they want. Most of us wouldn't want to encourage our kids to develop the skills they'd need to be feared rather than liked. But helping them develop more empathy and impulse control, as well as remembering to reward them for being cooperative and kind, benefits everyone.

It's also important to know—as child psychologists do—that "popular" kids often need adult help and empathy, too. Popularity itself, research has long shown, can be a risk factor for unhappiness. Maintaining "popular" status takes real effort, particularly when it's based on power rather than likability. It's often cyclical, as the sociologist Donna Eder noted in a much-cited article on the "cycle of popularity" back in the 1980s. Being a popular girl in middle school, she wrote, usually requires a big sacrifice of likability because, to ascend to the summit of social desirability, you have to snub the lesser mortals who used to be your friends. In doing so, you set yourself up for the permanent risk of falling from the pinnacle of power to the total no-friend zone.

All this is no doubt why, as I heard repeatedly in my interviews, popular kids of the status-derived, rather than the well-liked, variety generally don't have happy memories of middle school. The dynamics of popular crowds are notoriously damaging. The values these groups espouse don't lead to good things. In addition, while it takes a certain social acumen to get into the popular crowd, staying there, experts say, can actually prevent kids from developing other, more positive friendship skills that can keep them happy in the long term. And this is undoubtedly why popular middle school kids often find themselves socially adrift in high school and early adulthood. The skills that work at 12 don't get you very far after 15.

I heard this directly in the stories of several women who had crested a personal wave in middle school and then struggled to find their place socially starting in tenth grade. And I saw it in the relationship trajectory of a self-avowed former "mean girl," whose middle school friendships soured as she and her friends moved up into high school. Her work history was littered with treacherous power plays involving other women, and her adult friendships were full of the back-and-forth of competition and envy. "To this day, I have few female friends," she told me. "I'm worried still if somebody's hanging out with somebody else without me. . . . That feeling of exclusion has followed me."

Beyond the schadenfreude of hearing how the "cool" kids eventually come to bad ends, there are some very good reasons why acquiring a bit of expert knowledge about the dark side of popularity is extremely helpful. Intellectual distance helps defang the monsters of middle school past *and* present. It's emotionally liberating, for example, to be able to bear in mind that the "mean girls" in your child's class who register in the 12-year-old part of your brain as mortal threats are actually kids scientifically proven to be more lonely, more depressed, and more isolated-feeling than others. They may seem on the surface to be less awkward, ungainly, and self-conscious—more mature and together—than their less popular peers, but their relational aggression is a "tell" that they actually have some skill deficits that will trip them up later if they don't learn the error of their ways.

Specifically, "mean girls" tend to have problems with what experts call a negative attribution style and social information processing skills. This means that they interpret other people's intentions and behavior in a mistakenly hostile way. They also, very often, have distorted beliefs about what normal behavior is—thinking, perhaps from having grown up in an aggressive home, that relationally aggressive behavior is far more common, acceptable, and normal than it really is. They tend to be more reactive than other kids—even physically aggressive kids—in situations where their relationships feel threatened. In all, they generally misread what's going on socially around them and calibrate their own responses based on that false information. In other words, while their current victims may see or their adult victims may remember them as evil, they really are somewhat impaired. Which means, with the proper guidance, they can change.

"I was one of those kids," Karen, the former popular girl who'd become the head of a middle school in Massachusetts, told me. "I get where some of the bravado is coming from and what some of the vulnerabilities are." She grew up in a fancy Chicago suburb. She attended private school. She had her own brand-new car at 16. She was outgoing, athletic, funny, smart, and attractive, and she had all the right clothes. Everyone wanted to be around her. But she was one of few African American girls in the school, and that didn't make life easy. "The vulnerabilities of kids—of the popular kids, or the kids who can be unkind or less empathetic—comes from a desire to belong or fit in. That's where it came from for me," she said.

Having been a "popular girl"—even a "mean girl," she admitted, with a great deal of embarrassment—she now has some strong feelings about the way schools should deal with kids accused of "bullying," particularly when it takes place online. Where parents of a hurt child generally see pure meanness, she sees skill deficits—and those, she believes, have to be addressed as much through education as through discipline. Rather than rushing in to "label someone a bully," she said, we should "unpack what a kid's motivation is," because it often isn't malicious at all. Hurtful behavior, especially online, can indicate that "a kid is coming to understand the power of language and the power of groups," she said, and that this understanding still needs a lot of work.

It can be very helpful to realize that kids who are "unpopular" most often have social skills problems, too. They may have trouble entering, exiting, or keeping up with conversations, or with "reading" tone of voice, facial expressions, or other subtle social cues. They may have poor self-regulation skills that trip them up socially—like difficulty reining in strong emotions or restraining themselves from blurting out less-than-palatable opinions. "Relationship blindness"—an inability to accurately see what other people find displeasing in you—can be a big problem. So can being overly aggressive or overly submissive, withdrawn, shy, or "inhibited"; being uncooperative or unhelpful; or showing high levels of "negative affect" (being down and grumpy, critical, or irritable) or disagreeableness.

Interestingly enough, like "popular" kids of the "mean girl" (or boy) variety, "unpopular" kids may be hobbled by a negative attribution style, too. Another trait that serves kids really badly likability-wise is "rejection sensitivity," a tendency to be devastated by rejection (real or perceived) and to always expect to be rejected. Rejection-sensitive kids often go to great ("annoying") lengths to get others to like them. Because they perceive rejection even when it's not happening, they can be inappropriately defensive and aggressive. For a rejection-sensitive person (kid or adult), a friendship breakup—or a romantic breakup later on—can feel like a cosmic confirmation of their worst fears about their own worthlessness. All of which can cause what some psychologists have called "self-fulfilling prophecy effects"—a spiral of more and more relationship pain, not just in the middle school years but in high school and beyond.

Kids who have untreated mental health issues such as an anxiety disorder or depression are often unpopular in middle school. Battling mental illness (which kids do on average for *eight years* before getting a proper diagnosis and starting treatment) can make kids withdrawn, aggressive, or submissive, or make them come across as "weird" or just kind of *off*. They tend to be at very serious risk of being bullied. In my interviews, a striking number of the adults who recalled having been bullied, rejected, or otherwise miserable in middle school realized, in retrospect, that they were suffering from the first major flare-ups of the depression, bipolar disorder, obsessive-compulsive disorder, or other anxiety disorder that would stay with them for the rest of their lives.

IF IT SEEMS like I'm blaming the victim—if the patent unfairness of all this seems overwhelming (it's not enough for a kid to be anxious or depressed; they have to pay for it socially as well?)—my intent is only to inspire parents to take action and get help for their kids. The skill deficits that keep some kids socially sidelined in middle school can be overcome or, at least, greatly lessened. They can be learned, and are every bit as worth learning as English or math. Perhaps they're even more important.

Listening for the deeper meanings behind the words our middle schoolers use and responding to the emotions buried there are just about the most important things parents can learn to do. Because things in middle school are very often far more complicated than they seem. And, to borrow some popular terminology from the psychologist and author Carol Dweck, thinking less like middle schoolers and more like the experts who study and work with them can help us go from our traditional "fixed mindset" about these kids ("they're awful, they're hopeless, they're irredeemable") to one that's "growth" oriented ("they're still learning, they need help, and they're full of potential").

Perhaps most valuable of all: Doing this can help us feel compassion. And compassion is the salve of the middle school parent's soul. Teaching it, modeling it, and getting your middle schoolers to expand their thinking and feeling beyond the bounds of their own minds are by far the best gifts you can give them.

The takeaways are clear: Instead of spiraling down into the affective realm of middle schoolers, we adults can—and must—raise our own level of emotional functioning. We have to learn to listen without immediately rushing in to fix things. We must be able to tolerate distress—our own distress—without falling to pieces.

We have to figure out how to acknowledge, without excessively dwelling on, the bad things that happen in middle school. That means, when we can credibly do so without sounding ridiculous, trying to give things a positive spin. Or, at the very least, finding a way to bring a light touch and a sense of humor to middle school's dark places, always bearing in mind that few social situations—in middle school as in the rest of life—are black-and-white. This is all incredibly hard to do. But if we can pull it off, even imperfectly, it will send a message to our kids that they are competent and capable and that their friendship losses or dramas are problems to be solved, rather than existential catastrophes. And that is extremely empowering—for them *and* for us.

We can't save our children from the miseries of middle school. But we can save ourselves from the pain of experiencing our own miseries over and over again. And we have to. Because something astonishing happens when we are finally able to take a critical, and compassionate, look at middle school and middle schoolers, past and present.

We instantly grow up.

CHAPTER 9

Forgetting and Remembering

Whatever your current assessment and memories of your
adolescence, it is helpful to recognize that they are probably
only partially true.

—DR. ROBERT C. KOLODNY AND
NANCY J. KOLODNY, ET AL.,
How to Survive Your Adolescent's Adolescence

NOTHING TELESCOPES PAST and present more powerfully than our
own super-vivid memories from the sixth, seventh, and eighth
grades.

But what if those memories are not as accurate as they feel?

When I started this book, I had little, if any, desire to spend
time with real-life, current-day middle schoolers. At that point, I
thought it was just because I didn't like them—with the exception
of my own, of course, and the friends who were loyal to them.
That's not a hard thing to admit. People say it to middle school

teachers all the time: "How can you do your job?" they ask. "I would want to shoot myself!"

The truth, I realized when I started to actually visit schools to do research, was that I was afraid of middle schoolers. Or of some of them, at least: the straightened-hair, North Face–wearing, attractive, charismatic, slightly swaggering, posse-surrounded "popular" kids.

That insight came to me one morning when I was invited to park myself for a few minutes in the back of an eighth-grade classroom while waiting for an administrator to be ready for an interview. It was an English class. The kids were facing one another, their desks arranged in a big open square, and they were working on grammar. That was super-boring, for them and for me, as they realized, to their delight, when the teacher called on me to answer a question that had stumped everyone else. I was so far away in my head that he had to re-explain everything before I could answer.

"Space cadet," I thought, words I probably hadn't heard, or used, since my own eighth-grade year.

While mentally absenting myself from the grammar lesson, I'd been watching the social dynamics of the classroom. A boy and a girl sat together like a king and a queen, radiating star energy. It wasn't necessarily a bad energy—they weren't snarly or mean. The class was working through the grammar questions, bantering lightly, and everyone seemed engaged. Except for one girl, who seemed to be in a bad way.

She was dressed just like all the "popular" girls I'd seen in the hallways. She was attractive and polished. And yet she seemed to wear some sort of shroud that made her invisible to the others. Her expression was perfectly neutral, but everything about her conveyed carefully controlled misery—her downcast eyes, her frozen face, the extreme economy of her movements. She was there, but not there. When the teacher told everyone to look to their left or their right to find a partner, she looked down, and no one looked her way. No one reacted when she was left to do the partner work alone. The teacher told her to join a neighboring duo, and she sort of vaguely oriented herself in their direction. And then she disappeared inside herself again.

The kids were about to embark upon "passion projects," special research papers on topics of their own choosing, with which they'd cap off their time at the school. When the grammar exercise was over, the teacher invited me to share my research methods with the students and give them some advice. My stomach flipped and knotted, in part because, at that point, I was pretty much throwing thought spaghetti against the walls of my skull and seeing what would stick, and partly because joining the group meant standing up, walking, and sitting back down at one of the desks in the square—in the empty spot next to the silent girl and directly in front of the royals.

Once I'd moved, I stalled for a while by asking the students to tell me the subjects of their projects so that I could issue some completely useless pieces of advice: "You'll probably want to narrow that down." "*Definitely* try *The New York Times*."

And then, out of sheer nervousness, I started babbling. I told them about the week that I'd been shunned in eighth grade.

This interested them.

I told them about how the effects of that shunning had stayed with me, and how, in the past, I'd always carried the memory of having been a victim of bullying in middle school. (Although the word "bullying," I told them, had only presented itself after the Columbine massacre, because everyone had started using it then.) In fact, I added, a little bit of the book I was writing had been born in the period right after Columbine, when I'd tried to write a magazine article in which I was going to confront my eighth-grade "bully," Marci.

This interested them even more.

I'd run into a big problem, I said. This was just before you could hunt people down by Google-stalking them online, and so (now I could take a truly instructional tone) I'd had to call my old school, which only had a phone number for one of my former classmates, Mary, who had not been a bully. She had, in fact, been one of my best friends in seventh grade. That wasn't great, but it was something. And so I called her.

She was minimally friendly as I explained what I was doing. And then she said: "Funny, I don't remember Marci 'bullying' you. What I do remember is you dumping Olivia and me."

I had nothing to say to that. I was shocked. Not because I didn't recall or believe her version of events; what she'd said was absolutely true. Sometime toward the middle of eighth grade, I had "dumped" her and Olivia to hang out with the "popular" girls. That action, arguably, had kind of set everything else in motion. But prior to speaking with Mary, that part of the story had just sort of disappeared from my mind.

The point being, I told the kids, that often, in middle school, *things are not what they seem.*

I felt, rather than saw, the presence on my left grow a little bit brighter. The others were staring at me wide-eyed.

Then the door flew open. The administrator I was supposed to be interviewing called me out for our meeting. She looked a bit annoyed. I realized, in retrospect, that I hadn't been cleared to talk to the kids.

When I stood up, shouts of protest came from the square.

When I thought back on this later, I realized that those friendly cries were very likely due to the fact that my departure would mean more grammar. But at the time, I thought: *They like me. They're actually being nice to me.*

And I felt a joyful surprise that was only slightly less embarrassing to acknowledge to myself at that moment than it is to admit here.

HAD I BEEN able to stay longer, there were more stories I could have told. There was the time I was in New York with my family, staying in my mother's apartment. My daughter was digging through boxes in my old room. "Treasure" boxes from when I was very little: round cookie tins of letters saved from sleepaway camp, and a small orange canister that had once held animal crackers.

"What's this?" my daughter asked, a strange accusatory tone in her voice. She was in fifth or sixth grade. She'd found a note. It had been folded many times over.

"I don't know what I've done to make you mad at me," the spindly handwriting read. *"You don't have to be my friend if you don't want to. But please just let me know what I've done."*

I recognized the handwriting immediately. "It was from Olivia," I said. "She was my friend in sixth and seventh grades."

"Why were you mad at her?" she asked.

"I wasn't," I said.

"So why did you stop being friends with her?" she asked.

"I don't know," I said. "I just did."

Olivia had come to my school in sixth grade. We'd spent many Saturdays on the floor at the Brentano's bookstore on Eighth Street, reading depressing YA fiction about teenage boys becoming drug addicts and teenage girls having sex and getting pregnant. After sitting on the floor for hours, I would get up feeling sick. We'd stumble out into the sunlight, walk past the head shops and shoe stores, and buy an Orange Julius. Sometimes we spent entire afternoons in her room, playing the game Life and listening to the rock opera *Tommy*. She lived in a loft with bare wood floors, along with a dog, an older sister, and a stepmother she called by her first name. All of that was very exotic to me.

In seventh grade, we went on a "double date" to the original

Star Wars, where I had popcorn with butter for the first time. My "date"—a boy I'd known since kindergarten, and who was a good head shorter than me—said I could rub the grease off my hands on his pants leg.

We organized games of Spin the Bottle. I lent her my copy of *Wuthering Heights,* and her dog chewed it up. She bought me another one—"bigger and better, new and improved," she said, but it wasn't the same, and I held it against her.

It was odd: I could remember being friends, and I could remember not being friends. But I couldn't remember any transition. No fight, no falling-out—nothing. Somehow, over the course of eighth grade, I'd switched friend groups. I'd gone from being part of Judy-Mary-and-Olivia—top of the class, editors of the school literary magazine, teacher's pets (except in science, where Mary was the only one the teacher liked)—to hanging out with Anna, who was skinny and smelled of strawberry lip gloss; Jill, who was funny; and Kelly, who reminded me of Olivia Newton-John.

"I don't think I would have liked you very much when you were my age," my daughter said.

Memory is such a strange thing. What sticks and what doesn't. What becomes part of the story of your life—the story by which you know yourself—and what gets thrown away.

Rachel Simmons, the author of the 2002 bestseller *Odd Girl Out,* writes of having been so consumed by her own story of ostracism in third grade that she entirely forgot (or "I remembered . . . but I didn't remember," as she put it to me) having dropped her best friend from elementary school, Anne, when a more powerful girl in the popular clique they'd both joined in middle school decided that Anne had to go. She "remembered but didn't remember," in fact, right up to the moment when, in her mid-20s, she actually ran into Anne and excitedly shared with her the news that she was writing a book on girl exclusion.

"And she just was sort of like, 'Uh, hello?'" Simmons told me. "It was like a slo-mo, horrifying realization."

A number of other women I interviewed for this book—all former "popular" girls who self-identified as having been "mean"—had memories that they had "unremembered," too. Megan, a Unitarian minister, had compartmentalized her horribleness so completely (and she had, she said, been really awful) that when she ran into the mother of a girl she and her clique had cruelly mocked for years, the memory seemed so remote that, in making light conversation, she simply talked about how much she'd loved the school. When the mom set her straight, the onslaught of memories was absolutely devastating.

She almost started crying when I told her about the "I don't know" conversation I'd had with my daughter. "We spend so much energy trying to teach our kids how to be compassionate, loving, generous, whatever—all these *words*," she said with a sigh. "Then when we connect it to our own experiences"—her words faltered—"it's such a profound mismatch between our aspirations and our reality."

Her son was a ninth grader at the time we spoke. Ever since middle school, she said, he'd been the odd kid out—"a geeky, nerdy, awkward kid." The other kids weren't cruel to him, as far as she knew. They just ignored him. After his one good friend dropped him, he'd spent every weekend at home. "He doesn't even reach out to kids anymore," she told me, "because kids are not available."

It was hard to tell how much this upset him. But it tortured her. "Maybe, inside, he's carrying a tremendous amount of shame. Or sadness," she said. Worse still was the question she asked herself all the time: "Would *I* have been friends with this kid?" She did not like the answer.

We all have a "narrative identity"—a story through which we know ourselves, present ourselves to others, and give ourselves a coherent history. It's a human universal, although culture plays a role in shaping our stories' narrative form. There are archetypal sagas that we fit ourselves into—subconsciously, most of the time—and they give us a way to make sense of our experiences and find community.

People's middle school stories, I've seen time and again, very often have a disproportionate impact on the narratives of self that they carry through adulthood. And that's a huge problem. When it comes to our middle school selves, the narratives on offer from our culture—"I was a popular kid," "I was a nerd," "I was a bully," "I was the victim of a bully or 'mean girl' "—aren't very helpful from a psychological growth and long-term well-being perspective. They promote black-and-white thinking. They can take away our sense of agency.

In addition—as I would have gone on to tell the class of eighth graders I visited—there is so much more to our middle school experiences than we remember. We form our memories, our stories of self, based on very partial, and often very poor, information. We don't see the big picture. Sometimes—at least in the past this was true—that's because adults don't want us to see it. But it's also because, at the ages of 11 through 14, we're not yet capable of seeing it. Not without adult help, anyway.

It's awful when people move through life with negative stories of self based on decades-old, immature perceptions that they find fully credible. One woman I interviewed, who was in her early 30s, described everyone's nightmare scenario: When she turned 11, she had a birthday party, and no one came.

"I was not destined to be a popular person," she said. She spoke in a matter-of-fact tone.

"Did your mom get in touch beforehand with the other parents?" I asked. "Did you send invitations to their houses? Did they know for sure that it was really happening?"

No to mom. No to mailed invitations. She had asked the girls herself at school.

"They probably didn't remember," I said. "They probably didn't realize it was really a *thing*."

But she shrugged that off. No, it was her own fault, she insisted. She'd just been blind. "Some of my intense undesirability as a friend and person in the world I didn't realize until later," she said.

Is it possible to rewrite a narrative once you've based your identity on it for decades? I know that it is.

Had I been allowed to stay longer in that eighth-grade class, I would have told one other story. It dates back to 2010, when my mother called me one afternoon to say that a women's magazine had published a big article about Marci's sister. I looked online, and there she was—a very pretty young woman with long brown hair, in a black-and-white photo that looked familiar, even though I hadn't seen it in over thirty years. It had been in the newspapers at the time, and on small posters plastered on lampposts.

She was really Marci's half sister, but Marci always just said "sister," with awe and admiration. I didn't know her. I think I saw her once or twice in Marci's apartment, in the brief period, at the start of sixth grade, when we were best friends.

Yes—best friends. It's a detail that tends to drop out of my "I was a victim of a 'mean girl'" story. We'd become close when we'd landed in the same homeroom that September. I'd been kind of at loose ends, in the market for new friends, after the two girls I'd been closest to since kindergarten had left our school unexpectedly at the end of fifth grade.

Ours was not a natural friendship. Marci and I were very different. She was loud and athletic; I was quiet and read all the time. She was wealthy; I was not. She was pretty; I was not. Her wavy hair held a perfect Dorothy Hamill haircut; I was lucky if mine could manage the most anemic semblance of "wings." For a year or two, she'd been paired up in everyone's mind with a boy who was, in looks and in general level of cool, her male equivalent:

a Jared-Leto-as-Jordan-Catalano type nicknamed "Izzy," with whom I'd never exchanged a single word.

And then, of course, there had been that shunning incident on the Girl Scout camping weekend back in third grade. I'd always been on my guard with Marci after that, even as we started to spend more and more time together in early sixth grade. We hung out together after school, listening to music in her room with the floral color scheme I admired so much that I copied it almost exactly when I redid my own room in seventh grade. I even went with her family to her country house one weekend. In the picture her father took of us by the pool, she looks like a real teenager. I look like a little kid. We went out to dinner with her parents, and we briefly walked in the woods—not all that far, it turned out, from where her sister's remains would be found two summers later.

Marci's sister is believed to have been one of the first victims of a serial killer—one of a number of charming, attractive, psychopathic men who roamed the United States in the late 1970s, taking advantage of the new anything-goes, rules-up-for-grabs culture of the time, the lack of coordinated information sharing among police departments, and the shockingly short prison sentences for sex offenders.

She disappeared the summer after our sixth-grade year. Marci and I were no longer best friends by that time. I had a new best friend, Francesca, who was two years older than me and who, as far as I was concerned, walked on air. Once again, I can't remember a transition out of my friendship with Marci. My memories jump from early sixth grade at her country house to the point in eighth grade when Anna told me that Marci had said that her mother had said that I "ate like a dog."

Eighth grade had begun just a few months after Marci's sister's bones were recovered from under some brush on the grounds of an old private estate. Did it go through my mind at all during that school year that Marci might have had other things working on her when she decided to send some hate my way? Did it dawn on me that some kind words, or perhaps just an absence of malice, might have helped pave the way—for both of us—to a more harmonious eighth-grade year?

No, it did not. Not for a second. And not only because my head was so filled with my self-obsessions. Marci's sister's death just wasn't acknowledged. We attended a tiny church school, where our entire graduating class had only twenty-two students, many of whom, like Marci and me, had been there since kindergarten. We went to chapel twice a week; we took an ethics class where a hopeful-looking teacher made us imagine that we were on a lifeboat with one person too many and had to decide whom to pitch over the side. But there were no admonitions from adults that we needed to understand that our classmate was going through a rough time and the one way we could help was by being extra kind.

Nobody said anything. Maybe it was because there was a tinge of shame that clung to the story, as though the fault had been, somehow, Marci's sister's for going off with a strange guy with long hair in the first place. That attitude did exist among some older adults at the time. We were still fighting the sixties culture wars, after all. And the complexities of that culture—so full of anger and ugliness—were no help when it came to making sense of our lives.

IT'S EASY *NOT* to see how much our middle schoolers need our help. They're very vocal about not wanting it, and—as I hope I've made clear—many of the ways that we try to give it are patently destructive. Seventh and eighth graders can sound quite grown-up when they talk. In fact, when they're not flipping out over something inane, they sound like they're more or less operating in the same universe as we are.

But they are not.

A year or two before starting this book, I happened to come across something I'd written two weeks before eighth-grade graduation (I was counting the days). The handwriting looked like it belonged to a different person; in fact, it was so inconsistent that it looked like it could have belonged to a couple of different people. In a way, it did. In seventh grade, I'd made myself unlearn the way I'd been forming letters since childhood and tried instead to develop a new handwriting style that looked like it might have come from the pen of the sort of girl I wanted to be.

More than the look of the handwriting, however, what struck me most about this piece of writing was the sound. It was eerily similar to that of my writing today. *"I alienate myself from people in that I create situations in my mind, such as that all my friends hate me, or something similar (situations that have no bearing on reality),"* I'd written, as part of what seemed to be a set of answers to some kind of questionnaire. *"I then get angry at myself, and at those around me for hating me, and I pull into myself. In that way, I remove myself from my friends, not the other way around. If I actually take time to look, I see that my friends act the same to me as ever. Luckily, so far, I have found the truth before pulling away too much, and no one ever notices the difference."*

My powers of observation were good, but my understanding of what I saw around me lagged far behind. Reading 13-year-old me reminded me of what it had been like at that age to read books that were too hard for me: I'd understand all the words but miss the true meaning, because I didn't have the life experience to make good sense of the material.

That sense-making is what our middle schoolers need from us. They need context, insight into what other people's lives might be like, a way of entertaining different theories of what someone else's behavior might mean. They sometimes need suggestions as to what their own odd behaviors mean. If we can provide them with this, we can nudge them in a compassionate direction. We can, perhaps, spark some empathy. Given that we are the most annoying people on earth, they may shrug us off. But whether or not our efforts are acknowledged, the fact of simply trying to broaden the scope of their thinking might be enough to make a difference.

"I couldn't believe it when I looked at the eighth graders' yearbook page," my now-young-adult daughter said to me the other day after babysitting a current student at the school where she was abjectly miserable in seventh and eighth grade. "They are *kids*. *We* were *kids*."

ACKNOWLEDGMENTS

THIS VERY PUBLIC acknowledgments page is not the place where I can express the full depth of my gratitude to the friends, family members, and colleagues who sustained their belief in me during the very, *very* long four years I spent reporting and writing this book. I have expressed my profound thanks to them privately many times before, and trust that they know just how precious their support has been. So I'll keep my thanks here quick and to the point:

I am very grateful to my agent, Amy Williams, for her energy, enthusiasm, wit, wisdom, and professionalism. She pumped me up and brought my ideas to life. And she retaught me that writing can be fun.

Amanda Cook was not just a wonderful editor and intellectual guide; she displayed a level of kindness and generosity of spirit that both humbles and inspires me. I consider myself extremely lucky to have come into her orbit. If I can, with this book, pass on to others even a fraction of the goodwill that she has shown me, then I'll consider this joint venture a very great success indeed.

I want to thank Max Berley for reminding me of my voice and keeping me fortified with puddings (for better or for worse). I would not have been able to write this book without his clarity of vision. And I owe a special debt of gratitude to Julia and Emilie Berley for many hours of research, fact-checking, wool-gathering, bullshit-catching, chili-making, *Big Mouth*–watching, and general creativity and inspiration.

I want to thank Barb Jatkola for deftly bringing order to the book's unruly places, and also thank Zach Phillips for his steady help along the way. I am always thankful for the love and support of my mother, Zelda Warner, to whom I now owe a special shout-out for her sharp-eyed proofreading skills. She is a lifesaver.

I was very fortunate in the course of writing this book to have been able to draw upon a voluminous body of published work on early adolescence, past and present. Linda Perlstein was the first person to spark my interest in taking a skeptical look at how we talk and think about 11-to-14-year-olds; her 2003 book, *Not Much Just Chillin': The Hidden Lives of Middle Schoolers,* is a myth-busting classic. Rosalind Wiseman, Rachel Simmons, and Peggy Orenstein have set the gold standard for all the popular and jour-nalistic writing about this age group that has come into being over the past two decades. They have been extremely gracious and helpful to me, and I hope that my work can join theirs in its sense of higher purpose.

And, last but by no means least, I am deeply grateful to all the parents, experts, educators, and grown-up middle schoolers of all ages who so generously shared their time, thoughts, and memories with me for this book. I was not aware, when I started doing my interviews, that asking people to tell me their middle school sto-ries would bring me so quickly and deeply into the heart of their lives. I greatly appreciated their openness and honesty, and hope I've been able to do justice here to the rich worlds of meaning they revealed to me.

INTRODUCTION: TRIGGER WARNING

xi   The seventh and eighth grades": Anne Lamott, *Operating Instructions: A Journal of My Son's First Year* (New York: Anchor, 2005), 10.

xvii   *"interview for pain"*: Michael Thompson and Catherine O'Neill Grace with Lawrence J. Cohen, *Best Friends, Worst Enemies* (New York: Ballantine, 2001), 250. This phrase is well loved by school administrators in my area.

xxii   "secondary trauma": Brené Brown, cited in Jennifer Senior, "Why You Truly Never Leave High School," *New York,* Jan. 20, 2013.

1. MIDDLE SCHOOL IN OUR MINDS

3   "those deep emotional scars": Judith Martin, "Suffer the Little Children—It's a Rite of Passage," *The Washington Post,* Feb. 18, 1979.

7   "the Bermuda Triangle of public education": "Joel Klein's First Day of School," *The New York Times,* Sept. 5, 2002.

8   Donald Trump's "sophomoric" behavior: "CNN Reagan Library Debate: Later Debate Full Transcript," CNN.com, Sept. 16, 2015,

cnnpressroom.blogs.cnn.com/2015/09/16/cnn-reagan-library-debate
-later-debate-full-transcript/.

8   "grabbed by the pussy": After Donald Trump's election, I heard or
saw this phrase a number of times in casual conversation, in an interview for this book, and in, for example, Jia Tolentino, "On the
Streets," *The New Yorker,* Nov. 21, 2016.

8   "There was nothing they could do to me": Sallie Krawcheck, cited in
Tara Parker-Pope, "How to Build Resilience in Midlife," *The New
York Times,* July 27, 2017.

8   a self-described "nerdy" 11-year-old: Rebecca Milzoff, "A Choreog-
rapher Takes Her Daughter to Work, with a Famous Friend," *The
New York Times,* Jan. 21, 2007.

8   the same bully: Philip Galanes, "'Homeland' Times Two: Claire
Danes and Jeh Johnson," *The New York Times,* Oct. 18, 2015.

8   "She was not cool": John Lahr, "Varieties of Disturbance," *The New
Yorker,* Sept. 9, 2013.

9   "the lack of ankles": Hillary Rodham Clinton, *What Happened* (New
York: Simon & Schuster, 2017), 116.

9   the "Magnificent Seven": Carly Pifer, "I Was a Mean Girl," *Slate,*
Feb. 19, 2013, https://slate.com/human-interest/2013/02/i-was-a
-mean-girl-and-i-didnt-need-the-internet-to-bully-other-kids.html.

10   the "unjoined" feeling: Carson McCullers, *The Member of the Wedding* (1946; Boston: Houghton Mifflin, 2004), 3.

10   "a clutch of nausea": Ayelet Waldman, *Bad Mother: A Chronicle of
Maternal Crimes, Minor Calamities, and Occasional Moments of Grace*
(New York: Broadway Books, 2009), 104.

11   "regularly scheduled torture": Miley Cyrus, *Miles to Go* (New York:
Disney Hyperion, 2009), 11, 20ff.

14   "looking-glass self": Charles Horton Cooley, *Human Nature and the
Social Order* (1902), cited in David A. Kinney, "From Nerds to Nor-

mals: The Recovery of Identity Among Adolescents from Middle School to High School," *Sociology of Education* 66 (Jan. 1993): 21–40.

14 "the mirror of their peers": Madeline Levine, *The Price of Privilege: How Parental Pressure and Material Advantage Are Creating a Generation of Disconnected and Unhappy Kids* (New York: HarperCollins, 2006), 116.

14 "major spiritual crisis": Bill Clinton, *My Life* (New York: Knopf, 2004), 47.

14 "Some of what came into my head": Ibid., 40.

15 "heavy brainwashing": Amy Schumer, *The Girl with the Lower Back Tattoo* (New York: Gallery, 2016), 59–61.

16 "imaginary audience": David Elkind, "Egocentrism in Adolescence," *Child Development* 38 (Dec. 1967): 1025–34.

17 an ultra-extreme example: Domingo Martinez, "Middle School: Mimis in the Middle," *This American Life,* WBEZ Chicago/PRX, Oct. 28, 2011.

20 A similar drop-off in popularity: Joseph P. Allen, Megan M. Schad, Barbara Oudekerk, and Joanna Chango, "What Ever Happened to the 'Cool' Kids? Long-Term Sequelae of Early Adolescent Pseudomature Behavior," *Child Development* 85 (Sept.–Oct. 2014): 1866–80; Michael Thompson, interview with author, Dec. 19, 2016.

25 *Slender Man stabbing*: In 2014, two 12-year-olds, Morgan Geyser and Anissa Weier, lured their friend Payton Leutner into the woods in a Milwaukee suburb after a sleepover and stabbed her nineteen times with a kitchen knife. The girls said they attacked Leutner, who survived after crawling to a nearby road, because they wanted to please a fictional character called Slender Man, whom they believed was real. See, for example, Ivan Moreno, "Wisconsin Girl Gets Maximum 40 Years in Mental Hospital for Slender Man Stabbing," *Chicago Tribune,* Feb. 2, 2018.

2. WHEN FAMILIARITY BRED CONTEMPT

26 Caitlin Teagart: "Brain Dead Teen, Only Capable of Rolling Eyes and Texting, to Be Euthanized," *The Onion,* Jan. 31, 2012, https://www.theonion.com/brain-dead-teen-only-capable-of-rolling-eyes-and-texti-1819595151.

27 the average age of menarche: Joan Jacobs Brumberg, "'Something Happens to Girls': Menarche and the Emergence of the Modern American Hygienic Imperative," in *The Girls' History and Culture Reader: 20th Century,* ed. Miriam Forman-Brunell and Leslie Paris (Urbana: University of Illinois Press, 2011), 15–42.

27 eighteen months to two years later: Elizabeth J. Susman and Lorah D. Dorn, "Puberty: Its Role in Development," in *Handbook of Adolescent Psychology,* ed. Richard M. Lerner and Laurence Steinberg, 3rd ed., vol. 1 (Hoboken, N.J.: Wiley, 2009), 116–51.

27 economics trumped biology: In the early nineteenth century, "a young person did not achieve full adult status until marriage and establishment of an independent farm or entrance into a full-time trade or profession. Full adulthood might be attained as early as the mid- or late teens, but usually did not occur until the late twenties or early thirties." Steven Mintz, "The Changing State of Childhood: American Childhood as a Social and Cultural Construct" (paper presented at the Restaging Childhood Conference, Utah State University, Bear Lake, Utah, Aug. 7, 2009).

27 an adult's load of work: In the colonies and early United States, "contemporaries associated puberty with rising power and energy rather than with the onset of an awkward and vulnerable stage of life." Joseph F. Kett, *Rites of Passage: Adolescence in America, 1790 to the Present* (New York: Basic Books, 1977), 17.

27 Puritan children: Steven Mintz, *Huck's Raft: A History of American Childhood* (Cambridge, Mass.: Harvard University Press, 2004), 23.

28 no longer entirely dependent: Kett, *Rites of Passage,* 13–16.

28   attended school only sporadically: The shift toward graded educa-
      tion happened much faster in cities than in rural areas. In the 1850s,
      urban schools began to be divided by age group, each with a different
      teacher. By the 1880s, this was standard, and by the late nineteenth
      century, almost all children stayed in urban schools until age 13.
      Some poor families withdrew their children for good as early as age
      10, but children usually stayed until they became basically literate,
      which happened by 11 or 12. Priscilla Ferguson Clement, *Growing
      Pains: Children in the Industrial Age, 1850–1890* (New York: Twayne,
      1997), 112.

28   a humiliation: Throughout the late nineteenth century, 6-to-14-year-
      olds were educated together in the same elementary school build-
      ings. Before about 1875, they were not even separated by grade. In
      the last twenty-five years of the century, graded elementary schools
      were established around the country, and by the 1870s, it was more
      or less standard for students to enter the first grade around age 6 and
      leave the eighth grade around age 14. Joseph E. Kett, "Reflections on
      the History of Adolescence in America," *History of the Family* 8
      (2003): 355–73.

28   wealthy white planters: White children in the South were sent away
      starting as young as age 10 to make sure they didn't spend their most
      impressionable (and sociable) early adolescent years in the company
      of slaves. Clement, 96.

28   smart wealthy boys: Kett, "Reflections on the History of Adoles-
      cence in America," 360.

28   Firefighters: Kett, *Rites of Passage,* 91.

28   teenagers as young as 13: Ibid., 38.

28   Johnny Walker: Emmy E. Werner, "Children's Voices from the Civil
      War," in *Childhood in America,* ed. Paula S. Fass and Mary Ann Mason
      (New York: NYU Press, 2000), 129–31.

29   "strong enough to hold a plow": Ulysses S. Grant, *Personal Memoirs*
      (1885), cited in Paula S. Fass, "The Child-Centered Family? New

Rules in Postwar America," in *Reinventing Childhood After World War II,* ed. Paula S. Fass and Michael Grossberg (Philadelphia: University of Pennsylvania Press, 2012), 1–18.

29   girls in the early to mid-nineteenth century: Constance A. Nathanson, *Dangerous Passage: The Social Control of Sexuality in Women's Adolescence* (Philadelphia: Temple University Press, 1991), 78.

29   "blank slates": The Puritan idea of childhood was infused with a preoccupation with original sin. John Locke's very different vision of the child as a blank slate to be shaped through experience spread throughout Europe after the publication of his 1689 treatise, *An Essay Concerning Human Understanding.* His ideas didn't reach North America until the 1750s, but then spread in the United States after the Revolutionary War. At the same time, Americans fell under the sway of Jean-Jacques Rousseau, whose 1762 book, *Emile,* had established that children came into the world pure and innocent and were corrupted only by the influence of society. Preserving childhood innocence continued to be a major concern for American adults throughout the nineteenth century. Beth Bailey, "The Vexed History of Children and Sex," in *The Routledge History of Childhood in the Western World,* ed. Paula S. Fass (London: Routledge, 2013), 191–210.

30   rapidly changing times: Many historians have made this point, but all seem to refer back to the still-foundational work of Joseph Kett, who put it thus in "Reflections on the History of Adolescence in America": "The emphasis on opportunity replaced the older link between status and specific social ranks with spatial definitions of status (the young man 'away from home' or 'on the rise')." The University of Texas at Austin historian Steven Mintz, whose work I always admire, has said this: "Because parents in the emerging middle class could not automatically transfer their societal status to their children through bequests of family lands, transmission of craft skills, or selection of a marriage partner, they adopted new strategies to give

their children a boost by limiting the number of their offspring through birth control and prolonging the transition to adulthood through intensive maternal nurturing and extended schooling." Steven Mintz, "American Childhood as a Social and Cultural Construct," in *Families as They Really Are,* ed. Barbara J. Risman (New York: Norton, 2010), 50–51.

30   a decisive turning point: According to the Columbia University sociologist Constance Nathanson, for boys the years 12 to 14 became nothing less than a period "of moral crisis in which life's future prospects would be decided." As part of this development, adults began to worry about whether the boys entering this crucial period were up to the task. Girls did not encounter this particular "moral crisis." "Insofar as girls' prospects were decided at birth, a period of struggle with life's purpose was difficult to imagine." Nathanson, 77. For more on this period as a new turning point, see Mintz, *Huck's Raft,* 134ff.

31   sisters who'd grown up playing freely: In "The Caddie Woodlawn Syndrome," Anne Scott MacLeod describes how, with puberty, all that was free and fun in nineteenth-century girlhood ended. "The door closed," she writes, and "the claims and constraints of nineteenth century womanhood" began. Anne Scott MacLeod, "The Caddie Woodlawn Syndrome," in *The Girls' History and Culture Reader: 19th Century,* ed. Miriam Forman-Brunell and Leslie Paris (Urbana: University of Illinois Press, 2011), 206.

31   two to one: Forman-Brunell and Paris, "Introduction," *The Girls' History and Culture Reader: 19th Century,* 8.

31   an unsigned article: "Concerning Some of the Pitfalls of the Way of Home Life in America," *Ladies' Home Journal,* Dec. 1887.

32   the greatest sexual threat: Mary E. Odem, *Delinquent Daughters: Protecting and Policing Adolescent Female Sexuality in the United States, 1885–1920* (Chapel Hill: University of North Carolina Press, 1995), 39.

32   Joel Hawes: Joel Hawes, *Lectures to Young Men* (1829), cited in John

Demos and Virginia Demos, "Adolescence in Historical Perspective," *Journal of Marriage and Family* 31, no. 4 (Nov. 1969): 632–38.

32   "pliant" and "plastic": These terms from early-to-mid-nineteenth-century writings are cited in Demos and Demos, 634.

32   "most particularly sexual innocence": Bailey, "The Vexed History of Children and Sex," 192.

32   the average age of menarche declined: Jane H. Hunter, *How Young Ladies Became Girls: The Victorian Origins of American Girlhood* (New Haven, Conn.: Yale University Press, 2002), 131.

32   Working-class girls: Ibid.

33   a new sexual precocity: Ibid., 131–32.

33   a heightened concern: "A huge new concern about masturbation revealed the rising level of anxiety about sex and childhood." Peter N. Stearns, *Childhood in World History* (New York: Routledge, 2007), 79.

33   dispersal of the "energies": Kett, *Rites of Passage,* 134.

33   John Harvey Kellogg . . . Will Kellogg: Hillel Schwartz, *Never Satisfied: A Cultural History of Diets, Fantasies, and Fat* (New York: Macmillan, 1986), 184.

33   "idiots" worthy of the "insane asylum": John Harvey Kellogg, *Plain Facts for Old and Young* (Burlington, Iowa: Segner & Condit, 1881), ebook.

34   put an end to apprenticeships: "Adolescence was created and democratized (at least in Britain and the United States) when child labor laws, industrialization and union organizing gutted apprenticeships, which had been the conventional way for youth to move from dependency to independence." Nancy Lesko, *Act Your Age! A Cultural Construction of Adolescence,* 2nd ed. (New York: Routledge, 2012), 6.

34   an abominably low 10 or 12: Odem, 9.

34   "Even the little child": Harriet Jacobs, *Incidents in the Life of a Slave Girl: Seven Years Concealed,* in *Through Women's Eyes: An American*

History, ed. Ellen Carol DuBois and Lynn Dumenil, 4th ed. (New York: Bedford/St. Martin's, 2015), 183.

34 such legislation was opposed: Bailey, "The Vexed History of Children and Sex," 199.

35 few black girls: According to Beth Bailey, "Age of consent laws rendered underage girls legally innocent, no matter their behavior, and placed responsibility for illegitimate sexual conduct on men." This was considered an intolerable risk by many lawmakers in the South. Beth Bailey, "Sexuality," in *Encyclopedia of Children and Childhood in History and Society,* ed. Paula S. Fass, vol. 3 (New York: Macmillan, 2004), 743–51.

35 age of consent: Ibid., 749.

35 until the 1930s: Even though most states around the nation had passed compulsory attendance laws in the 1880s and 1890s, requiring kids to stay in school at least until age 12 or 14, those laws varied a great deal and lacked enforcement power. M. S. Katz, *A History of Compulsory Education Laws* (Bloomington, Ind.: Phi Delta Kappa Education Foundation, 1976). After World War I, a federal child labor law was declared unconstitutional, so reformers shifted their strategy to compulsory school attendance laws. This led to a decline in child labor but not its disappearance. Joseph M. Hawes, *Children Between the Wars: American Childhood, 1920–1940* (New York: Twayne, 1997), 7–13. The childhood historian Paula Fass has noted that many immigrant families resisted sending their children for extended schooling, wanting them to work instead and also wanting to keep them close to home so that they would not be unduly influenced by American culture. "Not until the 1930s," she writes, "in the context of the extreme limitations of the economy, did Italians compromise and send their adolescent children to high school in response to their understanding of what seemed economically necessary, not just a state requirement." Paula Fass, *The End of American Childhood: A History of*

Parenting from Life on the Frontier to the Managed Child (Princeton, N.J.: Princeton University Press, 2016), 151.

35 African American children: Although African American parents were, along with Scots and eastern European Jews, the most ardent supporters of public education in the late nineteenth century, by 1880 only 20 percent of black children ages 5 to 19 in the South were able to spend their days in school. Clement, 98.

35 "relatively unmarked by psychological traumas": John Modell and Madeline Goodman, "Historical Perspectives," in *At the Threshold: The Developing Adolescent,* ed. S. Shirley Feldman and Glen R. Elliott (Cambridge, Mass.: Harvard University Press, 1990), 93–122.

36 the wife of a school principal: Stephen M. Frank, *Life with Father: Parenthood and Masculinity in the 19th Century American North* (Baltimore: Johns Hopkins University Press, 1998), 131.

36 "perfect in every way": Edna Ormsby, cited in Linda W. Rosenzweig, *The Anchor of My Life: Middle Class American Mothers and Daughters, 1880–1920* (New York: NYU Press, 1993), 70–71.

36 some scholars say: See, for example, Mintz, *Huck's Raft,* 196.

36 "The term *adolescence*": Ibid.

37 Middle-class mothers knew: Ann Hulbert notes that the rise of the scientific parenting expert and the ideal of a new, "scientific" form of child-rearing occurred around the turn of the twentieth century, at a time when modern life became more complex in terms of the life path that a teen might take. She quotes one top expert of the time, Dr. L. Emmett Holt, as saying that a parent's job had become that of equipping children with the means "to grapple successfully with the complex conditions and varied responsibilities which will be their lot." Mothers needed the advice of experts because the skills and knowledge they needed to impart weren't things their own mothers had passed down. Ann Hulbert, *Raising America: Experts, Parents, and a Century of Advice About Children* (New York: Knopf, 2013), 36.

37   new medical specialty of pediatrics: G. Stanley Hall, *Adolescence: Its Psychology and Its Relations to Physiology, Anthropology, Sociology, Sex, Crime, Religion, and Education,* vol. 1 (New York: Appleton, 1904), 237.

37   vaporous terms: The reformer Ellen Key provided one example of this tone in 1909: "This devotion, much more than the hours immediately given to one's children is the absorbing thing; the occupation which makes an earnest mother always go to any external activity with divided soul and dissipated energy." Ellen Key, *The Century of the Child* (New York: G. P. Putnam's Sons, 1909), 102. For an extended exploration of the turn-of-the-century cult of motherhood, see Judith Warner, *Perfect Madness: Motherhood in the Age of Anxiety* (New York: Riverhead, 2005), 65ff.

38   "race suicide": Many writers in the late nineteenth century based their opposition to women's higher education on the grounds that when young women applied themselves to intellectual pursuits, they squandered precious stores of energy they truly needed for their reproductive organs. That the women in question were almost always white, Protestant, native-born, and upper-middle-class, at a time of massive immigration by Catholics and Jews, was no coincidence. See, for example, Hall, *Adolescence,* 236. Most famously in this context, President Theodore Roosevelt repeatedly warned that American Anglo-Saxons were committing "race suicide" by using birth control and allowing their fertility rate to drop well below that of immigrants and nonwhite Americans. See, for example, Thomas G. Dyer, *Theodore Roosevelt and the Idea of Race* (Baton Rouge: LSU Press, 1992), 143ff.

38   a prominent women's magazine writer: Alice D. Kelly, "Why Adolescence Is Hard on Parents," *Parents' Magazine,* Dec. 1931, 26.

39   an avid audience: The mothers who took part in these study circles—formally known as the parent education movement—were avid to

use their minds and find in child-rearing the "challenging career" they couldn't otherwise hope for. Jeanne Brooks-Gunn and Anna Duncan Johnson, "G. Stanley Hall's Contribution to Science, Practice and Policy: The Child Study, Parent Education, and Child Welfare Movements," in "G. Stanley Hall's *Adolescence:* A Centennial Reappraisal," ed. Jeffrey Jensen Arnett and Hamilton Cravens, special issue, *History of Psychology* 9, no. 3 (2006): 247–58.

3. THE HORMONE MONSTER EMERGES

40   "Psychoses and neuroses abound": G. Stanley Hall, *Adolescence: Its Psychology and Its Relations to Physiology, Anthropology, Sociology, Sex, Crime, Religion, and Education,* vol. 1 (New York: Appleton, 1904), 266.

41   He learned about sex: G. Stanley Hall, *Life and Confessions of a Psychologist* (New York: Appleton, 1923), 131–35.

42   "age of puberty": For Hall, the "age of puberty" marked the beginning of adolescence. "Physical puberty" began sometime between the ages of 11 and 14 and was followed by the challenges of "moral puberty . . . when all the greatest problems of life present themselves simultaneously; the choice of a career and the anxiety about making a living; all the problems of love, and for some the religious problems." This more existential aspect of puberty, he believed, hit between the ages of 16 and 20. Other experts, he noted, situated them earlier, between 11 and 15. Hall, *Adolescence,* 277.

42   published his own thinking on adolescence: Sigmund Freud published "The Transformations of Puberty," the last piece in his *Three Essays on the Theory of Sexuality,* in 1905, just one year after Hall published *Adolescence.* The first English translation of Freud's essay, by A. A. Brill, appeared in 1910. Sigmund Freud, *Three Contributions to the Sexual Theory* (New York: Journal of Nervous and Mental Disease, 1910).

42   "Sex asserts its mastery": Hall, *Adolescence,* xiv.

42   dense and almost lurid pages: Ibid., 415–24.

42   an extended discussion: Ibid., 432–37.

42   a bit of a quack: "A wonderful creature," the philosopher-psychologist William James, who had overseen Hall's doctorate at Harvard, wrote in one of a number of nasty letters about his former student. "Never an articulate conception comes out of him." William James to Croom Robertson, Nov. 9, 1887, in *The Thought and Character of William James,* ed. Ralph Barton Perry, vol. 2 (London: Humphrey Milford Oxford University Press, 1935), 85. James also wrote, "Mystification of some kind seems never far distant from everything he does." William James to Hugo Münsterberg, Aug. 21, 1893, in Laurence R. Veysey, *The Emergence of the American University* (Chicago: University of Chicago Press, 1970), 151.

42   "Chock full of errors": Edward Thorndike, cited in Ellen Condliffe Lagemann, *An Elusive Science: The Troubling History of Education Research* (Chicago: University of Chicago Press, 2002), 57. "The feature of style is a baffling conjunction within the same paragraph, or even sentence, of statements which to the commonplace mind have no logical connection," Thorndike wrote in a not-untypical review, cited in James Younnis, "G. Stanley Hall and His Times: Too Much So, Yet Not Enough," in "G. Stanley Hall's *Adolescence:* A Centennial Reappraisal," ed. Jeffrey Jensen Arnett and Hamilton Cravens, special issue, *History of Psychology* 9, no. 3 (2006): 224–35.

43   "recapitulation": This was an idea associated with the French naturalist Jean-Baptiste Lamarck, which has been neatly summarized by Robert Epstein, the former editor in chief of *Psychology Today,* as "a theory from biology that asserted that individual development (ontogeny) mimicked evolutionary development (phylogeny)." For Hall, Epstein says, adolescence was "the necessary and inevitable reenactment of a 'savage, pigmoid' stage of human evolution." He notes that this theory was "completely discredited" in biology by the

1930s, and yet Hall's notion that "teen turmoil is an *inevitable* part of human development" (his italics) still endures. Robert Epstein, "The Myth of the Teen Brain," *Scientific American,* June 1, 2007.

43   questionnaire effort: Jeanne Brooks-Gunn and Anna Duncan John-son, "G. Stanley Hall's Contribution to Science, Practice and Policy: The Child Study, Parent Education, and Child Welfare Movements," in "G. Stanley Hall's *Adolescence:* A Centennial Reappraisal," ed. Jef-frey Jensen Arnett and Hamilton Cravens, special issue, *History of Psychology* 9, no. 3 (2006): 247–58.

43   "the intellectual twilight zone": A psychologist cited as "one of our most respected technologists" in Edward L. Thorndike, "Biographi-cal Memoir of Granville Stanley Hall, 1846–1924," *National Acad-emy of Science* 12 (1925): 135–80.

43   an enormous number: The Clark University psychologist Jeffrey Jensen Arnett and the Iowa State University historian Hamilton Cravens make this point, calling the sales figures "astonishing" given the size of the American reading public. Jeffrey Jensen Arnett and Hamilton Cravens, "Introduction," in "G. Stanley Hall's *Adoles-cence:* A Centennial Reappraisal," ed. Jeffrey Jensen Arnett and Ham-ilton Cravens, special issue, *History of Psychology* 9, no. 3 (2006): 165–71.

43   a heavily edited, condensed, and cleaned-up version: In a brief for-ward to *Youth,* Hall wrote, "I have often been asked to select and epitomize the practical and especially the pedagogical conclusions of my large volumes on *Adolescence* published in 1904, in such form that they may be available at a minimum cost to parents, teachers, reading circles, normal schools, and college classes." He claimed that the book had undergone relatively minor changes, but I noted that it did now contain a much-needed glossary and also lacked the long disqui-sitions on onanism and puberty's physical effects. G. Stanley Hall, *Youth: Its Education, Regimen, and Hygiene* (New York: Appleton, 1907), ebook.

43   "a more careful and painstaking study": G. Stanley Hall, "How and When to Be Frank with Boys," *Ladies' Home Journal,* Sept. 1907, 26.

43   valued Hall's thinking: Brooks-Gunn and Johnson, 253.

44   an enormous impact: John Demos and Virginia Demos, "Adolescence in Historical Perspective," *Journal of Marriage and Family* 31, no. 4 (Nov. 1969): 632–38. They note that Hall's work on adolescence since the 1880s had "quickly" been extremely influential on "general texts on psychology, studies of education, the new literature on child-rearing, and a variety of books on child labor, religious training, vocational guidance, and the like."

44   "rapid fluctuations of mood": Hall, *Adolescence,* xv.

44   wretchedly self-conscious: "Reflectiveness often leads to self-criticism and consciousness that may be morbid." Ibid., 314.

44   confused and unmoored: "Youth awakes to a new world and understands neither it nor himself." Ibid., xv.

44   "the subject becomes dumb-bound, silent": Ibid., 318.

44   "an inverse ratio": Ibid.

44   "abjectly dependent": Ibid., 84.

45   "imitation reaches its acme": Ibid., 316.

45   "stormy revolution": Jean-Jacques Rousseau, *Émile ou De l'éducation,* in *Oeuvres Complètes* (Paris: Editions Gallimard, 1969), 489–90.

45   "Very terrible convictions": Increase Mather, cited in David L. Larsen, *The Company of the Preachers* (Grand Rapids, Mich.: Kregel, 1998), 296. In May 1655, a month before he turned 16, Mather underwent what he later described as a painful adolescent moment of religious awakening. Given that puberty happened so much later in the colonies, it's fair to think of this as happening right around what we now think of as middle school age.

45   "a tinge of melancholy": It was his opinion that dramatic mood swings could, for some children, begin as early as age 10 or 11. Isaac Taylor, *Home Education* (New York: Appleton, 1838), 132.

45   "wild desires, restless cravings": Henry Ward Beecher, *Lectures to Young Men* (1844), cited in Demos and Demos, 634.

46   For Freud's daughter Anna: Anna Freud, "Adolescence," *Psychoanalytic Study of the Child* 13, no. 1 (1958): 255–78. Unlike Hall, the Freudians did not believe that human sexuality came to life in one huge burst at puberty, but Anna Freud's conception of the phase was in other ways very similar. She saw adolescence as a period when the "ego" had to use all its most desperate defense mechanisms to ward off the incredible anxiety caused by the ramping up of the "drives" (which meant, in particular, the forbidden erotic desires of early childhood). However convoluted its articulation ("Defense Motivated by Fear of the Strength of the Instincts Illustrated by the Phenomena of Puberty" was how Freud subtitled her section on adolescence in her first major book, *The Ego and the Mechanisms of Defense,* in 1936), this view, like Hall's, essentially came down to the Hormone Monster and the good child battling it out, with parents caught in the crossfire. Indeed, she and other psychoanalysts believed that problems arose if adolescents weren't able to fully explore all the contradictory and often unpleasant aspects of being their age. Parents, she cautioned, might be tempted to celebrate if their offspring turned out to be docile in the years around puberty. After all, she sympathized in 1958, "there are few situations in life which are more difficult to cope with than an adolescent son or daughter during the attempt to liberate themselves."And yet, she warned, adolescents who *weren't* difficult, who continued to be " 'good' children" and to get along with their parents with no "outer evidence of inner distress," were exhibiting a "delay of normal development" that was deeply problematic. "They are, perhaps more than any others," she wrote, "in need of therapeutic help to remove the inner restrictions and clear the path for normal development, however 'upsetting' the latter may prove to be." Adults might well "deplore" the adolescent passage, but they had to allow it to run its course. And as part of that,

they had to be prepared to respond to adolescent obnoxiousness with understanding rather than repression.

47   "wearisome and annoying repetition": "And thus was committed the cardinal sin of boring adolescent boys and girls, who are not naturally interested in nonproductive efforts," Pringle wrote of the causes of school attrition. "The boys especially were able to find occupations more congenial. They soon discovered more novelty and more opportunities to exercise their spirit of adventure in driving delivery wagons." Ralph W. Pringle, *The Junior High School: A Psychological Approach* (New York: McGraw-Hill, 1937), 4.

47   One contemporary study: Edward L. Thorndike, *The Elimination of Pupils from School* (Washington, D.C.: U.S. Government Printing Office, 1908), 10–11. Thorndike's study was based on statistics from U.S. cities with populations over 25,000. He noted that the attrition numbers were probably a bit higher than those in smaller cities or rural areas.

48   "Never again": Hall, *Adolescence*, xii.

48   a rapid uptick: See Jeffrey Jensen Arnett, "G. Stanley Hall's *Adolescence*: Brilliance and Nonsense," in "G. Stanley Hall's *Adolescence*: A Centennial Reappraisal," ed. Jeffrey Jensen Arnett and Hamilton Cravens, special issue, *History of Psychology* 9, no. 3 (2006): 186–97.

48   an increase in myelination: "Although Hall reviewed anatomical data of the day showing that much of the physical growth of the brain was complete before adolescence, he also drew attention to studies by Cajal (1896) and Flechsig (1898) indicating late myelination of neuronal processes within the brain," the adolescent development experts Ronald Dahl and Ahmad Hariri wrote in a 2005 reappraisal of Hall's legacy. "Hall highlighted the emerging evidence that the gradual accrual of myelin coating around nerves—which was understood at that time to increase the speed of neural transmission and thus connectivity—is a maturational process that begins peripherally and progresses centrally. The implications, Hall recognized, sug-

gested that complex mental processes—those requiring efficient connectivity across different regions within the brain—were likely to be developing late and improving well through adolescence." Ronald E. Dahl and Ahmad R. Hariri, "Lessons from G. Stanley Hall: Connecting New Research in Biological Sciences to the Study of Adolescent Development," *Journal of Research on Adolescence* 15 (2005): 367–82.

48   the onset of mental illness: "During the tumult of the first stages of puberty, which often threatens decomposition of the personality, and before the new orientation, the psycho-physic organism is peculiarly sensitive," Hall wrote. ". . . So great is the vulnerability, that outside influences which would be ordinarily healthful, may break up the slow progress toward reorganization and leave their mark in exaggerated religiosity, or paranoeic symptoms and perversion of many kinds. . . . Especially in natures of morbid heredity, the soul seems to lapse to a lower plane and ordinary prudence and judgment are superseded. [The Scottish psychiatrist T. S.] Clouston said that if fifty such individuals were on a savage island, they would not sow or reap and would die of hunger." Hall, *Adolescence,* 269. Jeffrey Jensen Arnett has noted that Hall even rightly identified that the depressive feelings that overwhelm some adolescents tend to follow a "curve of despondency" that begins at about age 11, hits its worst point around age 15, and then slowly resolves into something like a child's pre-puberty levels of happiness. Arnett, "G. Stanley Hall's *Adolescence: Brilliance and Nonsense,*" 186–97.

48   he rather remarkably anticipated: "It has taken nearly 100 years for MRI studies to firmly ground these ideas in developmental neuroscience," Dahl and Hariri wrote. While Hall linked these brain changes to so-called late-developing "reason, judgment, moral, and esthetic feelings," they noted, scientists today think of adolescence as the time when "inhibitory control, self-regulation capacities, and other

'executive functions'" develop, including "emotion regulation, action monitoring," and "self-control." Dahl and Hariri, 367–82.

48   Aristotle: Descriptions of pubescent "youth" (which really meant only boys, beginning at puberty) in classical antiquity contain many elements that are familiar today: intense emotion, existential angst, surging (male) desire, and all the other forms of generalized insanity that we tend to sum up, with a sigh, as "raging hormones." Expanding further upon the "youthful type of character" that emerges at puberty, Aristotle wrote: "Of the bodily desires, it is the sexual by which they are most swayed and in which they show absence of self-control. . . . They are fonder of their friends, intimates, and companions than older men are, because they like spending their days in the company of others, and have not yet come to value either their friends or anything else by their usefulness to themselves. All their mistakes are in the direction of doing things excessively and vehemently. . . . They love too much and hate too much. . . . They think they know everything, and are always quite sure about it." Aristotle, *Rhetoric,* book 2, trans. W. Rhys Roberts (Adelaide: University of Adelaide eBooks@Adelaide, 2015).

48   conscious choices: Rolf E. Muuss, *Theories of Adolescence,* 6th ed. (New York: McGraw-Hill, 1995), 5. Muuss also notes that, like many other thinkers from classical antiquity through the Middle Ages, Aristotle believed that early human development was divided into three seven-year stages: birth to age seven was called "infancy"; seven to the start of puberty was "boyhood," and puberty to age twenty-one was "young manhood."

48   Locke . . . Rousseau: Muuss, 11–13.

49   "remarkable faculties": Taylor, 132.

49   "period of functional acquisition and readjustment": William H. Burnham, "Suggestions from the Psychology of Adolescence," *School Review* 5, no. 10 (Dec. 1887): 652–83.

49   "judge, inquire, reason": Aubrey Augustus Douglass, *The Fifteenth Yearbook of the National Society for the Study of Education Part III: The Junior High School* (Bloomington, Ill: Public School Publishing, 1916), 28. Douglass put the start of adolescence by common agreement at age 12. He noted that experts formerly thought it started at 14.

50   woefully unprepared: The push to improve schooling for this age group began in 1888 with a speech by Harvard University president Charles Eliot to the National Education Association, in which he complained that college freshmen were not being adequately prepared by their four years of high school. In 1893, the NEA recommended that kids begin studying secondary-school-level academic subjects in what were then the upper elementary grades. P. Gayle Andrews, "Junior High School," in *Encyclopedia of Children and Childhood in History and Society,* ed. Paula S. Fass, vol. 2 (New York: Macmillan, 2004), 511–12.

50   some higher-level academic subject matter: James Bryant Conant, *Recommendations for Education in the Junior High School Years* (Princeton, N.J.: Educational Testing Service, 1960), 9.

50   "enjoy the feast": G. Vernon Bennett, *The Junior High School* (Baltimore: Warwick & York, 1919), 8.

50   "the mother of the race": Ibid., 8.

50   "vocation" of homemaking: Ibid., 23.

51   "vita sexualis": Hall declared it the "plain path of life" for adolescence. Hall, *Adolescence,* 413.

51   "peculiarities of disposition": Thomas H. Briggs, *The Junior High School* (Boston: Houghton Mifflin, 1920), 83–84.

51   "the possibility of evil": Burnham, 659.

51   all the forms of "evil": Bennett, 6–7. Bennett's full tally of the "evils growing out of adolescence" was so impressive that I'm including the whole thing here. The "physical evils" comprised "(a) Arrested development, caused by some disease, from overstudy, fright, etc.;

(b) perverted sex habits, as self-abuse; (c) habits arising out of the adolescent's sudden induction into manhood which gives him the adult's desires and freedom to satisfy them but not the adult's restraining will power, such as the habit of keeping late hours, smoking, chewing tobacco, drinking liquor, eating rapidly, and choosing irregular diet; (d) a reaching and straining to do things that their elders do, without proper judgment, such as running endurance races; and (e) improper actions by girls at delicate bodily periods and neglect of bodily needs through a prudish sense of modesty." The "mental evils" consisted of "(a) Arrested mental development caused by the physical changes incident to adolescence or caused by worry over those changes; (b) mental weakness caused by excessive indulgence in sex thoughts and habits; (c) habits arising out of the adolescent's sudden induction into manhood which gives him freedom to do much as he pleases, such habits as idleness, irregularity in work, fickleness, weakness of will; (d) mental stagnation resulting from the youth's leaving school and entering unskilled work; (e) the 'bighead,' contempt for the opinions of others, unwillingness to learn, a feeling of 'knowing it all.'" And the "moral evils," in full, were: "(a) Lying to parents and weaving webs of deceit; (b) disobedience to parents and general outlawry against the home; (c) playing 'hookey' from school, cutting classes, chafing against restraints of any kind; (d) habits arising out of the freedom and independence that come with adolescence, such as the reading of trashy novels, frequenting bad moving picture houses, smoking, gambling, drinking, staying out late at night, indulging in excessive social affairs, stealing to meet the unusual need for spending money; (e) perverted sex habits (ranging from mere 'looseness' of actions to downright 'shamelessness')." Bennett's somewhat obsessive fascination may very likely, like G. Stanley Hall's preoccupation with "self-abuse," have had more to do with his own life story than with any actual observed behaviors in junior high school students. He himself struggled with what were called "perverted sex habits" in his time. After a long and prominent career, which eventually led to a seat on the Los Angeles City Council, he was forced to abruptly end his public life in 1951 after having been arrested in a park on a "morals" charge. "Councilman Bennett Asks Jury Trial," *Los Angeles Times,* Oct. 5, 1950.

52   The first of the grade 7–9: "Indianola Junior High," Ohio History Connection, ohiohistorycentral.org/w/Indianola_Junior_High_School.

52   The second opened: "A Brief History of Willard Middle School," Willard Middle School, Berkeley, Calif., willardpta.org/centennial /brief-history/.

52   the schools proliferated rapidly: By 1922, there were 387 junior high schools, and by 1938 that number had increased more than sixfold. Thomas H. Peeler, "The Middle School: A Historical Frame of Reference," in *Reading in the Middle School,* ed. Gerald G. Duffy (Newark, Del.: International Reading Association, 1971), 8. The earliest schools taught health, hygiene, and personal grooming and offered lessons in proper diction and etiquette to immigrant children. Some schools, in large urban areas, served essentially as community centers and social service agencies, providing showers and healthcare facilities and running "Americanization programs" for the newly arrived. All of this, reformers hoped, would help convince immigrant parents to keep their children out of work and in school, and to a large extent, over time, it did. Jaana Juvonen et al., *Focus on the Wonder Years: Challenges Facing the American Middle School* (Santa Monica, Calif.: RAND, 2004), 10–11.

52   more time with their peers: The historian Howard Chudacoff makes the point that by the 1920s, "most adolescents spent more waking hours with peers than with family." Howard P. Chudacoff, "Adolescence and Youth," in *Encyclopedia of Children and Childhood in History and Society,* ed. Paula S. Fass, vol. 1 (New York: Macmillan, 2004), 15–17.

52   over three-quarters of U.S. students: Conant, 10–11.

52   Some worked in factories: Kriste Lindenmeyer, *The Greatest Generation Grows Up* (Chicago: Ivan R. Dee, 2005), 49.

52   it was still rare: Joseph M. Hawes, *Children Between the Wars: American Childhood, 1920–1940* (New York: Twayne, 1997), 30.

52   "tuition plan": Lindenmeyer, 136.

53   "individual transformation": Paula S. Fass, *The End of American Childhood: A History of Parenting from Life on the Frontier to the Managed Child* (Princeton, N.J.: Princeton University Press, 2016), 157. Fass is talking about both junior high and high school.

53   "miserably self-conscious period": Dorothy Canfield Fisher, "As the Twig Is Bent: The French Bend It One Way; We Bend It in Another," *Good Housekeeping,* Sept. 1922, 36. This article compared American children with their same-age French peers and found the latter to be almost uncannily self-possessed and well mannered.

53   They teased one another: D. A. Thom, *Guiding the Adolescent* (Children's Bureau Publication No. 225, U.S. Department of Labor, Washington, D.C., 1933), 11.

53   she noted in her diary: Coco Irvine, *Through No Fault of My Own: A Girl's Diary of Life on Summit Avenue in the Jazz Age* (St. Paul: University of Minnesota Press, 2011), 14. This is the 1927 diary of a girl who grew up in an extremely wealthy family in St. Paul, Minnesota. She received the diary as a Christmas present the year she was in seventh grade and continued writing in it for about a year.

53   wrote to Eleanor Roosevelt: Lindenmeyer, 145.

54   "I don't like my mother": Irvine, 66.

54   "restless, unsympathetic": Jessica Cosgrave, "Mothers and Daughters: No. 1. The Conflict of the Generations," *Good Housekeeping,* Sept. 1925.

54   "blind love, fear and protest": Jessie Taft, "Adolescence: A Critical Period in Your Child's Development," *Children: The Magazine for Parents,* Feb. 1928.

54   "scathing remarks": Alice D. Kelly, "Why Adolescence Is Hard on Parents," *Parents' Magazine,* Dec. 1931.

55   "good-natured contempt": Leta S. Hollingworth, *The Psychology of the Adolescent* (New York: Appleton, 1928), 13.

55   "half-grown children": Barbara Beattie, "The Ups and Downs of Adolescence," *Parents' Magazine,* May 1929.

55   an expert on boys: Edwin F. Patton, "Getting Your Boy Ready for Adolescence," *Parents' Magazine,* Nov. 1929.

55   a laundry list: Winifred Richmond, "Meeting the Problems of Youth," *Parents' Magazine,* March 1933. Things would get better in middle adolescence, Richmond promised parents.

55   "hard to control": Gladys Denny Shultz, "A Preview of Your 12-to-18-Year-Old," *Better Homes and Gardens,* May 1933.

55   a real gulf: William H. Burnham, "Cultivating Wholesome Personality," *Parents' Magazine,* Sept. 1931.

55   "a totally new environment": Cosgrave.

56   "dirty" talk: Thom, 15.

56   "sex-saturated environment": Emily V. Clapp, *Growing Up in the World Today* (Boston: Massachusetts Society for Social Hygiene, 1932). The Massachusetts Society for Social Hygiene, seeing a need for some quality public education on the lived reality of adolescence in a fast-changing world, held an open competition, and this was the prizewinning entry. The pamphlet was written for parents, teachers, counselors, clergy, and "the young people themselves" who were looking "to reach sound and practical solutions of the many perplexing problems to be met in these times."

56   "wholesome solidarity": Pringle, 29.

56   a new category of potential shoppers: The media scholars Daniel Thomas Cook and Susan B. Kaiser note that advertisers targeted "teen-agers" for the first time in the 1940s as retailers, hurting for sales after the Great Depression, scrambled to find new consumers wherever they could. Daniel Thomas Cook and Susan B. Kaiser, "Betwixt and Be Tween: Age Ambiguity and the Sexualization of

the Female Consuming Subject," *Journal of Consumer Culture* 4, no. 2 (2004): 203–27.

4. PARTY HOUNDS AND VIXENS

57   *"TOO MANY SUBTEENS"*: This is the cover blurb for an article by Burk Uzzle, "Boys and Girls: Too Old Too Soon," *Life,* Aug. 10, 1962, 54–64.

58   reasonably conservative: Marjorie Lederer, "We're Telling You!," *Ladies' Home Journal,* Dec. 1944, 20–21. Starting in the late 1920s, *Ladies' Home Journal* designated a group of its readers "sub-debs"— upper-middle-class white girls who hadn't yet made their debut in society. By the 1940s, that group had greatly democratized to include "The Sub-Deb of America, aged 12 to 18—that bizarre species of fauna which flaunts its spirit in bobby socks and drowns its seething sorrows in colas and Crosby": the American everygirl. "Listen, mother—bounce the frown," Lederer's article began, with the author writing in the collective voice of the junior readers. "Though we're very well aware of all the possible menaces to the present and future 'purity' of our tender existences, we want you to know that there isn't half as much danger along those lines as you think there is."

58   the "right" way to behave: Social status for this age group was all about "wealth, personal appearance, social background, and conformity to group rules," as the University of Memphis historian Joseph Hawes has put it. See Joseph M. Hawes, *Children Between the Wars: American Childhood, 1920–1940* (New York: Twayne, 1997), 27.

58   At the bottom: D. A. Thom, *Guiding the Adolescent* (Children's Bureau Publication No. 225, U.S. Department of Labor, Washington, D.C., 1933), 79. Being supersensitive and hyper-analytic made such kids too "self-centered" for social success, Thom wrote. For this he blamed the home environment—because a too-happy household

made kids insufficiently motivated to lose themselves in their peer group. Introverted parents, just by being themselves, set a bad example, too.

58   a 1951 study: Travis L. Hawk, "The Relationship of Certain Factors to Popularity in Students of the Eighth Grade of the Junior High School at Ozona, Texas" (master's thesis, North Texas State College, Ozona, Aug. 1951), 42. "The timid, shy boy is not popular," Hawk wrote. "The boy who indulges in the most classroom misbehavior enjoys the greatest degree of popularity with other boys." One notable attribute that made boys popular with girls at this age was "freedom from nervous symptoms," according to Hawk. "The girls seem to recognize a well-adjusted individual and like him." Girls admired smart boys, but the feeling was not reciprocated by the boys, who liked them best for their looks. And girls were most liked by other girls because of their "school relations" and because "they are attractive; they have adjusted well to school life; they feel worthy and important; they have good personal and social adjustment."

59   spied on some older kids: Coco Irvine, *Through No Fault of My Own: A Girl's Diary of Life on Summit Avenue in the Jazz Age* (St. Paul: University of Minnesota Press, 2011), 31.

59   Coco obsessed: Ibid., 6.

59   "This sounds like a childish game": Ibid., 49. On another occasion, when her mother forbade her to continue reading the "funnies" in her older brother's bed, she was deeply insulted, first by the suggestion that she might be up to something untoward, and then by the suggestion that she might not know what untoward behavior actually was. "Then a sinister thing occurred," she wrote. "Mother called me into her room and wanted to talk about the facts of life, of all things. She asked me if I knew where babies come from. I told her disdainfully that I did. (I have for ever so long, through no fault of hers.)" Ibid., 13.

59   "Boy-Friends Book": Julia Heller, *Boy-Friends Book* (1932; Alexandria, VA: Alexander Street Press, 2001), ebook.

61   Sally Horner: Heller McAlpin, " 'The Real Lolita' Investigates the True Crime Story of Sally Horner," book review, NPR.org, Sept. 11, 2018, npr.org/2018/09/11/646656280/the-real-lolita-investigates-the-true-crime-story-of-sally-horner.

61   "She was viciously mocked": Sarah Weinman, "The Last Days of the Real Lolita: What Happened After Sally Horner, Whose Story Helped Inspire the Novel, Returned Home," book excerpt, *The Cut,* Sept. 6, 2018, thecut.com/2018/09/excerpt-the-real-lolita-by-sarah-weinman.html. See also Sarah Weinman, "The Real Lolita," Hazlitt, Nov. 20, 2014, hazlitt.net/longreads/real-lolita.

62   "What 'everybody' does": Frances Drewry McMullen, "Age Thirteen . . . Doorway to Adolescence," *Parents' Magazine & Family Home Guide,* Nov. 1954.

62   "I can forgive her": Weinman, "The Real Lolita."

62   "coerced conformity": Stephanie Coontz, *The Way We Never Were: American Families and the Nostalgia Trap* (New York: Basic Books, 1992), 33.

62   "good homes": Hawk, 11–13. Hawk found that the factors most strongly correlated with being popular had more to do with the home and parents than with the child. As he put it, "Good homes produce well-adjusted children." The biggest factor in popularity among boys was the socioeconomic status of their parents, because these kids "have cars to drive, dress better, and are taught better manners in the home." Next came "community relations" (meaning the child's and the family's relationships to others in the community) and then the "feeling of belonging to the group."

63   "entertaining squirrel cage": Annie Winsor Allen, "Boys and Girls," *The Atlantic Monthly,* June 1920, 796–804. Frustratingly, Allen and her contemporaries consistently defined "adolescence" as the period

between 12 and 20—an age span that, in fact, contains radically different stages of life and levels of maturity. I have tried, whenever possible, to cite sources that refer directly to "early adolescence" (which was extremely rare at this point) or to life in the age around puberty, or that speak specifically of 12-to-15-year-olds, whose lives paralleled those of today's middle schoolers.

63   "cause much trouble": Leta S. Hollingworth, *The Psychology of the Adolescent* (1928), cited in Thom, 32.

63   "The thing that gets us down": Lederer, 21.

64   "the conventional feeling": Hawk, 24.

64   "extreme resentment": Eric W. Johnson, *How to Live Through Junior High School* (New York: Lippincott, 1959), 29.

64   "unwittingly hastened the disrespect": William M. Alexander, "The Junior High School: A Changing View" (address to the Tenth Annual Conference for School Administrators, Cornell University, July 1963), in *The Legacy of Middle School Leaders: In Their Own Words,* ed. Tracy W. Smith and C. Kenneth McEwin (Charlotte, N.C.: Information Age Publishing, 2011), 6–15. ncmle.org/docs/alexander.pdf.

65   Could middle schoolers actually learn: Ibid.

65   a majority of older teens: Paula S. Fass, "The Child-Centered Family? New Rules in Postwar America," in *Reinventing Childhood After World War II,* ed. Paula S. Fass and Michael Grossberg (Philadelphia: University of Pennsylvania Press, 2012), 1–18.

65   almost 90 percent: Ibid., 6.

66   a kind of transaction: Hawes, 26. Kriste Lindenmeyer adds this nice detail: "Going dutch" took off in the 1930s both because boys didn't have any money and also because it could take "some of the pressure off a girl to provide sexual favors." Kriste Lindenmeyer, *The Greatest Generation Grows Up* (Chicago: Ivan R. Dee, 2005), 194–95.

66   a trial run for marriage: The "steady" relationship in the late 1940s "almost mimicked the marriages of the steadies' slightly older peers."

Beth Bailey, "Sexuality," in *Encyclopedia of Children and Childhood in History and Society,* ed. Paula S. Fass, vol. 3 (New York: Macmillan, 2004), 743–51.

66　"necking and petting": Ibid., 750.

66　average age of first marriage: The percentage of female 15-to-17-year-olds who were married increased from 4.6 percent in 1940 to 7.2 percent in 1950, then fell a bit to 6.8 percent in 1960. The percentage of 15-to-17-year-old boys who were married increased from 0.4 percent in 1940 to 1.1 percent in 1950, and then, unlike for girls, rose to 1.2 percent in 1960. U.S. Department of Health, Education, and Welfare, "Teenagers: Marriages, Divorces, Parenthood, and Mortality," Aug. 1973. Between 1940 and 1959, the percentage of girls ages 14 to 17 who were married increased by a third. Bailey, 749–50.

66　unplanned pregnancy: Chad Gordon, "Social Characteristics of Early Adolescence," in "Early Adolescence," ed. Stephen R. Graubard, special issue, *Daedalus* 100 (Fall 1971): 931–60.

66　"Elvis' gyrations": Esther Schattman and Lucy Kavaler, "They're Growing Up Faster Nowadays," *Parents' Magazine,* Sept. 1958.

66　"leerics": *Variety,* cited in Dwight Macdonald, "A Caste, a Culture, a Market. II," *The New Yorker,* Nov. 29, 1958.

67　"rowdyism, riot and revolt": *Daily News* (New York), cited in "Education: The New Three R's," *Time,* March 15, 1954.

67　"Within the memory": Dr. Robert M. Lindner, cited in Macdonald.

67　"The first association": Teenagers, Macdonald noted, were spending an "appalling number of hours hooked up to some kind of communications machine," whether the telephone, radio, or a new form of mass media, the TV. Macdonald.

67　"anxiety-drenched obsession": Peter N. Stearns, *Childhood in World History* (New York: Routledge, 2007), 93–94.

67　girls wearing makeup: Eleanor Roosevelt, "If You Ask Me," *Ladies' Home Journal,* Feb. 1942. Daniel Thomas Cook and Susan B. Kaiser note that by the 1940s, mothers were writing to advice columnists about their daughters wanting to wear makeup and "'adultlike'" clothing by age 12 or 13. Daniel Thomas Cook and Susan B. Kaiser, "Betwixt and Be Tween: Age Ambiguity and the Sexualization of the Female Consuming Subject," *Journal of Consumer Culture* 4, no. 2 (2004): 203–27.

67   A definitive *no*: Eleanor Roosevelt, "If You Ask Me," *Ladies' Home Journal,* Dec. 1946.

67   Retailers, eager to rev up their sales: Cook and Kaiser, 208.

68   "urge to all look alike": *Earnshaw's Infants' and Children's Merchandiser,* cited in Cook and Kaiser, 211.

68   an archetypal, hypersexual bad boy: Edgar Z. Friedenberg, *The Vanishing Adolescent* (New York: Dell, 1959), 176–77. "The 'teen-ager,'" Friedenberg wrote, "seems to have replaced the Communist as the appropriate target for public controversy and foreboding."

68   teen pregnancy articles: See, for example, Glenn Matthew White, "Teen-Age Illegitimate Pregnancy: Why Does It Happen?," *Ladies' Home Journal,* Aug. 1958.

69   eleven were just 13 or 14: "These Marauding Savages," *Time,* April 28, 1958.

69   goings-on at John Marshall Junior High: "Undercover Teacher," *Time,* Nov. 24, 1958; "Education: Outrage in Brooklyn," *Time,* Feb. 10, 1958.

69   "undercover" as a substitute teacher: George N. Allen, "'Don't Let 'Em See You're Afraid,' Writer Told by School Official," *New York World-Telegram,* Nov. 13, 1958. Allen also discovered that many teachers at John Marshall Junior High in Brooklyn were teaching subjects about which they knew nothing, as in the case of a gym teacher saddled with an additional triple load of art, social studies, and English.

69   common points of reference: Young adolescents like those at John

Marshall Junior High "yield to no authority and treat all sympathetic attempts to work with them as signs of weakness which they exploit to their advantage," a soon-to-be-retired New York City public school guidance counselor wrote in 1956. Elizabeth R. Roby, "Blackboard Jungle, Jr.," *Ladies' Home Journal,* Sept. 1956.

69   "teenage terrorism": Macdonald.

70   "wedding like bands": Jean Anderson, "Teen-Age Marriage Craze," *Ladies' Home Journal,* March 1963.

70   seventh graders: Schattman and Kavaler.

70   "jilted": "Teen-Agers Draft a Code," *Ladies' Home Journal,* Sept. 1958.

70   "better off dead": Selma Fraiberg, "The Trouble with Early Dating," *Parents' Magazine & Better Homemaking,* Sept. 1961.

70   "too tolerant altogether": Nan Harrison and Joan Younger, "What's a Mother to Do?," *Ladies' Home Journal,* Oct. 1956.

70   " 'I don't want to *be* changed' ": Norman M. Lobsenz, "The Plot to Abolish Childhood," *Redbook,* June 1962.

71   timetables for dating: Ruth Imler, "It's About Time: THE SUB DEB," *Ladies' Home Journal,* Nov. 1953.

71   "strictly taboo": "GUIDEPOST for Youth Conduct."

71   *Beginning to Date*: By the short film's end, George is well on his way to a successful life in society, having learned the all-important first rule of etiquette: "consideration for the feelings of others." *Beginning to Date,* Encyclopaedia Britannica Films, 1953, archive.org/details /Beginnin1953.

72   knowing how to curry favor: Hawk, 47. After trying to identify the factors behind popularity so that "aid may be given the unpopular child," Hawk also recommended that teachers highlight the strengths of boys from low socioeconomic backgrounds, who were otherwise, his research showed, destined to be unpopular.

72   The whole concept of popularity: There are many examples from

the popular media through the mid-twentieth century showing that popularity was an unquestioned virtue and unpopularity was seen as a sign of physical or psychological deficiencies that parents could, and should, address. In 1937, the psychologist Elizabeth Hurlock wrote, "It is not at all an uncommon thing for both boys and girls to break away from their former play companions, and spend their leisure time alone." Don't force them to play with others, she counseled, because if you do, they might be bad companions, and this may "lead to an unpopularity which it will take years to overcome." Elizabeth B. Hurlock, "Just Before the Teens," *Parents' Magazine,* Jan. 1937. A 1936 article titled "What Price Popularity?" was not, as might be expected, an exploration of the hidden costs of popularity, but rather a warning to parents against the ravages of going it alone, and it included what one could do as a parent to help adolescents avoid "pangs of loneliness and unpopularity." Dorothy Canfield Fisher, "What Price Popularity?," *Parents' Magazine,* Oct. 1936. And in 1944, Marjorie Lederer, writing in the voice of *Ladies' Home Journal*'s "sub-debs," took a teasing tone as she conveyed their request that parents lighten up on curfews, using language that she (and her under-18 constituents) must have known would be most convincing: "You don't want us to be unpopular, do you?" Lederer.

72   "well-adjusted": According to one definition, "Adjustment is accommodating or fitting oneself to circumstances, as when we say that a student is adjusted to or gets along well with the group in which he finds himself." N. L. Munn, *The Fundamentals of Human Adjustment* (London: George Harp, 1956), 21. The link between popularity and adjustment runs throughout Hawk's 1951 thesis. After socioeconomic status, he found the factors most important in boys' popularity with other boys had to do with how well connected they were and how possessed they were of a "feeling of belonging to the group." Both, he believed, were taught by example in their

homes: "Good homes produce well-adjusted children." And while girls were most liked for their looks among boys, their popularity among other girls was based on their "total adjustment," which included the quality of their relationships at school. Again, this consisted of both feeling like they fit in and being the kind of person who knows how to fit in. Hawk, 23. In 1953, *Parents' Magazine* advised that it was never too early to start children on the road to understanding and mastering their expected sex roles. In fact, it was a key part of the learning that was meant to take place in the single-sex activities typical of the preadolescent "gang age": "Boys learn to act, think and feel like men," author Constance Foster wrote, while girls "play at femininity until it becomes second nature." It was extremely important that parents encourage this, she noted, lest an improperly gender-trained boy or girl may become "queer or different," "unpopular," "a little odd," or "sissies." Constance Foster, "The Tween-Age Child," *Parents' Magazine,* June 1953.

The idea that a child should above all be true to himself or herself doesn't really show up until the 1960s and is probably of a piece with the refusal of African Americans and then women to continue adjusting themselves to the realities of life as they found it. In fact, I was struck by this 1966 quote in *Parents' Magazine* from a former junior high principal and the author of the 1959 book *How to Live Through Junior High School,* because its tone was so dramatically different from anything I had encountered before: "The bases for social success in junior high school are narrow and superficial. . . . Good looks, the right clothes, having enough pocket money, success in sports, and an easy line of chatter count more than anything else. . . . Not everyone will be popular, and not infrequently the most popular boys and girls turn out to be less interesting and less profound adults. . . . Certainly it is better for a child to stand for his own convictions and standards, and to pursue his own interests, than to subordinate everything to the wish to be popular." Eric W. Johnson, "What to Do for the Child Who Has No Friends," *Parents' Magazine & Better Homemaking,* Aug. 1966.

72   heterosexuality: According to the author Linda Rosenzweig, a "distinctly new heterosexual imperative" took root very strongly starting in the 1920s. Linda W. Rosenzweig, "Friendship," in *Encyclopedia of Children and Childhood in History and Society,* ed. Paula S. Fass, vol. 2 (New York: Macmillan, 2004), 372–74.

73   a huge photo spread: Uzzle.

74   12 percent of female respondents: *Sexual Behavior in the Human Female* (1953), cited in Peter J. Pecora et al., *The Child Welfare Challenge: Policy, Practice, and Research,* 2nd ed. (New York: Aldine de Gruyter, 2000), 176.

74   "no public interest": Steven Mintz, "Placing Childhood Sexual Abuse in Historical Perspective," *Immanent Frame,* July 13, 2012. The family historian Stephanie Coontz has also noted that when girls or women in the 1950s reported sexual abuse to therapists, their memories were often written off as expressions of "their unconscious oedipal desires." Social workers who did believe that something sexual had taken place, she noted further, were more likely at mid-century than in decades past to categorize those experiences as instances of "female 'sex delinquency.'" She cites the historian Linda Gordon in relation to the point about caseworkers, saying that Gordon's work shows that "though incest cases were common throughout the records of caseworkers from 1880 to 1960 . . . the problem was increasingly redefined as one of female 'sex delinquency.'" Coontz, 35.

75   his findings were very much at odds: Johnson, *How to Live Through Junior High School,* 209–12.

75   A ninth-grade boy: Ibid., 208.

76   "the usually innocent activity": Ibid.

76   "moral panic": Steven Mintz, *Huck's Raft: A History of American Childhood* (Cambridge, Mass.: Harvard University Press, 2004), 340.

76   the boys wreaking havoc: "These Marauding Savages," *Time*. The
     boys who set upon Michael Farmer—who was white—were mem-
     bers of two black and Puerto Rican gangs, the Egyptian Kings and
     the Dragons, who were seeking revenge against an Irish gang, the
     Jesters, who had been harassing black and Hispanic kids all summer
     when they tried to use the pool. Mara Bovsun, "Two Victims of
     Early Gang Violence Pummeled, Stabbed by the Egyptian Kings and
     Dragons, Mostly Puerto Rican and African American Warring Fac-
     tions at New York City Pool," *Daily News* (New York), July 9, 2017.
     Untrained George Allen, assigned to teach a special "adjustment
     class" of low IQ ninth graders—"a euphemism for the worst kids in
     school," as he put it—judged his students to be both irredeemable
     and uneducable, while noting that they were not native-born whites:
     "I wanted to taste the rewards of being able to impart learning to
     students who sought knowledge. But I couldn't. The makeup of the
     class was against it. The register contained 24 Negroes, one student
     of foreign descent, and five of Puerto Rican parentage." George
     Allen, " 'Hey Teach' Is Signal for Classroom Bedlam," *New York
     World-Telegram,* Nov. 20, 1958.

77   doctors found ways to prescribe it: As *The Saturday Evening Post* noted
     in 1966, "whether by legitimate or underground routes," the Pill did
     find its way to college campuses and even to some high school stu-
     dents. Steven M. Spencer, "The Birth Control Revolution," *The
     Saturday Evening Post,* Jan. 15, 1966.

77   only 4 percent of whom: Lawrence B. Finer, "Trends in Premarital
     Sex in the United States, 1954–2003," *Public Health Reports* 122,
     no. 1 (Jan.–Feb. 2007): 63–78.

77   a junior high schooler who was on the Pill: Spencer.

78   "mature" themes and content: Peter Bunzel, "Shocking Candor on
     the Screen, a Dilemma for the Family," *Life,* Feb. 23, 1962.

78   "sinful and immoral": Vladimir Nabokov, cited in Peter Bunzel,
     "Yes, They Did It: 'Lolita' *Is* a Movie," *Life,* May 25, 1962.

78   "ten, or earlier": Vladimir Nabokov, *Lolita* (1955; New York: Vintage, 1997), 43.

78   "debauched": Ibid., 135.

78   "hopelessly depraved": Ibid., 133.

79   "All righty then": Cited in "Filmsite Movie Review: *Lolita* (1962)," AMC Filmsite, filmsite.org/loli4.html.

79   "pitiable, not hateful": Bunzel, "Yes, They Did It."

80   a new kind of animal: The University of Iowa media studies professor M. Gigi Durham has written that the "Lolitas" who lived on from the film were "deliberate sexual provocateurs, turning adults' thoughts to sex and thereby luring them into wickedness, wantonly transgressing our basic moral and legal codes." M. Gigi Durham, *The Lolita Effect: The Media Sexualization of Young Girls and What We Can Do About It* (New York: Penguin, 2008), 25–26.

5. INTO THE ABYSS

81   "first 'sexually obligated' generation": Kathleen Fury, "Sex and the American Teen-Ager," *Ladies' Home Journal,* March 1980.

83   "an authentic nymphet": David Rosenthal, Growing Pains: 'Lolita' Comes to Broadway," *New York,* March 16, 1981.

83   "shy, enchanting creatures": "Photography View," *The New York Times,* Jan. 1, 1978.

83   accused Hamilton of rape: Emily Langer, "David Hamilton, Photographer Celebrated as Artist and Condemned as Pornographer, Dies at 83," *The Washington Post,* Nov. 30, 2016; Sam Roberts, "David Hamilton, Photographer Known for Nude Images of Girls, Dies at 83," *The New York Times,* Nov. 28, 2016.

83   "preteen sex symbol": "America's Newest Sexy Kid Star," *New York,* Jan. 31, 1977.

83   Dr. H. Jon Geis: Mel Juffe and Anthony Haden-Guest, "Pretty Babies," *New York,* Sept. 29, 1980.

84   "slower, safer and less sexualized": Mary Pipher, *Reviving Ophelia: Saving the Selves of Adolescent Girls* (New York: Putnam, 1994), 241.

84   "I spent my days": Ibid., 233–34.

84   "blissfully uncomplicated": Judy Mann, "Way Beyond Spin the Bottle," *The Washington Post,* July 14, 1999.

84   "She thinks it's swell": Cover blurb, *New York,* Sept. 26, 1977.

84   "The dregs of the sexual revolution": Rebecca Solnit, cited in Jia Tolentino, "What Should We Say About David Bowie and Lori Maddox?," *Jezebel,* Feb. 16, 2016, https://jezebel.com/what-should -we-say-about-david-bowie-and-lori-maddox-1754533894.

85   "as young as young girls used to be": Juffe and Haden-Guest.

85   The onset of puberty: Grace Wyshak and Rose E. Frisch, "Evidence for a Secular Trend in Age of Menarche," *The New England Journal of Medicine* 306 (1982): 1033–35. The authors note that at the time of the study, the average age at which girls were starting their periods was 12 years 8 months.

85   it leveled off: The average age of a girl's first period changed only slightly, from 12 years 9 months in the 1970s to 12 years 6 months in 2011. But breast development—a basic marker of the start of puberty, as opposed to the start of reproductive maturity—has followed a very different trajectory in recent decades, Louise Greenspan and Julianna Deardorff argue in *The New Puberty: How to Navigate Early Development in Today's Girls* (New York: Rodale, 2014). Their book details their own research that tracked breast development among 1,329 ethnically diverse girls between the years 2004 and 2011. They found that the average age when breast development began was approximately 8 years 9 months for African American girls, 9 years 3 months for Hispanic girls, and 9 years 8 months for white and Asian American girls. By 2011, the age when breast devel-

opment began had fallen "significantly" since the 1970s, they wrote. Louise Greenspan and Julianna Deardorff, *The New Puberty: How to Navigate Early Development in Today's Girls* (New York: Rodale, 2014), xx. It's long been known that African American girls get their periods earlier than white girls. But it's only in recent years that the numbers have been consistently disaggregated. In 2009, the average age of first period for white, African American, and Latina girls was 12.6 to 12.9 years, 12.1 to 12.2 years, and 12.2 to 12.3 years, respectively. Elizabeth J. Susman and Lorah D. Dorn, "Puberty: Its Role in Development," in *Handbook of Adolescent Psychology,* ed. Richard M. Lerner and Laurence Steinberg, 3rd ed., vol. 1 (Hoboken, N.J.: Wiley, 2009), 116–51.

85   "Human sexuality is governed": Albert Bandura, "The Stormy Decade: Fact or Fiction?," *Psychology in the Schools* 1 (July 1964): 224–31. In *At the Threshold: The Developing Adolescent,* ed. S. Shirley Feldman and Glen R. Elliott (Cambridge, Mass.: Harvard University Press, 1990), 22–31.

85   subsequent repetition and reinforcement: After a period of emphasis on social factors above all, an exhaustive empirical literature review in 2001 stated that both hormonal and social factors contribute to sex differences in sexual desire. Lisa M. Diamond and Ritch C. Savin-Williams, "Adolescent Sexuality," in *Handbook of Adolescent Psychology,* ed. Lerner and Steinberg, 479–523.

85   "brave, sometimes bewildering new world": David Gelman et al., "The Games Teen-Agers Play," *Newsweek,* Sept. 1, 1980. Over the decades, *Newsweek* has consistently distinguished itself for its fascination with, and stylistic flair with which it covers, the issue of young teen sexuality.

88   "they pretended to believe me": Ayelet Waldman, interview with author, Oct. 7, 2015.

88   mean-spirited puerile behavior: The author and longtime researcher on youth Mike Males is convinced that hate was at the root of all the

insanity that was (and continues to be) said about teenagers, and I think he has a good point. Mike A. Males, *Teenage Sex and Pregnancy: Modern Myths, Unsexy Realities* (Santa Barbara, Calif.: ABC-Clio, 2010), 95ff.

91   "societal narcissisms": Rob Ribera, "The Ice Storm: An Interview with Rick Moody," *Confluence,* Oct. 16, 2013, http://blogs.bu.edu /confluence/2013/10/16/ice-storm-rick-moody.

93   the first wave of baby boomers: A fair bit has been written about the split in sensibility and experiences between baby boomers born just after the Second World War and those born in the late 1950s and early 1960s, with the latter group once characterized by the cultural commentator and author Jonathan Pontell as "Generation Jones," due to their "Jonesing" for some notice and recognition. Jeffrey J. Williams, "Not My Generation," *Chronicle of Higher Education,* March 31, 2014.

93   hit such a low point: Daniel Offer, *The Psychological World of the Teenager* (1969), cited in Joan Lipsitz, *Growing Up Forgotten: A Review of Research and Programs Concerning Early Adolescence* (New Brunswick, N.J.: Transaction Books, 1980), 163–64.

93   "the great wasteland": Edward C. Martin, "Reflections on the Early Adolescent in School," in "Early Adolescence," ed. Stephen R. Graubard, special issue, *Daedalus* 100 (Fall 1971): 1087–103.

93   "eerily quiet generation": Lipsitz, 6.

94   "no one cares . . . blatant void": Ibid., 121.

94   "so-called 'middle school movement'": Ibid., 94.

94   measured by new or reconfigured buildings: In the 1965–66 school year, there were only about five hundred middle schools in the United States; in 1967–68, there were more than a thousand; and in 1969–70, there were at least thirteen hundred. As had been the case in the creation of the junior high school, logistical necessity played a big role in their growth. The massive baby boom generation was moving up through the elementary schools, and school districts

around the country were adding kindergarten classrooms, both leading to severe overcrowding in existing school buildings. Formerly
segregated school systems, too, were scrambling for space, requiring
new buildings or reconfigurations of old ones. Thomas H. Peeler,
"The Middle School: A Historical Frame of Reference," in *Reading
in the Middle School,* ed. Gerald G. Duffy (Newark, Del.: International
Reading Association, 1971), 11. Large-scale change took quite a
while, though. By 1971, 23 percent of schools for these grades were
organized as middle schools; by 1981, middle schools accounted for
33 percent of these schools; by 1991, 51 percent; and by 2000,
69 percent. "Middle Schools: The Emergence of Middle Schools,
Growth and Maturation of the Middle School Movement," *Education Encyclopedia,* education.stateuniversity.com/pages/2229/Middle
-Schools.html.

95   "a time of tumultuous upheaval": Lipsitz, xvi.

95   "the most maligned": John E. Schulenberg et al., "School from the
Young Adolescent's Perspective: A Descriptive Report," *The Journal
of Early Adolescence* 4, no. 2 (1984): 107–30.

95   "copulating schoolgirl": Karen Houppert, *The Curse: Confronting the
Last Unmentionable Taboo—Menstruation* (New York: Farrar, Straus
and Giroux, 1999), 56. There seems to have been far less contemporary criticism of the fantasy than there would be decades later. It was,
however, interesting to find the following, written by a self-identified
baby boomer man, in a women's magazine from about that time:
"Lord knows, if the fantasies our (mostly male-dominated) media
throw up to us are any indication (designer jean ads, all those teenage jailbait movies), then American men of my generation have an
obsession with barely pubescent women that's straight out of *Lolita*.
It is no accident that novelist Thomas McGuane once allowed publicly that he preferred young girls because 'their stories are shorter.'
So seemingly, does everybody." Steven Simels, "I Want a Woman—
Not a Girl," *Redbook,* Feb. 1984, 78.

95   problems that had long worried adults: Beatrix Hamburg, "Early Adolescence as a Life Stress," in *Coping and Health,* ed. S. Levine et al. (New York: Plenum Press, 1980), 121–43.

96   empirical studies were sorely lacking: When the adolescent psychologist Laurence Steinberg was a PhD student, he recalled in a 2014 autobiographical essay, the field of developmental psychology was an "empirical wasteland." He observed that what studies there were from the 1950s through the 1980s were generally purely descriptive and interested particularly in what went wrong with kids—notably, delinquency. Laurence Steinberg, "The Importance of Serendipity," in *The Developmental Science of Adolescence: History Through Autobiography,* ed. Richard M. Lerner, Anne C. Petersen, Rainer K. Silbereisen, and Jeanne Brooks-Gunn (New York: Psychology Press, 2014), 495.

96   "the drive derivatives": Anna Freud, "Adolescence," *Psychoanalytic Study of the Child* 13, no. 1 (1958): 255–78.

96   "identity vs. role confusion": Erik H. Erikson, *Childhood and Society* (London: Paladin,1977), 234. Fascinatingly, in 1968, Erikson wrote that the end of childhood brings a "crisis of wholeness" as young adolescents struggle to "become whole people in their own right." He viewed junior high school–age conformity and the obsession with fitting in as the modern, Western version of traditional societies' initiation rituals; it's all about the creation of "insiders," he wrote. Erik H. Erikson, *Identity: Youth and Crisis* (New York: Norton, 1968), 77–78.

96   "a healthy preparation for marriage": Jerome M. Seidman, ed., *The Adolescent: A Book of Readings,* rev. ed. (1953; New York: Holt, 1960), 385. This is from an editor's note summarizing a selection from John Levy and Ruth Munroe, *The Happy Family* (New York: Knopf, 1938).

96   "their reluctance to cooperate": Freud.

97   "especially disappointing": Arthur Witt Blair and William H. Burton, *Growth and Development of the Preadolescent* (New York: Appleton-Century-Crofts, 1951), 10.

97   "divested of the halo": Blair and Burton, 4.

97   a dark continent: In 1971, when the journal *Daedalus* devoted an entire issue to early adolescence, many of the authors admitted that
when it came to hard-and-fast data about kids of junior high school
age, they could do nothing more than extrapolate from studies of
high schoolers; rely on "casual observation and hearsay evidence," as
the issue editor, Stephen Graubard, put it; and make a plea to their
colleagues in psychology and related fields to do much more. Stephen R. Graubard, "Preface," in "Early Adolescence," ed. Stephen
R. Graubard, special issue, *Daedalus* 100 (Fall 1971): v. In 1983, re-
flecting back on this history, the Virginia Commonwealth University psychologist John Hill characterized the resistance by researchers
to study this group as a feeling that they were "too volatile and
socially, cognitively, and affectively disorganized to permit developmental generalizations." John P. Hill, "Early Adolescence: A Research Agenda," *The Journal of Early Adolescence* 3, nos. 1–2 (1983):
1–21.

98   the reality of sex was greatly exaggerated: Of the cohort of women
who went through junior high between the early 1970s and early
1980s, only 10 percent had had sex by age 15. Lawrence B. Finer,
"Trends in Premarital Sex in the United States, 1954–2003," *Public
Health Reports* 122, no. 1 (Jan.–Feb. 2007): 63–78.

98   not sexually active, not taking drugs: By way of a close age comparison, in 2010, 10 percent of 14-to-15-year-old boys and 12 percent of 14-to-15-year-old girls had ever had intercourse. J. Dennis
Fortenberry, "Puberty and Adolescent Sexuality," *Hormones and Behavior* 64, no. 2 (July 2013): 280–87. Rates of intercourse for middle
schoolers, however, are lower. One 2010 study of four thousand
sixth, seventh, and eighth graders in urban public schools in Southern California found that 9 percent had had intercourse. Christine J.
De Rosa et al., "Sexual Intercourse and Oral Sex Among Public
Middle School Students: Prevalence and Correlates," *Perspectives on*

Sexual and Reproductive Health 42 (Sept. 2010): 197–210. A 2011
study of rural white youth in the Midwest showed that 8 percent had
had intercourse. J. A. Dake et al., "Midwestern Rural Adolescents'
Oral Sex Experience," *Journal of School Health* 81 (March 2011):
159–65. A 2017 analysis combining seven large national surveys con-
ducted over multiple decades found some marked declines in adolescent behaviors since the early 1990s (when statistics permitting direct
comparison first became available), including those that adults most
fear, such as drinking, taking drugs, and having sex. The percentage
of eighth graders who had tried alcohol declined from 56 percent in
1990–94 to 29 percent in 2010–14. The percentage of eighth graders
who'd ever gone on a date declined from 51 percent in 1990–94 to
43 percent in 2010–16. The percentage of ninth graders who'd had
sex (some, presumably, in middle school) declined from 38 percent in
1990–94 to 29 percent in 2010–16. Overall, the researchers noted,
kids ages 11 to 18 in the late 2010s were on a "slower developmental
pathway" toward adulthood and sexual maturity than were their
same-age peers in the early 1990s. "Late adolescents look more like
middle adolescents once did, and middle adolescents look more like
early adolescents once did," they wrote. Ironically, the researchers
suggested that one explanation for this trend could be increased In-
ternet use. If kids are spending so much time online, they're not
going out and having sex, they reasoned. They also noted that all of
this occurred despite an increased incidence of early puberty in the
same time frame, with the ostensible risk, in the popular mind at
least, of bringing on the behaviors that those extra years of "raging
hormones" might unleash. Jean M. Twenge and Heejung Park, "The
Decline in Adult Activities Among U.S. Adolescents, 1976–2016,"
Child Development 90, no. 2 (2017): 1–17.

99   scary and salacious phenomena: Peggy Mann, "Do You Know
Where Your Children Are (and What They're Doing)?," *Ladies'
Home Journal,* Oct. 1979.

6. MOMMY & ME 2.0

101   "my heart has been ripped out": Melissa Taylor, "Middle School Drama and Mean Girls and What I Want My Daughter to Know About Friends," *SheKnows,* 2014.

102   "sexual acceleration" of childhood: Nina Darnton, "The End of Innocence," *Newsweek,* June 1, 1991.

102   "significant rise in the prevalence of oral sex": Tamar Lewin, "Teenagers Alter Sexual Practices, Thinking Risks Will Be Avoided," *The New York Times,* April 5, 1997.

102   new "prodigies" of sex: Ron Stodghill II, "Where'd You Learn That?," *Time,* June 15, 1998.

102   "crowded study hall": Laura Sessions Stepp, "Parents Are Alarmed by an Unsettling New Fad in Middle Schools: Oral Sex," *The Washington Post,* July 8, 1999.

102   "Mr. Pimp": Victoria Benning, "Uncle Disputes Charge Against Girl," *The Washington Post,* April 14, 1998.

102   "shattering insights": Judy Mann, "Way Beyond Spin the Bottle," *The Washington Post,* July 14, 1999.

103   "epidemic": Cited in Caitlin Flanagan, "Are You There God? It's Me, Monica," *The Atlantic,* Jan./Feb. 2006, theatlantic.com/magazine/archive/2006/01/are-you-there-god-its-me-monica/304511/.

103   "rainbow parties . . . pervasive": "Is Your Child Leading a Double Life?," *The Oprah Winfrey Show,* first aired Oct. 2, 2003, cited in Joel Best and Kathleen A. Bogle, *Kids Gone Wild: From Rainbow Parties to Sexting: Understanding the Hype over Teen Sex* (New York: NYU Press, 2014), ebook.

103   no hard evidence: In fact, there really wasn't any evidence at all. Not for the rainbow parties, not for any of it. There was no reliable research on middle schoolers and oral sex in the 1990s. In 1992, a group of conservative senators led by Jesse Helms managed to kill funding for the American Teenage Study, which was supposed to

have been the first longitudinal survey of adolescent sexual behavior. Inveighing against "reprehensible sex surveys" that, they claimed, aimed "to legitimize homosexuality and other sexually promiscuous lifestyles," the senators had, unsurprisingly, a major chilling effect on other research as well. Lisa Remez, "Oral Sex Among Adolescents: Is It Sex or Is It Abstinence?," *Family Planning Perspectives* 32, no. 6 (Nov. 2000): 298–304. There were no reputable numbers on oral sex, and the limited data available from the Centers for Disease Control and Prevention actually shows that, as the level of national panic over the sex lives of middle schoolers rose over the course of the 1990s and early 2000s, the percentage of those kids having sex— based on high schoolers' recollections of when they had first had intercourse—actually *decreased*. According to CDC data, the percentage of high schoolers who reported having had sex at least one time before age 13 had declined from a high of 10.2 percent in 1991 to 8.3 percent in 1999 and 7.1 percent in 2007. In Mike A. Males, *Teenage Sex and Pregnancy: Modern Myths, Unsexy Realities* (Santa Barbara, Calif.: ABC-Clio, 2010), 90. The latest numbers from the CDC indicate that only 3.6 percent of high schoolers report having had sex before age 13. Centers for Disease Control and Prevention, "Had Sexual Intercourse Before Age 13 Years (for the first time) Among 12th-Grade Students," *High School Youth Risk Behavior Survey, 2015.*

103 Or not doing: There was, for example, the boy who told *The Washington Post*'s Laura Sessions Stepp about the girl who'd told everyone that she'd given him a blow job but really hadn't. Stepp. There were the girls who'd bragged to *The Washington Post*'s Liza Mundy that they were going to have a weekend party with "sex games" such as "runnin' a train" ("serial sex," Mundy explained), but whose plans, in the end, had fizzled: "Somebody brought a 24-pack of condoms, somebody else brought a couple bottles of alcohol, but apparently the mom had checked on them more often than they'd expected," Mundy learned in a follow-up interview. "At any rate, there had been

some freak dancing" (that is to say: "where a guy stands behind a girl and dances close to her, his crotch against her bottom," Mundy specified), "but then things calmed down, the boys went home and the girls went to sleep." Liza Mundy, "Sex & Sensibility," *The Washington Post Magazine,* July 16, 2000. And the aforementioned "Mr. Pimp" never managed to get his sex-for-money scheme off the ground. Benning.

103   pretty rare: A 1994 study, for example, found that only 9 percent of 12-year-olds had had sex, compared with 16 percent of 13-year-olds, 23 percent of 14-year-olds, 30 percent of 15-year-olds, and 71 percent of 18-year-olds. Alan Guttmacher Institute, *Sex and America's Teenagers* (New York: Alan Guttmacher Institute, 1994).

103   nonconsensual: A 1994 study revealed that 74 percent of women who said they had first had intercourse before the age of 14 had done so "involuntarily," as had 60 percent of those who said they had first had intercourse before age 15. Ibid. A 1998 study found that 24 percent of women who had been younger than 14 when they'd first had sex reported that it had been nonvoluntary. In addition, 44 percent of women who said they'd first had sex *voluntarily* before age 14 ranked their first intercourse as very low—at levels 1–4—on a 10-point "wantedness" scale the researchers employed to capture the experiences of girls who had not consented to sex (wholeheartedly or at all) but did not view what had happened to them as "rape." Joyce Abma, Anne Driscoll, and Kristin Moore, "Young Women's Degree of Control over First Intercourse: An Exploratory Analysis," *Family Planning Perspectives* 30, no. 1 (1998): 12–18. This is an analysis of the 1995 National Survey of Family Growth.

103   "No one, least of all Oprah": Peggy Orenstein, *Girls & Sex: Navigating the Complicated New Landscape* (New York: Harper, 2016), 50. Amy Benfer, writing in *Salon* in 2000, had choice words about the coverage at the time. Amy Benfer, "Talking Trash," *Salon,* Jan. 25, 2000, https://www.salon.com/2000/01/25/kid_sex.

103 a form of "hysteria": Jennie Yabroff, "The Myths of Teen Sex," *Newsweek,* June 9, 2008.

103 a "myth": Tara Parker-Pope, "The Myth of Rampant Teenage Promiscuity," *The New York Times,* Jan. 26, 2009.

104 "relational aggression": Bad behavior has long been a big part of the study of adolescence, whether in the form of worries about gangs in the early twentieth century, concern about juvenile delinquents in the decades following the Second World War, or research on "conduct" problems in the late 1970s through the mid-1980s. But prior to the 1990s, aggression had always been considered almost exclusively a boy problem. In the 1990s, that began to change, as female researchers pointed out that psychological studies were consistently defining aggression through behaviors such as fighting or vandalism that were most typically seen in boys. Because the ways of doing harm that girls commonly used—spreading rumors, shunning, ostracizing, and the like—didn't show up on behavioral questionnaires, they hypothesized, girl aggression had effectively been written out of the picture. When those sorts of emotionally violent acts were included in tests to measure aggressive behavior, researchers at the University of Illinois Urbana-Champaign found that all the results changed. Suddenly, rather than one gender being far more aggressive than the other, girls and boys turned out to be aggressive in different ways. This study put the term "relational aggression" on the map. Nicki R. Crick and Jennifer K. Grotpeter, "Relational Aggression, Gender, and Social-Psychological Adjustment," *Child Development* 66 (June 1995): 710–22.

105 a way of getting weaponized: All that was not lost on Wiseman, who told me that in more recent years, she has been trying to shift the conversation, to give it added nuance, and to lead kids—and parents in particular—to see other kids as complex people who might temporarily occupy roles like "queen bee," "wannabe," or "messenger," but who are much more than those labels and who can, above all,

grow and change. "A label ideally is something you can look at when there's a pattern of behavior you're seeing or exhibiting. It can give you insight . . . and that should give you the ability to step away and question yourself," she told me. "But because of the way people's brains compartmentalize—and also because it's an easy way not to reflect on one's own behavior—it becomes really easy to say that girl's this, that girl's that—and then it locks these girls into roles that nobody wants to be in. And it does not allow for reflection."

111   "tormented": Mary Pipher, *Reviving Ophelia: Saving the Selves of Adolescent Girls* (New York: Putnam, 1994), 11.

111   "concerned with their femininity": Ibid., 12, 18–19.

111   "Everyone is grieving": Ibid., 24.

111   "splendid generation": Lucinda Franks, "Little Big People," *The New York Times Magazine,* Oct. 10, 1993. "The parents of many of these children—those of us who began our families later in life—came of age in the Vietnam War years," Franks wrote. "Our ideas of child rearing were like our ideas about everything else: radically different from our parents, who thought a child was just a child. . . . Those of us who were veterans of the 60s and 70s swore that we would treat our children with respect . . . like 'little people,' empowering them with the rights, the importance and the truth telling we had been denied."

111   "trains of girls": "Lucinda Franks, Author of 'The Sex Lives of Your Children,' and Dr. Harold Koplewicz, Psychiatrist, on Sex Games Young Children Play," *The Early Show,* CBS, Jan. 10, 2000.

112   "I wept": "Lucinda Franks: The Sex Lives of Your Kids," *Richard Heffner's Open Mind,* PBS, April 13, 2000.

112   the sense of loss: Many parents became more anxious and depressed. Their self-esteem plummeted. They developed a whole array of somatizing symptoms, like headaches, insomnia, and gut pain. They became dissatisfied with their jobs and marriages. Their children's growing independence made them feel "powerless, nervous and out

of control," the Steinbergs noted. In fact, they wrote, more than one parent described the pulling away of their pubescent kids as nothing less than an "involuntary divorce." And this, the authors observed, brought on "an array of disturbing emotions." "Many felt a painful sense of loss, depression, envy, jealousy, anger, and frustration—and often regret," they wrote. "And not surprisingly, these negative emotions spilled over into other aspects of parents' lives, creating a domino effect. Many reported feeling for the first time a keen dissatisfaction with themselves, with their job and career, with their marriage, and with parenting." Laurence Steinberg with Wendy Steinberg, *Crossing Paths: How Your Child's Adolescence Triggers Your Own Crisis* (New York: Simon & Schuster, 1994), 67, 29.

112   "a cruel contrast": Ibid., 15.

112   "alongside Adonis or Venus": Ibid., 51.

122   In a suburb of St. Louis: Judith Warner, "Helicopter Parenting Turns Deadly," *The New York Times*, Nov. 29, 2007, opinionator.blogs .nytimes.com/2007/11/29/helicopter-parenting-turns-deadly/.

122   "Build a wall!": Kelly Wallace and Sandee LaMotte, "The Collateral Damage After Students' 'Build a Wall' Chant Goes Viral," CNN, Dec. 28, 2016.

125   A generation ago: Joan Lipsitz, *Growing Up Forgotten: A Review of Research and Programs Concerning Early Adolescence* (New Brunswick, N.J.: Transaction Books, 1980), 163ff.

7. LOOKING FOR CONTROL IN ALL THE WRONG PLACES

127   "by leaving center stage": Jennifer Senior, "The Collateral Damage of a Teenager," *New York*, Jan. 20, 2014.

127   parents' feelings of "self-efficacy": Terese Glatz and Christy M. Buchanan, "Change and Predictors of Change in Parental Self-Efficacy from Early to Middle Adolescence," *Developmental Psychology* 51 (2015): 1367–79.

129   puberty actually starts in the brain: Frances E. Jensen with Amy Ellis Nutt, *The Teenage Brain: A Neuroscientist's Survival Guide to Raising Adolescents and Young Adults* (New York: HarperCollins, 2015), 21; Louise Greenspan and Julianna Deardorff, *The New Puberty: How to Navigate Early Development in Today's Girls* (New York: Rodale, 2014), 6.

129   Boys' testosterone levels: Jensen and Nutt, 21.

129   a kind of overall tune-up: Laurence Steinberg, *Age of Opportunity: Lessons from the New Science of Adolescence* (Boston: Houghton Mifflin, 2014), 42.

129   "all sorts of environmental influences": Ibid., 43. See also Richard A. Friedman, "Return to the Teenage Brain," *The New York Times*, Oct. 8, 2016, and Daniel J. Siegel, *Brainstorm: The Power and Purpose of the Teenage Brain* (New York: Jeremy P. Tarcher, 2013), 2.

129   "sensitivity thresholds": Tom Hollenstein and Jessica P. Lougheed, "Beyond Storm and Stress: Typicality, Transactions, Timing, and Temperament to Account for Adolescent Change," *American Psychologist* 68, no. 6 (2013): 444–54. These authors caution, however, that the role of the sex hormones is somewhat indirect, and they now believe it's an adolescent's environment that determines how much of a role the hormones play and also how they affect behavior.

129   more reactive to stress: "What this means is that adolescents have it rough: more vulnerability to stress and fewer tools to deal with it." William Stixrud and Ned Johnson, *The Self-Driven Child: The Science and Sense of Giving Your Kids More Control over Their Lives* (New York: Viking, 2018), 23.

130   "react differently": Jensen and Nutt, 21.

130   "under conditions of perceived social threat": Hollenstein and Lougheed, 448.

130   done by age five: Jensen and Nutt, 3. Through much of the second half of the twentieth century, the Swiss psychologist Jean Piaget's

enormously influential theory of cognitive development taught that the stage of "formal operational thought"—the ability to think abstractly and logically, to think about your thinking, and to differentiate your own point of view from other people's—emerged right around age 12. After that, teenagers would continue to acquire knowledge and grow more mature in their cognition, but as a structural matter "formal operational thought" was an end point: "No new mental systems develop and the mental structures of adolescence must serve for the rest of the life span," the child psychologist David Elkind, who in the 1960s studied Piaget's work at the Swiss psychologist's International Center for Genetic Epistemology in Geneva, once explained. David Elkind, "Egocentrism in Adolescence," *Child Development* 38 (Dec. 1967): 1025–34.

130   a major uptick in brain development: National Institute of Mental Health, "Teenage Brain: A Work in Progress" (NIH Publication No. 01-4929, January 2001), psychceu.com/Brain_Basics/teenbrain.pdf.

131   the fMRI study: Ibid.

132   more intense and detailed: Steinberg, 21.

132   particularly susceptible to cultural messages: Eileen L. Zurbriggen, Rebecca L. Collins, Sharon Lamb, Tomi-Ann Roberts, Deborah L. Tolman, L. Monique Ward, and Jeanne Blake, *Report of the APA Task Force on the Sexualization of Girls* (Washington, D.C.: American Psychological Association, 2007), apa.org/pi/women/programs/girls /report-full.pdf.

133   "second critical period": See, for example, Deanna Kuhn, "Adolescent Thinking," in *Handbook of Adolescent Psychology,* ed. Richard M. Lerner and Laurence Steinberg, 3rd ed., vol. 1 (Hoboken, N.J.: Wiley, 2009), 152–86.

133   " 'social rewards' ": Mitch Prinstein, *Popular: The Power of Likability in a Status-Obsessed World* (New York: Viking, 2017), 56–59.

134   "virtually addicted to popularity": Ibid., 60.

134   mental health issues . . . spike: Jacquelynne S. Eccles, "The Development of Children Ages 6 to 14," *Future of Children* 9 (Fall 1999): 30–44.

134   the peak age: Jay N. Giedd et al., "Why Do So Many Psychiatric Disorders Emerge During Adolescence?," *National Review of Neuroscience* 9, no. 12 (Dec. 2008): 947–57.

134   Suicide attempts and successes: Eccles, 37.

134   relational aggression and bullying: Joni D. Splett, Melissa A. Maras, and Connie M. Brooks, "GIRLSS: A Randomized, Pilot Study of a Multisystemic, School-Based Intervention to Reduce Relational Aggression," *Journal of Child and Family Studies* 24, no. 8 (2015): 2250–61.

135   A 2010 study: Martin H. Teicher et al., "Hurtful Words: Exposure to Peer Verbal Aggression Is Associated with Elevated Psychiatric Symptom Scores and Corpus Callosum Abnormalities," *The American Journal of Psychiatry* 167 (Dec. 2010): 1464–71. The researchers found that the brains of subjects who had been verbally abused were different in a few specific ways from those of subjects who had not been: Their brains showed alterations to the corpus callosum, a connective area through which the two hemispheres of the brain communicate, and the corona radiata, a part of the brain involved in communication between the brain stem and the cerebral cortex. They also found that those who had suffered verbal abuse in childhood showed symptoms of anxiety, depression, and disassociation and engaged in drug use in young adulthood. The extent of these problems was dependent on the degree of verbal abuse. Peer verbal abuse appeared to be as damaging as earlier studies had shown parental verbal abuse to be.

135   moving . . . in childhood: Roger T. Webb, Carsten B. Pedersen, and Pearl L. H. Mok, "Adverse Outcomes to Early Middle Age Linked with Childhood Residential Mobility," *American Journal of Preventive*

Medicine 51, no. 3 (2016): 291–300. Although the study couldn't provide answers to why families moved, leaving open the possibility that some kind of family turbulence, as opposed to the relocations themselves, was really behind kids' problems later in life, it was able to control for socioeconomic status and for parental psychiatric history. And, significantly, it showed that the elevated risks for kids that accompanied moving during the early adolescent years held true independently of family income level.

135   don't all mature at the same time: Jensen and Nutt, 21.

136   the field of evolutionary psychology: Evolutionary psychology took off in the early to mid-1990s, with evolutionary developmental psychology building in the decade after. According to three key thinkers in the field, we face many of the same challenges as our ancestors did, "especially in the social realm," despite massive changes in humans' material culture. Their interest (and that of evolutionary psychologists like them) is in how cognitive structures developed in humans as they adapted to their environment and why. David F. Bjorklund, Bruce J. Ellis, and Justin S. Rosenberg, "Evolved Probabilistic Cognitive Mechanisms: An Evolutionary Approach to Gene x Environment x Development Interactions," in *Advances in Child Development and Behavior,* ed. R. V. Kail, vol. 35 (London: Academic Press, 2007), 1–36. See also David M. Buss, "Evolutionary Psychology: A New Paradigm for Psychological Science," *Psychological Inquiry* 6, no. 1 (1995): 1–30, and Greenspan and Deardorff, 157.

136   all in preparation for mating: Elizabeth J. Susman and Alan Rogol, "Puberty and Psychological Development," in *Handbook of Adolescent Psychology,* ed. Lerner and Steinberg, 15–44.

136   the gap between puberty and "mating": Laurence Steinberg notes that the "menarche to marriage" stretch grew from about five years in the mid-nineteenth century to fifteen years in 2010. Steinberg, 48.

136   "collective autonomy": Fize calls the years 11 to 15, corresponding

to *le collège* (junior high) in France, a moment of *"autonomie collective."* Michel Fize, cited in Emmanuelle Lucas, "Ces étiquettes qui collent à la peau des ados," *La Croix,* Sept. 12, 2017.

137   right where they're most vulnerable: Splett, Maras, and Brooks, 2251.

137   the best shot: After all, writes Laurence Steinberg, mating is "the point of adolescence." Steinberg, *Age of Opportunity,* 74.

138   aggression toward outsiders: Beatrix Hamburg and David Hamburg, "Afterword: On the Future Development of Adolescent Psychology," in *Handbook of Adolescent Psychology,* ed. Lerner and Steinberg, 815–19.

138   high in "allocentrism": Joseph P. Allen, Bert N. Uchino, and Christopher A. Hafen, "Running with the Pack: Teen Peer-Relationship Qualities as Predictors of Adult Physical Health," *Psychological Science,* Aug. 19, 2015.

138   social rejection acts: Prinstein, 110.

139   "'the pain of independence'": Gregory S. Berns et al., "Neurobiological Correlates of Social Conformity and Independence During Mental Rotation," *Biological Psychiatry* 58 (2005): 245–253, cited in Allen, Uchino, and Hafen, "Running with the Pack."

139   were successfully "autonomous": Joseph P. Allen, Joanna Chango, and David Szwedo, "The Adolescent Relational Dialectic and the Peer Roots of Adult Social Functioning," *Child Development* 85, no. 1 (Jan.–Feb. 2014): 192–204.

139   Finding a new "tribe": Lisa Damour, *Untangled: Guiding Teenage Girls Through the Seven Transitions into Adulthood* (New York: Ballantine, 2016), 50.

139   "at its peak": Lyn Mikel Brown, *Girlfighting: Betrayal and Rejection Among Girls* (New York: NYU Press, 2003), 102; "follow the rules just right": Brown, *Girlfighting,* 115.

139   active among boys as well: Pamela Orpinas, Caroline McNicholas, and Lusine Nahapetyan, "Gender Differences in Trajectories of Relational Aggression Perpetation and Victimization from Middle to High School," *Aggressive Behavior* 41 (2015): 401–12.

140   notoriously short-lived: Amy C. Hartl, Brett Laursen, and Antonius H. N. Cillessen, "A Survival Analysis of Adolescent Friendships: The Downside of Dissimilarity," *Psychological Science* 26, no. 8 (Aug. 2015): 1304–15.

141   "attract mates": Bruce Ellis, cited in Greenspan and Deardorff, 42.

142   the worst years: Daniel Offer, *The Psychological World of the Teen-ager* (1969), cited in Joan Lipsitz, *Growing Up Forgotten: A Review of Research and Programs Concerning Early Adolescence* (New Brunswick, N.J.: Transaction Books, 1980), 163ff.

143   "deflation of childhood happiness": Reed Larson and Maryse H. Richards, *Divergent Realities: The Emotional Lives of Mothers, Fathers, and Adolescents* (1994), cited in the psychologist Jeffrey Jensen Arnett's incredibly useful article "Adolescent Storm and Stress, Reconsidered," *American Psychologist* 54 (May 1999): 317–26. Arnett writes: "Comparing preadolescent fifth graders with adolescent ninth graders, Larson and Richards described the emotional 'fall from grace' that occurs in that interval, as the proportion of time experienced as 'very happy' declines by 50%, and similar declines take place in reports of feeling 'great,' 'proud,' and 'in control.' The result is an overall 'deflation of childhood happiness' as childhood ends and adolescence begins."

143   they bring on the very problems: These issues have been documented by academics since the 1970s. For a research review covering all of this, see Jacquelynne Eccles et al., "Development During Adolescence: The Impact of Stage-Environment Fit on Young Adolescents' Experiences in Schools and in Families," *American Psychologist* 48 (1993): 90–101.

143 the most unhappy mothers: Suniya Luthar and Lucia Ciciolla, "What It Feels Like to Be a Mother: Variations by Children's Developmental Stages," *Developmental Psychology* 52 (2016): 143–54.

144 "emotional labor": This phrase is now used frequently in all sorts of contexts, but it originated in the sociologist Arlie Hochschild's book *The Managed Heart* (Berkeley: University of California Press, 1983). In a 2018 *Atlantic* article that charted the term's "concept creep," Hochschild reiterated its original meaning as having been "the work, for which you're paid, which centrally involves trying to feel the right feeling for the job": friendliness on the part of flight attendants, for example; harshness in the case of bill collectors. These days, however, she noted (unhappily), it's more generally invoked to capture "the unpaid, expected, and unacknowledged work of keeping households and relationships running smoothly," which is how I'm using it here. Julie Beck, "The Concept Creep of 'Emotional Labor,'" *The Atlantic,* Nov. 26, 2018.

146 see their earnings actually fall: Gen X was also the first generation of Americans who, as young adults, were expected to have lower lifetime earnings than their parents. Ted Halstead, "A Politics for Generation X," *The Atlantic Monthly,* Aug. 1999.

147 fears of downward mobility: Marianne Cooper, "How the Middle Class Got Screwed: College Costs, Globalization and Our New Insecurity Economy," *Salon,* Aug. 2, 2014.

147 harder hit by the Great Recession: Erin Currier, "How Generation X Could Change the American Dream," *Trend* (Pew Charitable Trusts), Winter 2018.

147 life would be more difficult: "Is the American Dream Still Attainable?," McClatchy-Marist Poll, Feb. 14, 2014.

147 a different set of rules: Ibid.

148 college coaches recruiting middle schoolers: Rod Beard, "Colleges Want to Be First in Line with Middle-School Stars," *Detroit News,* May 11, 2015.

148   seventeen hundred middle schools: Laura Pappano, "Is Your First Grader College-Ready?," *The New York Times,* Feb. 4, 2015, https://www.nytimes.com/2015/02/08/education/edlife/is-your-first-grader-college-ready.html.

149   "Talk to your child": "Middle School Checklists," Federal Student Aid, U.S. Department of Education, studentaid.ed.gov/sa/prepare-for-college/checklists/middle-school.

149   a running head start: Arun Venugopal, "Being 12: The Most Awkward, Essential Year of Our Lives," WNYC (New York Public Radio), March 9, 2015.

149   epidemic on college campuses: B. Janet Hibbs and Anthony Rostain, *The Stressed Years of Their Lives: Helping Your Kid Survive and Thrive During Their College Years* (New York: St. Martin's, 2019).

149   Death rates from suicide: Sabrina Tavernise, "Young Adolescents as Likely to Die from Suicide as from Traffic Accidents," *The New York Times,* Nov. 3, 2016.

150   "winner-take-all society": I talk about this at length in *Perfect Madness: Motherhood in the Age of Anxiety* (New York: Riverhead, 2005), chap. 9, which was inspired by the economists Robert H. Frank and Philip J. Cook's excellent book, *The Winner-Take-All Society* (New York: Free Press, 1995).

151   "communitarian" values: See, for example, Juzhe Xi, Laurence Owens, and Huarun Feng, "Friendly Girls and Mean Girls: Social Constructions of Popularity Among Teenage Girls in Shanghai," *Japanese Psychological Research* 58 (2016): 42–53.

151   willing to officially acknowledge them: "School Pressure to Blame for Youth Suicides, Official Study Finds," AFP, *South China Morning Post,* May 14, 2014, https://www.scmp.com/news/china/article/1512032/school-pressure-blame-chinese-youth-suicides-official-study-finds.

151   "the Stanford prisoner experiment": In 1971, researchers at Stanford University, led by the professor Philip Zimbardo, paid subjects to

take on the roles of prison guards and detainees for what was supposed to be a two-week social psychology experiment. It was suspended, however, after less than one week, after subjects exhibited a shocking level of cruelty. The experiment has long been considered revelatory of the ease with which "ordinary people" can engage in brutal behavior. In recent years, however, questions have been raised about its basic validity. Greg Toppo, "Time to Dismiss the Stanford Prison Experiment?" *Inside Higher Ed,* June 20, 2018, insidehighered .com/news/2018/06/20/new-stanford-prison-experiment-revelations -question-findings.

152   the most unequal: Jeffrey Sachs, "Income Inequality Is a Structural Issue in U.S.: Columbia's Sachs," *Bloomberg Day Break: Americas,* Bloomberg TV, May 3, 2019, https://www.bloomberg.com/news /videos/2019-05-03/income-inequality-is-a-structural-issue-in-u-s -columbia-s-sachs-video.

152   "kind and helpful": Organisation for Economic Co-operation and Development, *How's Life? 2015: Measuring Well-Being* (Paris: OECD Publishing, 2015). This study investigated the well-being of 11-, 13-, and 15-year-olds in twenty-six advanced industrialized nations. The United States was ahead of only Poland and Greece in the degree to which this age group found their classmates "kind and helpful." China was not included in the study.

152   least likely kids their age: Jaana Juvonen, "Reforming Middle Schools: Focus on Continuity, Social Connectedness, and Engagement," *Educational Psychologist* 42 (2007): 197–208. In this study, the students were 11.5 to 14.5 years old. Twelve countries were surveyed.

153   "not universal problems": Ibid., 199.

153   "the ungrateful age": It's also sometimes called *l'âge bête,* literally "the stupid age." And before the translation police come out in force, I'll just quickly say that neither direct translation captures the words' full significance in this context. *L'âge ingrât* is typically translated into

English as "the awkward age," but I feel that has more to do with the search for an equivalent English-language expression than it does with the words' actual meaning. Fortunately (for me), France has a National Center for Textual and Lexical Resources, which defines *l'âge ingrât* as "the period of adolescence when one loses the grace of childhood, without having acquired the equilibrium that maturity can bring." Website for the Centre National de Ressources Textuelles et Lexicales: cnrtl.fr. Page for ingrât: cnrtl.fr/definition/academie9/Ingrat.

153   *el edad del pedo*: According to a twentysomething Costa Rican who was living and working in the United States when I interviewed her in 2016. The woman who taught me the expression entered private school for the first time in the sixth grade, at which point, surrounded by wealthy classmates, she encountered extreme pressure regarding looks and clothes, heady competition over boys, and a large dose of gossip and slut-shaming—all of which she now attributes to life in that particular upper-middle-class subculture.

153   "inevitable and ubiquitous": Hollenstein and Lougheed, 446.

8. WHAT WE VALUE

155   *don't go back to middle school*: Michael Thompson, phone interview with author, Dec. 19, 2016.

159   makes for good entertainment: Or not-so-good entertainment, as when a 2015 hour-long CNN special report analyzed about 150,000 Instagram, Twitter, and Facebook posts by 13-year-olds and found that they contained . . . not much of anything. The host, Anderson Cooper, nonetheless was scripted to hype the findings for all they were worth. "Do *you* know the secret language they're speaking to each other—that they don't want their parents and teachers to understand?" he earnestly deadpanned in a narrative that ranged over online predators, phone addiction, drugs, and sexting and included

the word "shock" many times. And yet the analysis of the posts showed them for the most part to be pretty tame—and pretty lame. There were no red flags for suicide—though the researchers had looked hard for such clues. Lots of kids were run-of-the-mill nasty— and some kids' posts were surprisingly nice. A "dick pick" was sent and received—although the girl's reaction, "I was like—aaah! Moom!" was actually more comforting than concerning. A girl posted an image of herself in a bikini; Anderson informed the girl's mother that, using geolocation, a predator could have been on her in a minute . . . though none had been. The one African American boy and his dad in the report—both dressed quite formally, both very nerdy—were roundly humiliated by blow-up quotes from the son's less-than-savory Instagram posts: pictures of pot captioned "Lemme hit," and in reference to some girls the words "goddam you dirty bitch, you dirty bitch, you dirty bitch." Confronted by Anderson about the discrepancy between those posts and his overall appearance, the boy embarrassedly explained, "Like, yeah, but at one point, I wasn't really using it and people would tell me, you know, you got to make your Instagram like useful or funny, so at one point I was like OK, I mean I could try." Anderson Cooper, "#BeingThirteen: Inside the Secret World of Teens," CNN Special Report, first aired Oct. 5, 2015.

159 cleaner, safer, more nurturing: "Eighteen-year-olds now act more like 15-year-olds used to, and 15-year-olds more like 13-year-olds," the San Diego State University psychologist Jean Twenge wrote in *The Atlantic* in 2017, after comparing survey results of teen attitudes and behaviors going back to the 1980s. "Childhood now stretches well into high school." Twenge suggested it was possible that the time young teenagers were spending online was contributing to the decline in their undesirable "adult" activities. *The Atlantic* nonetheless headlined her story "Have Smartphones Destroyed

a Generation?" Jean M. Twenge, "Have Smartphones Destroyed a Generation?," *The Atlantic,* Aug. 3, 2017.

159   a pretty marginal activity: The statistics on sexting vary enormously depending on the age of the kids surveyed (behavior at 10 to 13 looking extremely different from that at 14 to 19 and, in particular, 17 to 19) and how "sexting" is defined. Surveys that define the practice as including both sexually explicit verbal messages and sexual images find much higher rates of sexting than do those that define it only in terms of photos and videos. And surveys that ask teens if they've sent "sexually explicit" images that specifically showed naked breasts or genitals yield *much* lower numbers than those that ask about "nude or nearly nude" images. The first definitive poll on sexting, a December 2009 study by the Pew Research Center, found that only 4 percent of 12-to-17-year-olds had texted nude or nearly nude images or videos of themselves to someone else, and only 15 percent had received them. Twice as many 17-year-olds as 12-year-olds had sent sexts, and three times as many high schoolers as middle schoolers had received them. Amanda Lenhart, "Teens and Sexting," Pew Research Center, Dec. 15, 2009, pewinternet.org /2009/12/15/teens-and-sexting/. By 2014—with smartphone use really taking off—a study in the journal *Pediatrics* found that just 5 percent of middle schoolers had ever sent a sexually explicit message or photo, while 20 percent had received one. Eric Rice et al., "Sexting and Sexual Behavior Among Middle School Students," *Pediatrics* 134, no. 1 (July 2014). Other studies seeking to chart the prevalence of texting among teenagers in the past decade have yielded results ranging so wildly (between 1.3 and 60 percent in one 2018 international meta-analysis) as to render them all but useless. But some interesting trends have held up across studies and over time: Sexting activity is much higher among older teens than it is among middle schoolers; kids who sext are far more likely than those who don't to

be sexually active; and kids who sext are also far more likely to be very heavy users of texting generally, the 2018 meta-analysis showed. Perhaps most interesting of all, the study revealed that whether or not parents make a practice of going through their kids' phones to monitor their online activity makes no difference in terms of how likely their kids are to engage in sexting. The only thing that does: limiting how many texts kids are allowed to send. (And, yes, it is possible, if onerous, usually for a fee.) Sheri Madigan et al., "Prevalence of Sexting Behavior Among Youth: A Systematic Review and Meta-analysis," *JAMA Pediatrics,* Feb. 28, 2018, pediatrics .aappublications.org/content/134/1/e21.

159   psychologically damaging: Specifically, a whole body of research shows that people who live their lives in pursuit of "extrinsic goals"—like achieving high status, having a lot of money, or having great grades and impressive high school leadership positions to enter into their Naviance accounts—tend, despite their eventual accomplishments, to be less happy than those who do what they do for "intrinsic goals"—like enjoying an activity, spending time with others, or developing a feeling of mastery. Driving yourself to achieve for the sake of external rewards has been associated with chronic stress, lower well-being, and poorer physical and mental health. Lucia Ciciolla et al., "When Mothers and Fathers Are Seen as Disproportionately Valuing Achievements: Implications for Adjustment Among Upper Middle Class Youth," *Journal of Youth and Adolescence* 46 (2017): 1057–75.

159   hit middle schoolers extra hard: What happens just in sixth grade can determine the course of the rest of a student's academic life. Specifically, the Johns Hopkins University School of Education professor Robert Balfanz has found that if a sixth grader misses school more than 20 percent of the time, has relatively severe behavior problems, fails math or English, *and* doesn't get good help (an important caveat, since that lack of help is most likely to plague low-income kids), he

or she has a 75 percent chance of later dropping out of high school. For Balfanz's research, see, for example, Azmat Khan, "Dropout Nation: Middle School Moment," *Frontline*, PBS, July 17, 2012, pbs.org/wgbh/frontline/article/middle-schoolmoment/.

Unsurprisingly, the perils of early adolescence tend to have their most fateful impact on the most vulnerable kids—notably, those living in poverty or contending with poverty plus racism. Black middle schoolers in particular have long been perceived as being more "adult" and less "innocent" than white kids. They're often hypersexualized in adult eyes and viewed with suspicion. Black boys, starting at age 10, are more likely to be viewed with suspicion and suspected of crimes, as well as to face a violent response from police officers if accused of a crime, according to research by Phillip Atiba Goff, the co-founder and president of the Center for Policing Equity at John Jay College of Criminal Justice. Black girls are more likely than white girls to be perceived as needing less protection, support, and comfort; to be more independent; and to know more about sex and other adult topics. And that toxic process of "adultification," as a team of Georgetown University researchers showed in 2017, peaks for black girls between the ages of 10 and 14. The Georgetown research (in which Goff is cited) is reported in Rebecca Epstein, Jamilia J. Blake, and Thalia Gonzalez, "Girlhood Interrupted: The Erasure of Black Girls' Childhood" (report, Georgetown Law Center on Poverty and Inequality, Washington, D.C., June 2017). The term "adultification" is now widely used but originated in the Smith College professor Ann Arnett Ferguson's book *Bad Boys: Public Schools in the Making of Black Masculinity* (Ann Arbor: University of Michigan Press, 2001).

159   the sound of adult hypocrisy: Rick Weissbourd and Stephanie Jones, "The Children We Mean to Raise: The Real Messages Adults Are Sending About Values" (report, Harvard Graduate School of Education, Cambridge, Mass., 2014).

161   the meanest, most unhappy group: In fact, the stress placed on grades, success in impressive activities, and being part of the "right" crowd is so out of control in hard-driving upper-middle-class communities that psychologists have been surprised in recent years to find that well-off middle schoolers are *actually doing worse,* mental health–wise and happiness-wise, than kids their age from middle- or even low-income families.

Upper-middle-class kids basically look just like their low- and middle-income peers on measures of well-being early on. But in middle school, their emotional trajectory diverges, and from that point on, they're actually the group that's most at risk of anxiety, depression, rule-breaking (in the form of cheating), and substance abuse. There's also more meanness and envy in their schools. Popularity, among boys, is more likely to be tied to both substance abuse and being a jerk ("peer aggression"), while "mean girls" are admired in a way they are not in other communities. And although attractiveness is linked to popularity in middle schoolers at all income levels, Suniya Luthar and colleagues at Columbia University's Teachers College discovered in 2013 that it was "startlingly so" for upper-middle-class girls, after comparing adolescent life in upper-middle-class and inner-city communities. In other words, all that micromanaging, all that anxious concern to protect kids from the worst vicissitudes of middle school, is backfiring badly. Suniya Luthar, Samuel H. Barkin, and Elizabeth J. Crossman, " 'I Can, Therefore I Must': Fragility in the Upper Middle Classes," *Development and Psychopathology* 25 (2013): 1529–49.

The fact that well-off middle schoolers—the kids who supposedly have all the advantages—are also proving to be super-vulnerable to the vicissitudes of adolescence has led researchers to expand their notions of what it means to be "at risk" in America. They now identify as a "risk factor" the values that hold sway in upper-middle-class communities. Kids who believe that their parents most highly value

external achievements like grades, college acceptances, and, ultimately, money and career prestige have worse mental health than
those who believe that their parents place the greatest emphasis on
inner strengths like kindness, decency, respect for others, and integ-
rity. This means that the emphasis on top grades, athletic accolades,
and the brand names attached to college acceptances is all really bad
for kids' mental health, particularly when they're absorbed in too
high a dose during the critical period of early adolescence. For more
on this phenomenon, see Ciciolla et al.

Other research has suggested that middle schoolers of all social
classes who are extremely taken with status experience fallout long
after eighth grade ends. In 2014, the University of Virginia psychologist Joseph Allen found that 13-year-olds who were particularly
concerned with being "popular" and "cool" became young adults
who struggled to make and maintain strong relationships: By their
early 20s, the former "cool" kids were still evaluating themselves and
others by criteria like whether they were "popular enough" or "part
of the right crowd"—and these considerations, Allen suggested,
didn't lead to happy or solid friendships or romantic relationships.
Joseph P. Allen, Megan M. Schad, Barbara Oudekerk, and Joanna
Chango, "What Ever Happened to the 'Cool' Kids? Long-Term Sequelae of Early Adolescent Pseudomature Behavior," *Child Development* 85 (Sept.–Oct. 2014): 1866–80.

161 "stage-environment fit": Jacquelynne S. Eccles et al., "Development
During Adolescence: The Impact of Stage-Environment Fit on
Young Adolescents' Experiences in Schools and in Families," *American Psychologist* 48 (Feb. 1993): 90–101. In the early 1990s, Eccles and
colleagues published important research that detailed all the ways the
U.S. junior high and middle school experience was unsuited for the
developmental needs of students. Kids that age wanted—and were
ready for—a greater degree of autonomy in how they spent their
time and approached their schoolwork, Eccles said. Instead, as they

moved into junior high, their teachers tended to get stricter and more controlling, and the curriculum became more rigid. Sixth, seventh, and eighth graders were capable of more abstract and creative thinking, but they were given busywork that was often at a *lower* intellectual level than what they had encountered at the end of elementary school. Right at the time they were the most painfully self-conscious and most obsessed with how they measured up to others, there was suddenly more emphasis on grading (and harsher grading as well). And right when they were distancing themselves from their parents and needed strong and positive relationships with their teachers, they were put in classrooms that were far less supportive, led by adults who didn't like them, and, even worse, *blamed them* if they failed to thrive. Middle school teachers, Eccles wrote, were being undermined by the very same issues of bad "fit" that undercut middle schoolers' well-being: They were teaching too many different kids in too many different classes, and as a result had few opportunities to get to know the kids well or figure out how best to teach them. They felt bad about their work and in response reacted more negatively to the kids in their classrooms. They often became more rigid and controlling, setting themselves up for more student rebellion. Classroom conflict skyrocketed; the students "proved" themselves to be awful and conformed to every negative stereotype about impossible young teens. "Attributing one's teaching difficulties to characteristics of the students that are beyond one's control provides a convenient ego-saving explanation for lack of student progress," wrote Christy Miller Buchanan, Jacquelynne S. Eccles, Constance Flanagan, Carol Midgley, Harriet Feldlaufer, and Rena D. Harold in "Parents' and Teachers' Beliefs About Adolescents: Effects of Sex and Experience," *Journal of Youth and Adolescence* 19 (1990): 363–94.

161 a whole host of problems: In fact, the research by Jacquelynne Eccles and colleagues showed that the whole experience added up to a "regressive environmental change," bringing on "developmental de-

clines" in middle and junior high school students and putting into motion a downward spiral that could lead the most at-risk students to drop out altogether when they reached high school. Eccles et al., "Development During Adolescence."

That decline wasn't just a matter of negative self-perception. More recent studies have shown that American children who attend middle schools (as opposed to K–8 schools) consistently suffer a big drop in academic achievement between fourth and eighth grade. Jaana Juvonen et al., *Focus on the Wonder Years: Challenges Facing the American Middle School* (Santa Monica, Calif.: RAND, 2004), 31ff. See also Jonah E. Rockoff and Benjamin B. Lockwood, "Stuck in the Middle: How and Why Middle Schools Harm Student Achievement," *EducationNext* 10, no. 4 (Fall 2010): 68–75.

162 "educational wastelands": David C. Banks, "Why Middle School Should Be Abolished," *The Daily Beast,* July 12, 2014, http://www .thedailybeast.com/articles/2014/07/12/why-middle-school-should -be-abolished.html?source=TDB&via=FB_Page.

162 "you're sort of wasting your time": "Middle School," *This American Life,* WBEZ Chicago/PRX, Oct. 28, 2011.

162 the most commonly envisioned fix: See, for example, Philissa Cramer, "Worried About Little Children Attending School with Much Older Students? A Study Says They'll Be Better Off," Chalkbeat, Sept. 20, 2016, https://www.chalkbeat.org/posts/ny/2016/09/20 /worried-about-little-children-attending-school-with-much-older -students-a-study-says-theyll-be-better-off/. The article references Amy Ellen Schwartz, Leanna Stiefel, and Michah W. Rothbart, "Do Top Dogs Rule in Middle School? Evidence on Bullying, Safety, and Belonging," *American Educational Research Journal* 53 (2016): 1450–84.

162 Baltimore, Milwaukee, Philadelphia, and New York: Martin R. West and Guido Schwerdt, "The Middle School Plunge," *Education-*

Next 12, no. 2 (Spring 2012), https://www.educationnext.org/the
-middle-school-plunge/.

162   Boston, as this book went to press: James Vaznis, "Boston School
Committee Votes to Eliminate Middle Schools," *Boston Globe,* June 13,
2019.

162   the keys to happiness: "People want communion: They want to have
good relationships with other people. And they also want agency:
They want to feel that they are . . . competent and skilled in certain
things." Professor of psychology Antonius Cillessen of Radboud
University in Nijmegen, the Netherlands, phone interview with author, April 24, 2017.

162   lifelong resilience: Resilience is, simply put, the ability to bounce
back and move on after bad things happen (something that virtually
everyone needs to be able to do in middle school). We tend to talk
about kids "being" resilient (or not). But in reality, it's something
that they become—chiefly through living and learning in supportive
environments, with solid bonds to adults, really good friendships,
and a strong sense of belonging. Kids who are highly resilient tend to
have some characteristics in common: They feel confident and have
what psychologists call an "internal locus of control," which is, essentially, the belief that they control what happens to them, as opposed to feeling acted upon by external forces. There's a significant
body of literature showing that when kids have a strong sense of
agency and self-efficacy—a "belief that they can control their own
destiny," as opposed to a belief "that their destiny is determined by
external forces"—they have a really meaningful head start on a good
life. And, to put things more clinically, when they have this strong
sense of an "internal locus of control" as opposed to an "external
locus of control," they are less at risk of anxiety and depression. William Stixrud and Ned Johnson, *The Self-Driven Child: The Science and
Sense of Giving Your Kids More Control over Their Lives* (New York:
Viking, 2018), 2. Another interesting commonality is that they are

less likely to say they were bullied in middle school or high school. This was the finding of a 2017 study by cyberbullying experts Sameer Hinduja and Justin Patchin, who surveyed more than twelve hundred 12-to-17-year-olds in the United States and compared their experiences of bullying with how they scored on measures of resilience. The study was not able to say whether highly resilient kids were actually bullied less or whether they were simply less likely to describe what happened to them as bullying. But it almost doesn't matter; the fact that they walked away *feeling* like they hadn't been bullied meant they were happier. And highly resilient kids who were bullied, the study found, were able to recover from the experience with relative ease. Their resilience served as a kind of shield, protecting them against middle school's worst psychic ravages. How could other kids gain this magic strength? Adults needed to help them build it, Hinduja and Patchin wrote, by training kids to be "overcomers" rather than "'victims' who must rely on adults to always come to their aid." Sameer Hinduja and Justin W. Patchin, "Cultivating Youth Resilience to Prevent Bullying and Cyberbullying Victimization," *Child Abuse & Neglect* 73 (Sept. 2017): 51–62.

164 black afterschool program teacher: Unsurprisingly, there is solid evidence that afterschool programs and extracurriculars make kids feel more connected to school. But as the UCLA psychologist Jaana Juvonen, long a top expert in middle school education and development, has noted, those sorts of programs aren't valued—read: funded—by our metrics-based education system. Jaana Juvonen, "Reforming Middle Schools: Focus on Continuity, Social Connectedness, and Engagement," *Educational Psychologist* 42 (2007): 197–208.

166 *"zoom in . . . zoom out"*: Weissbourd and Jones, 2.

166 Taking action to benefit: Ciciolla et al.

166 these usually don't work: One-off training doesn't work without intensive follow-up and commitment on the part of the entire school

community, including the parents. Organized programs that focus on bullying have proved to be depressingly ineffective. Hinduja and Patchin's 2017 review found that despite a decade of efforts, U.S. schools had made only "modest progress" in lessening adolescent peer aggression. Hinduja and Patchin, 51. And a 2014 study found that, in general, antibullying programs don't work, especially in middle school. Dorothy L. Espelage, Joshua R. Polanin, and Sabina K. Low, "Teacher and Staff Perceptions of School Environment as Predictors of Student Aggression, Victimization, and Willingness to Intervene in Bullying Situations," *School Psychology Quarterly* 29 (2014): 287–305.

166   truly change the climate: Norm change, especially when efforts are aimed at a whole school and not just a specific instance of bad behavior, can change the middle school climate. Stephanie M. Jones and Suzanne M. Bouffard, "Social and Emotional Learning in Schools: From Programs to Strategies," *Social Policy Report* 26, no. 4 (2012). Studies have shown that when teachers don't take a problem like sexual harassment seriously, there's more of it, and that in schools where teachers have strong relationships with their students and are willing to intervene to fight bullying and general meanness, students are more willing to stand up for others as well. Espelage, Polanin, and Low, 298.

166   do better long-term: They have better self-regulation skills, fewer problem behaviors, and less depression, and they are more engaged at school and do better academically. Casta Guillaume, Robert Jagers, and Deborah Rivas-Drake, "Middle School as a Developmental Niche for Civic Engagement," *American Journal of Community Psychology* 56 (2015): 321–31. Studies also show that children in school learn best—and are most receptive to what adults are trying to tell them—when they feel cared about and respected. Richard Weissbourg, Suzanne M. Bouffard, and Stephanie M. Jones, "School Climate and Moral and Social Development," School Climate Practice

Brief No. 1, in "School Climate: Practices for Implementation and Sustainability," ed. T. Dary and T. Pickeral (National School Climate Center, New York, 2013).

167   " 'How do I represent the people who are part of my community?' " Rosalind Wiseman, phone interview with author, March 20, 2017.

168   test-crazy California school districts: Tim Walker, "Experts: Keep Social and Emotional Learning out of the Testing 'Quagmire,'" *NEA Today,* April 13, 2016, neatoday.org/2016/04/13/testing-grit -sel/.

169   "egalitarian classroom environment": Shannon Audley, Alexandra Singer, and Mary Patterson, "The Role of the Teacher in Children's Peer Relations: Making the Invisible Hand Intentional," *Translational Issues in Psychological Science* 1, no. 2 (June 2015): 192–200.

175   Melinda Gates: Nellie Bowles, "A Dark Consensus About Screens and Kids Begins to Emerge in Silicon Valley," *The New York Times,* Oct. 26, 2018.

178   "secondhand stress": Stixrud and Johnson, 85–87.

179   how well parents managed their own stress: Robert Epstein, "What Makes a Good Parent?," *Scientific American Mind,* Nov. 2010.

179   "sociometric" and "perceived" popularity: Steven R. Asher and Kristina L. McDonald, "The Behavioral Basis of Acceptance, Rejection, and Perceived Popularity," in *Handbook of Peer Interactions, Relationships and Groups,* ed. Kenneth H. Rubin, William M. Bukowski, and Brett Laursen (New York: The Guilford Press, 2009), 232–48.

179   a distinct set of skills: Joseph P. Allen, Joanna Chango, and David Szwedo, "The Adolescent Relational Dialectic and the Peer Roots of Adult Social Functioning," *Child Development* 85, no. 1 (Jan.–Feb. 2014): 192–204.

179   "positive affect": Jessica Kansky, Joseph P. Allen, and Ed Diener, "Early Adolescent Affect Predicts Later Life Outcomes," *Applied Psychology: Health and Well-Being* 8, no. 2 (July 2016): 192–212.

179   getting others to *do* what they want: The two categories of popularity are not always distinct. In fact, the University of Kansas psychologist Patricia Hawley has written that perhaps the most socially
successful middle schooler of all is the person she calls the "well-
adapted Machiavellian"—that is to say, someone who combines just
the right amount of "prosocial" behavior with the right dose of "co-
ercion," with the two administered so skillfully that the whole performance inspires admiration, not disapproval. "As in the adult
world, some children stand out as being especially effective at achieving their personal goals," she wrote in a much-cited 2003 journal
article. "Also as in the adult world, these effective competitors can be
aggressive, deceptive, and manipulative. Yet as we observe these individuals in action, we often can't help but be impressed by their
skills and perhaps even feel drawn to them even after having seen
their 'dark side.' " Such children, she hypothesized, may grow up to
be some of our most successful CEOs and politicians. Patricia H.
Hawley, "Prosocial and Coercive Configurations of Resource Control in Early Adolescence: A Case for the Well-Adapted Machiavellian," *Merrill-Palmer Quarterly* 49, no. 3 (2003): 279–309.

179   a risk factor for unhappiness: Donna Eder, "The Cycle of Popularity: Interpersonal Relations Among Female Adolescents," *Sociology
of Education* 58 (July 1985): 154–65.

181   more lonely, more depressed: In 1995, Nicki Crick and Jennifer
Grotpeter suggested in their seminal "relational aggression" paper
that these kids might be at risk for "serious adjustment difficulties"
later in life. Nicki R. Crick and Jennifer K. Grotpeter, "Relational
Aggression, Gender, and Social-Psychological Adjustment," *Child
Development* 66 (June 1995): 710–22. Later studies found that relationally aggressive kids tend to be less trusting of others and to have
an "aggressive attributional bias"—both of which set them up for
emotional and behavioral problems down the line. See, for example,
Pamela Orpinas, Caroline McNicholas, and Lusine Nahapetyan,

"Gender Differences in Trajectories of Relational Aggression Perpetration and Victimization from Middle to High School," *Aggressive Behavior* 41 (2015): 401–12.

181   false information: Joni D. Splett, Melissa A. Maras, and Connie M. Brooks, "GIRLSS: A Randomized, Pilot Study of a Multisystemic, School-Based Intervention to Reduce Relational Aggression," *Journal of Child and Family Studies* 24, no. 8 (2015): 2250–61.

182   poor self-regulation skills: Amy C. Hartl, Brett Laursen, and Antonius H. N. Cillessen, "A Survival Analysis of Adolescent Friendships: The Downside of Dissimilarity," *Psychological Science* 26, no. 8 (Aug. 2015): 1304–15.

182   "Relationship blindness": C. A. Hafen et al, "Conflict with Friends, Relationship Blindness, and the Pathway to Adult Disagreeableness," *Personality and Individual Differences* 81 (July 2015): 7–12.

182   "inhibited": Juvonen, "Reforming Middle Schools," 202.

182   "negative affect": Kansky, Allen, and Diener.

182   disagreeableness: Hafen et al.

183   "rejection sensitivity": Kathleen B. McElhaney, Jill Antonishak, and Joseph P. Allen, "'They Like Me, They Like Me Not'": Popularity and Adolescents' Perceptions of Acceptance Predicting Social Functioning Over Time," *Child Development* 79, no. 3 (May–June 2008): 720–36.

183   "self-fulfilling prophecy effects": Emily Loeb, Elenda T. Hessel, and Joseph Allen, "The Self-Fulfilling Prophecy of Adolescent Social Expectations," *International Journal of Behavioral Development* (2015): 1–10.

183   at very serious risk of being bullied: One study has even found that showing symptoms of psychological distress during the fall of sixth grade—notably, symptoms of social anxiety or depression—increased the chances that a student would be bullied by spring. Juvonen, "Reforming Middle Schools," 202.

184   "fixed mindset": Carol S. Dweck, *Mindset: The New Psychology of Success* (New York: Random House, 2006).

9. FORGETTING AND REMEMBERING

186   "only partially true": Dr. Robert C. Kolodny, Nancy J. Kolodny, Dr. Thomas Bratter, and Cheryl Deep, *How to Survive Your Adolescent's Adolescence* (Boston: Little, Brown, 1984), 12.

191   dropped her best friend: Rachel Simmons, *Odd Girl Out: The Hidden Culture of Aggression in Girls* (New York: Harcourt, 2002), 129–30. Phone interview with author, March 22, 2017.

192   "narrative identity": A "narrative identity" is how people "convey to themselves and to others who they are now, how they came to be, and where they think their lives may be going in the future." Dan P. McAdams and Kate C. McLean, "Narrative Identity," *Current Directions in Psychological Science* 22 (2013): 233–38.

193   aren't very helpful: Ibid. According to McAdams and McLean, people need "to control their world and make self-determined decisions." McAdams and McLean, 235.

ABOUT THE AUTHOR

Judith Warner is the author of the *New York Times* bestsellers *Perfect Madness: Motherhood in the Age of Anxiety* and *Hillary Clinton: The Inside Story,* as well as the highly acclaimed *We've Got Issues: Children and Parents in the Age of Medication.* A senior fellow at the Center for American Progress, Warner has been a frequent contributor to *The New York Times,* where she wrote the popular Domestic Disturbances column, as well as numerous other publications.

ABOUT THE TYPE

This book was set in Bembo, a typeface based on an old-style Roman face that was used for Cardinal Pietro Bembo's tract *De Aetna* in 1495. Bembo was cut by Francesco Griffo (1450–1518) in the early sixteenth century for the Italian Renaissance printer and publisher Aldus Manutius (1449–1515). The Lanston Monotype Company of Philadelphia brought the well-proportioned letterforms of Bembo to the United States in the 1930s.